URBAN DESIGN:
METHOD AND TECHNIQUES

Second Edition

URBAN DESIGN:
METHOD AND TECHNIQUES
Second Edition

Cliff Moughtin, Rafael Cuesta,
Christine Sarris and Paola Signoretta

OXFORD   AMSTERDAM   BOSTON   LONDON   NEW YORK   PARIS   SAN DIEGO
SAN FRANCISCO   SINGAPORE   SYDNEY   TOKYO

Architectural Press is an imprint of Elsevier
Linacre House, Jordan Hill, Oxford OX2 8DP, UK
30 Corporate Drive, Suite 400, Burlington, MA 01803, USA

First edition 1999
Reprinted 2000
Second edition 2003
Reprinted 2004, 2007

Notice
No responsibility is assumed by the publisher for any injury and/or damage to persons
or property as a matter of products liability, negligence or otherwise, or from any
use or operation of any methods, products, instructions or ideas contained in the material
herein. Because of rapid advances in the medical sciences, in particular, independent
verification of diagnoses and drug dosages should be made

British Library Cataloguing in Publication Data
A catalogue record for this book is available from the British Library

Library of Congress Cataloging-in-Publication Data
A catalog record for this book is available from the Library of Congress

ISBN–13: 978-0-7506-5718-1
ISBN–10: 0-7506-5718-9

For information on all Architectural Press publications
visit our website at www.architecturalpress.com

Printed and bound in *The Netherlands*

07 08 09 10 10 9 8 7 6 5 4 3

CONTENTS

PREFACE

In this book's First Edition's preface it was assumed that the case for sustainable development was proven. Most scientists working in the field of environmental management would still probably agree with that assertion. However, the present administration of the USA remains to be convinced: they have not signed the Kyoto Protocol, and largely due to their intervention, the latest Earth Summit did not achieve as much as many scientists think necessary to stem the tide of pollution, avert damaging climate change or conserve a fragile global environment. The complacent view of global environment which permeates the thinking of the 'right' of American politics and their allies was given some credibility with the publication of *The Skeptical Environmentalist* (Bjorn Lomborg, Cambridge University Press, 2001). Most reputable scientists in the field, however, have rebutted the optimistic view of the state of the global environment presented by Lomborg in his thought-provoking book; see, for example, *Misleading Math About the Earth* (Scientific American, January 2002). Here in Britain and indeed, in Europe, sustainable development still appears to be a major goal of urban planning. Lord Faulkner, in his response to some of the criticisms of the *Green Paper on Planning* (Planning, 22nd March, 2002) promised, to give more weight to sustainability as a goal of development in a future planning agenda. Until the international scientific community decides that it is safe to adopt policies that lead inevitably to an environmental 'free for all', it is wise to propose development strategies, which reduce, as far as possible, the pressures on a fragile global environment. This book and others in the series will continue to advocate 'the precautionary principle' as a guide for environmental design, a principle that is fundamental to the theory of sustainable development.

Since the publication in 1992 of *Urban Design: Street and Square* (Cliff Moughton, Architectural Press), the first book on urban design in this series, there have been considerable developments in the understanding and practice of urban design. These developments in urban design have been gathering momentum since this book was first published in 1999, hence the need for a new edition. Many of the ideas in the Report by Lord Rogers and his Urban Task Force, *Towards an Urban Renaissance*, also published in 1999, have been absorbed into local government thinking and may in part be responsible for the Planning Green Paper, *Planning: Delivering a Fundamental Change*, prepared in 2002 by the former Department for Transport, Local Government and the Regions. If implemented, ideas in the Green Paper could lead to an innovative planning system where urban design is elevated to a central role.

The types of development and planning tasks that have involved urban design skills have become more varied since the early 1990s and now include tasks of urban restructuring over large sub-regional areas. If the ideas encompassed by the Green Paper on planning are implemented, then it is likely that the workload of the urban designer will increase; he or she will also be engaged in a wide variety of tasks, once thought to be the province of other disciplines. To some extent urban design can quite simply be defined as the work carried out by urban designers. Nevertheless, throughout this series of books on urban design the core of the subject is considered to be the planning and design of the city quarter, district or neighbourhood. Clearly, the successful planning, design and development of large areas, such as the quarter, of any city involves the skills of other professionals working in the field of urban development. Here, we wish to reaffirm that the main concern of urban design is the creation of sustainable urban quarters of environmental quality. However, the method outlined in this book is general in nature and therefore applicable to a wide range of projects in which the urban designer may be involved.

There are four main changes in this book: Chapter 2 'Negotiating the Programme' now includes sections on regeneration initiatives, land assembly and the costing of development. Chapter 4 'Analysis' now has a section on the use of computers in urban design, concentrating on Geographic Information Systems and Space Syntax. Chapter 6 'Project Evaluation' has been updated with the latest information on Environmental Impact Analysis and has been strengthened with a section on financial appraisal of projects. Finally, Chapter 8 'Project Management' now includes a case study as an illustration of the use of this technique in urban design.

Cliff Moughton

NOTES ON THE AUTHORS

Emeritus Professor Cliff Moughtin is a consultant in Urban Design. He holds degrees in Architecture and Planning and was awarded the degree of Doctor of Philosophy by The Queen's University of Belfast. He worked for many years in developing countries both as an architect and as a planner. He was Professor of Planning in The Queen's University of Belfast and in the University of Nottingham. He is the author of a number of books, including *Hausa Architecture*, published by Ethnographica in 1985 and three other books in the current series on *Urban Design*, published by Butterworth-Heinemann's Architectural Press.

Rafael Cuesta is Programme Manager in the public sector with experience in transport planning and urban development. He studied Natural Resources Management in Norway and holds a Postgraduate Dilpoma in Project Management from the College of Estate Management at Reading University and an MA in Environmental Planning from the University of Nottingham. He is currently responsible for developing and implementing public transport policies and programmes in Birmingham and the West Midlands. He previously worked in the development and implementation of the Nottingham Express Transit and for some years was Special Lecturer in Environmental Impact Assessment with the Institute of Planning STudies at the University of Nottingham.

Christine Sarris received her undergraduate degree in Earth and Life Studies from the University of Derby and holds an MA in Environmental Planning from the University of Nottingham. Her specialism is in bringing forward major sites for development and regeneration, incorporating urban design principles and accepted development control practices. She has an extensive career in development control with the public sector and is presently Team Leader in Projects with Nottingham City Council.

Paola Signoretta is currently a Research Associate at the School of Geography, University of Nottingham. She has a degree in Town and Country Planning from the University of Reggio Calabria, Italy. She holds the Degree of Doctor of Philosophy awarded by the University of Nottingham. She has worked as a Research Fellow at the Sheffield Centre for Geographic Information and Spatial Analysis, University of Sheffield. She has extensive experience in the use of GI technologies in social science research.

ACKNOWLEDGEMENTS

The authors are greatly indebted to the Leverhulme Trust who gave generous financial support to Cliff Moughtin for the work involved in his contribution to this book. Cliff Moughtin also wishes to thank The Building and Social Housing Foundation for funding the public participation exercise in Newark and also the Reverend Vidal Hall and Dan Bone for their valuable contributions to that project. The authors wish to thank Michael Hopkins and Partners and the University of Nottingham for providing information about the new University Campus; Gale and Snowden for material on their permaculture project in Surrey; and Derek Latham and Company for information about their project, 'The Railway Cottages, Derby'. The authors wish to acknowledge the support of Leicester City Council, Nottinghamshire County Council and the City of Nottingham in the preparation of this book. We also thank Kirsten Arge for her introductions to those working on sustainable development in Norway and Kate McMahon Moughtin for her meticulous editing of the manuscript.

The views and opinions included in this book are those of the authors only and not of the organizations they represent.

DEFINITIONS

1

INTRODUCTION

The theme of this book is the Method of Urban Design. In particular the book will examine the techniques used in urban Design Method to achieve sustainable development. Dictionary definitions of method include a number of key words such as procedure, systematic or orderly arrangement together with the idea of a clearly defined goal as an end product. For example, *The Shorter Oxford English Dictionary* defines method as: 'procedure for attaining an object, a special form of procedure adopted in any branch of mental activity', or 'a way of doing anything, especially according to a regular plan'.[1] *The American Heritage Dictionary* defines method more simply as: 'The procedures and techniques characteristic of a particular discipline or field of knowledge - **the Method**'.[2] It is this definition which is taken as the starting point for the development of the argument in this book. Identifying and describing a unique **Method** for Urban Design, using this last definition of the word method, is central to the development of the subject as a discipline. Clearly, method, when used here, will include concepts such as procedures, objectives and plan.

The word technique has its origins in the Arts. It is defined as: 'Manner of artistic execution or performance in relation to formal or practical details (as distinct from general effect, expression, sentiment, etc.); the mechanical or formal part of an art, especially fine arts ... mechanical skill in artistic work'.[3] Technique is therefore related to specific tasks as opposed to Method which is the description of a total process. *The American Heritage Dictionary* includes a definition of technique which conforms more closely to the nature of Urban Design: 'The systematic procedures by which a complex or scientific task is accomplished'.[4] Technique, as used in the title of this book and as developed in the text, refers to the set of detailed operations used in the various stages of the Urban Design process. Method, on the other hand, refers to the structure and form of the Urban Design management process.

The title of this book elicits, by association, the words methodology and technology. The book, however, is not about either methodology or technology although the text does cover both topics. Methodology is: 'The science of method; a treatise or dissertation on method'.[5] The study of method is dealt with summarily in this chapter where the broad outlines of alternative methods adopted in the allied disciplines of planning and architecture are analysed. From this discussion, a broad method is outlined for urban design which aims at sustainable development. Technology is defined as: 'The terminology of a particular art or subject',[6] or 'the application of science, especially to industrial or commercial objectives ... the entire body of methods and materials used to achieve such objectives'.[7] At one level the menu of techniques outlined in this text could be described as the technology of urban design. Here, a more limited view of urban design technology is advocated. Howard's idea for the 'Garden City' is taken as an example of urban technology.[8] For the purposes of this book urban technology comprises major instruments or concepts advocated for the solution of problems associated with urban development. Urban design technology therefore would include, in addition to the Garden City, such ideas as the Urban Village or the Urban Transport Corridor. Urban design technology using this definition appears in Chapter 5, 'Generating Alternatives'.

GOALS OF URBAN DESIGN

There are three main goals of urban design: they are to design and build urban developments which are both structurally and functionally sound while at the same time giving pleasure to those who see the development. Sir Henry Wotton, like many writers since, defined architecture as consisting of 'commoditie, firmness and delight'.[9] Urban design shares with its sister art, architecture, these three qualities of utility, durability and the ability to bring to the user a sense of well-being and emotional satisfaction. The general method of urban design and the techniques used within that method have been developed to achieve these interconnected ends. This book, however, does not present the full range of techniques used in urban design. For example, it does not discuss in any depth the structural requirements of urban design nor does it deal with the

engineering requirements of urban infrastructure. This book does not deal with the legal requirements of urban development so important for implementation. These large topics of urban design deserve comprehensive treatment and, no doubt, will form the contents of further works in this field. This book, however, builds on the ideas in the first two volumes in this series, *Urban Design: Street and Square* and *Urban Design: Ornament and Decoration*, it will illustrate a design technology based upon the design concepts discussed in those two volumes as they are used to achieve urban development which is in keeping with a unique city context.[10] *Urban Design: Green Dimensions*, the third volume in this series, is the basis of the other main area covered in this book.[11] Techniques will be discussed which measure the effects of urban developments on city sustainability. The issue of sustainable development is the social foundation of urban design today. The social imperative is an environmental crisis of global proportions; it is in coming to terms with the effect of this crisis on cities which gives purpose and meaning to urban design.

There are those that remain to be convinced about the nature and extent of the environmental crisis facing humanity, the present administration of the USA being amongst the sceptics. The USA, the main polluter and user of scarce resources, failed to sign the Kyoto Protocol and it is due to the USA, and its allies in these matters, that the latest Earth Summit did not achieve as much as many scientists think necessary to stem the tide of pollution, avert damaging climate change or conserve a fragile global environment. The complacent view of global environment, which permeates the thinking of the 'right' of American politics was given some credibility with the publication of *The Skeptical Environmentalist*.[12] Most reputable scientists in the field, however, have rebutted the optimistic view of the environment presented by Lomborg in his thought-provoking book (see, for example, *Scientific American*,[13]). For a more detailed outline of the critique of Lomborg's work see *Urban Design:*

Street and Square, Chapter Seven.[14] Here in Britain and indeed, in Europe, sustainable development still appears to be a major goal of urban planning. Lord Faulkner, in his response to some of the criticisms of the *Green Paper on Planning*, promised to give more weight to sustainability as a goal of development in a future planning agenda.[15] Until the scientific community decides that it is safe to adopt policies, which lead to an environmental 'free for all' it is wise to propose development strategies, which reduce, as far as possible, the pressures on a fragile global environment.

Sustainability, that is, development which is non-damaging to the physical environment and which contributes to the city's ability to sustain its social and economic structures, is one important aspect of 'commoditie'. The pursuit of sustainable city structures is predicated on the development of a built environment of quality. The two goals, sustainable development and a built environment of quality, are mutually supportive. This book, therefore, aims to explore the method and techniques which will deliver both sustainable development and city environment of great quality. At the start of a new millennium, quality in urban design must be seen against a backcloth of current concerns for the global environment and in a context of sustainable development where the environment is of paramount importance and is given priority in design decisions.

There seems to be widespread agreement that solving global problems will mean the adoption of policies and programmes which lead to sustainable development. The pursuit of a sustainable future in an environment of quality will require the design of appropriate policies and programmes which address directly the related problems of unsustainable growth and environmental degradation. Part of this total agenda for sustainable development is the pursuit of non-polluting, energy efficient urban forms of quality. This book explores ways in which urban design method can be adapted to achieve this end and also examines the techniques available for

measuring and evaluating large-scale urban projects in terms of the contribution made to sustainable development.

A generally accepted definition of sustainable development is: '... development that meets the needs of the present generation without compromising the ability of future generations to meet their own needs'.[16] This definition has three key ideas: development, needs and future generations. Development should not be confused with growth.[17] Growth is a physical or quantitative expansion of the economic system while development is a qualitative concept: it is concerned with improvement or progress including cultural, social and economic dimensions. The term 'needs' introduces the idea of resource distribution: 'meeting the basic needs of all and extending to all the opportunity to satisfy their aspirations of a better life'.[18] These are fine sentiments but in reality the poor of the Third World are unable to achieve their basic needs of life while the more affluent effectively pursue their aspirations; many luxuries being defined by the wealthy as needs. There will naturally be environmental costs if the standards of the wealthy in the developed world are maintained while at the same time the aspirations of people in underdeveloped and developing countries are fulfilled. A choice may be inevitable: meeting needs and aspirations is a political, moral and ethical issue. Sustainable development means a movement towards greater social equity both for moral and practical reasons. Techniques for assessing the distribution of costs and benefits within and between groups are basic tools for assessing the effects of development and form the basis for evaluating the degree to which development can be described as sustainable.

The definition of sustainable development extends the concept of equity to future generations, it introduces the idea of inter-generational equity: 'We have a moral duty to look after our planet and hand it on in good order to future generations'.[19] This idea of stewardship was fostered by the United Nations Conference on the Human Environment in

1972.[20] Stewardship implies that mankind's role on this planet is one of caring for the earth and steering a path which as far as possible benefits the human and natural systems of the world. Mankind is viewed as the custodian of the earth for future generations. The aim therefore of development policy is not simply to maintain the *status quo* but for each generation to hand on a better environment particularly where it is degraded or socially deprived: it requires of any particular generation the wisdom to: avoid irreversible damage; restrict the degrading of environmental assets; protect important habitats, high quality landscapes, forests and non-renewable resources.

The application of this principle which places great premium on environmental protection means that all development proposals should include the real environmental costs. The true cost of all activities, whether they take place in the market or not, should be paid by the particular development through regulation and/or market-based incentives. Conserving the environment for future generations introduces the notion of maintaining a minimum of environmental capital, including the major environmental support systems of the planet such as the great river estuaries, together with the more conventional renewable resources such as the tropical rain forests. While it is difficult to identify the minimum environmental stock necessary to fulfil this requirement it is clear that 'current rates of environmental degradation and resource depletion are likely to carry us beyond that level'.[21] Sustainability constraints may be difficult to define with any precision. It is possible, however, to identify the direction of change in consumption patterns which are necessary to avoid breaching environmental thresholds. By applying the precautionary principle, where doubt and uncertainty exist, it may be possible to indicate the types of urban development which are more sustainable, or more accurately, less unsustainable. Environmental impact studies based upon accurate environmental audits, discussed in Chapter 6, are basic tools for

use by the urban designer in making proposals for any major sustainable development.

In summary, the definition of sustainable development by Grø Brundtland implies both inter- and intra-generational equity within a framework of development which does not destroy the planet's environmental support system.[22] As Brundtland points out, there are many problems in pursuing development without a high degree of democratic participation. Unless people as individuals and as members of groups can share in the decision making and in the actual process of development, that development is bound to be unsustainable. There must be the opportunity for individuals and communities to own any development; such ownership comes through action in the development process. The urban designer working in the field of sustainable development must be skilled in the process and techniques of public participation. Techniques of participation are used at many stages in the design process and consequently appear in a number of chapters of this book.

The pursuit of sustainable development gives to urban design its social purpose and acts as a goal which informs the design process. Subsumed within this goal of sustainable development is the aim to develop an environment of aesthetic quality. The concepts used to define quality in the urban environment have been discussed in detail elsewhere.[23] In this book they appear in the assumptions which determine the type of investigations carried out in assessing the form and character of the urban context for any development proposals. Chapter 3 deals with these techniques which are used to analyse townscape, the purpose of such contextual studies being to form the basis of sets of proposals which fit into and complement existing structures. The analyses are predicated upon such notions as compatible land uses, appropriate grain of development, buildings and spaces of human scale, together with ideas about the use of local materials, colour and decorative treatments of regional significance.

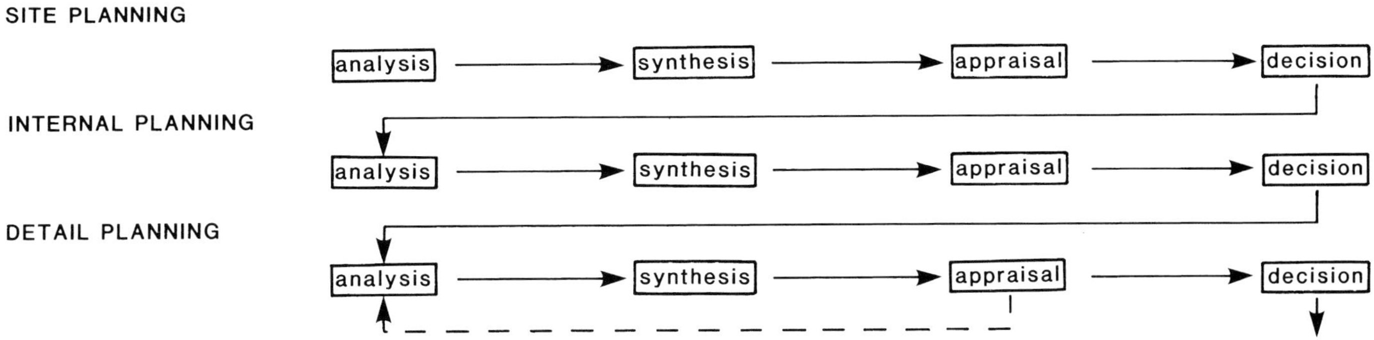

SITE PLANNING

INTERNAL PLANNING

DETAIL PLANNING

$$\boxed{\text{analysis}} \rightarrow \boxed{\text{synthesis}} \rightarrow \boxed{\text{appraisal}} \rightarrow \boxed{\text{decision}}$$

Figure 1.1 Architectural method.

URBAN DESIGN METHOD AND PEOPLE

Public participation in the process of design and implementation is a key factor in the definition of sustainable development. Sustainable urban development is the result of a process. It is a little simplistic to discuss participation in urban design unless that discussion includes a specific description of the type of participation and the techniques used at each stage of the process. The techniques of participation outlined in this book are based on the detailed analysis which appears in chapter 1 of *Urban Design: Street and Square.*[24]

Urban design, or the art of building cities, is the method by which man creates a built environment that fulfils his aspirations and represents his values. One value which is becoming increasingly important is care for the natural and built environment for the benefit of future generations. Urban design, therefore, can be described as a people's use of an accumulated technological knowledge to control and adapt the environment in sustainable ways for social, economic, political and spiritual requirements. It is the method learned and used by people to solve the total programme of requirements for city building. The city, therefore, is an element of a people's spiritual and physical culture and, indeed, is one of the highest expressions of that culture.

Central to the study of urban design is man, his values, aspirations and power or ability to achieve them. The task of the city builder is to understand and then express in built form, the needs and aspirations of the client group or citizens. How does the city builder design to best serve the community's needs? How can the designer ensure that the end product is both culturally acceptable and sustainable? What methods and techniques are best suited to this purpose? These are questions which are relevant considerations for those in the city-designing professions. An important aspect of a designer's skill is the development and use of a menu of techniques of public participation for incorporation into the design process. These techniques range from anthropological studies establishing essential cultural data, user studies and planning surveys, through informative techniques such as the exhibition, press notice and other media means of communication, to administrative procedures such as planning appeals and public inquiries. People's views can also be elicited at public meetings or sought through the electoral process by the inclusion of planning matters in political manifestos. Finally, there is a group of more active forms of participation, such as community design exercises, self-build operations and procedures for community administration and control.

THE URBAN DESIGN PROCESS

The RIBA practice and management handbook divides the design process into four phases:

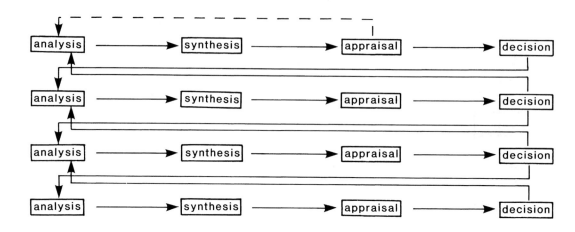

REGIONAL PLANNING

TOWN PLANNING

URBAN DESIGN

BUILDING DESIGN

Figure 1.2 Integrated design process for planning.

- Phase 1 *Assimilation*: the accumulation of general information and information specially related to the problem.
- Phase 2 *General Study*: the investigation of the nature of the problem: the investigation of possible solutions.
- Phase 3 *Development*: the development of one or more solutions.
- Phase 4 *Communication*: the communication of the chosen solution/s to the client.[25]

The description of design method is taken a little further by Markus and Maver. They argue that the designer goes through a series of linked decisions which form a clearly defined sequence.[26] This sequence is described as *analysis, synthesis, appraisal* and *decision*. The decision sequence is repeated for increasingly more detailed levels in the design process (Figure 1.1). During the analytical stage, goals and objectives are classified and patterns of information are sought. Synthesis is the stage where ideas are generated. It is followed by a critical evaluation of the alternative solutions against objectives, costs and other constraints. Decisions are made depending upon the findings of the evaluation. The decision process, however, is not defined as a simple linear progression: return loops between stages in the process are important, the process being iterative.

This way of looking at the design process for an individual building can be extended to urban design, city and regional planning (Figure 1.2). In this case, decisions at the higher level should inform the design process at the next lower order of design, for example, from regional to town planning. It makes most sense when each component of the environment fits consistently within the framework of a 'higher order' or contextual plan, for example, a building designed to fit within an urban design scheme which is determined by an urban structure plan based upon proposals for the region. It is, however, not simply a one-way process from large to small scale. It could be argued that each individual building should have some effect upon the larger urban grouping and that this three-dimensional design of large city areas should inform the planning of the city as a whole. Hence in Figure 1.2 there are return loops between the distinct facets of the development process for city planning.

In the discussion of design method so far there has been no overt mention of theory. Facts without theory have little or no meaning. Facts take on meaning when related to each other by a theoretical construct. Solutions to urban design problems, alternative ways of organizing city space, ideas about the relationship of function, urban structure and sustainability, have their origins in theory: in this book

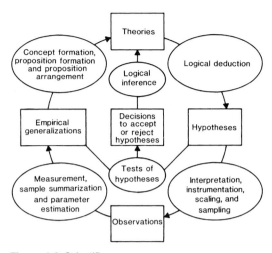

Figure 1.3 Scientific process.

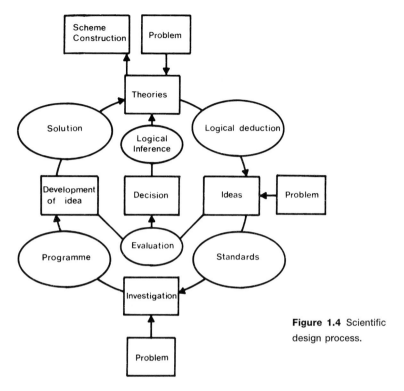

Figure 1.4 Scientific design process.

such concepts are considered as the technology of urban design. In order to understand the role of concepts in design and their relationship to theory it is useful to examine general scientific method. Scientific method is a direct analogy for the design process. The scientific process is illustrated in Figure 1.3: it involves five principal information components whose transformations into each other are controlled by six sets of techniques.[27] The information sets are the body of theory relating to the study area; the hypotheses thought to explain the phenomena studied; a set of observations from the specific environment and relating to the study subject; the fourth information component consists of empirical generalizations derived directly from the unique set of observations; and finally the body of decisions relating to the acceptance or rejection of the hypotheses. These information components are shown in rectangular boxes in Figure 1.3. The six groups of techniques which convert one information component to the next are shown within ovals on Figure 1.3. Theory, for example, is transformed into hypotheses through techniques of deductive reasoning. Observations are collected based on the hypotheses; the hypotheses being

interpreted using forms of instrumentation, scaling and sampling. The observations are then transformed into empirical generalizations through the process of measurement, gauging the parameters of the study and the analysis and summary of the sample of observations. The hypotheses can then be tested for the degree of conformity with the generalizations. The final information set, the decisions about the validity of the hypotheses, is derived from these tests. The last action in the process is the confirmation, modification or rejection of the theory through the technique of logical inference leading to concept or proposition formation and subsequent arrangement in new theoretical constructs.

This and other outlines of the scientific process appear clear, precise and systematic but, because of the pressures of time, money and politics, the scientific process is open to endless variation. Codifying method usually occurs after the event, the actual process being not always so precise as Figure 1.3 suggests. For example some elements of the process are more important for some research projects; some scientists practise a high degree of rigour in terms of method while others behave quite intuitively and informally, in a manner more usually associated with designers.

Figure 1.4 is a diagrammatic representation of the research process adapted to suit the needs of design. Entry into the design circle is possible at three points. Designers have been known to start the whole process with ideas for change and intervention, that is, they start at the point where in scientific method hypotheses are formed. Or they may start the design process with survey and data collection. The more usual, classic procedure is to start by trying to understand the theoretical nature of the problem, then to proceed through steps on Figure 1.4 in a clockwise direction. Nevertheless, it is possible to move directly from a statement of the problem to ideas and concepts for its resolution or to a search for data that will assist with finding a solution. Both these procedures, however, require some preliminary notions about theory however ill-informed or unexplicit they may be; it is only through theory that design concepts and data can be organized into coherent patterns.

At the core of scientific method is asking the right question or questions. In a similar way, it is defining the problem which is the art of design. This, however, is not the full explanation of a creative design process. There is a school of thought, not now as popular as it once was, which appears to infer that good design is simply the result of applying the correct method. The 'method school', in its more extreme forms, suggests that the study of the problem, followed by the logical evaluation of all possible solutions, would necessarily result in the best solution being discovered for the problem under investigation. In complex design situations it is not always possible to define the problem from the outset, nor to collect all the

relevant facts, nor is it possible to generate all possible solutions. This is to misunderstand the nature of most complex urban design problems and the process by which an attempt is made to change features of the environment. Most urban design problems are explored through an examination of solutions. An application of this style of design method may result in the redefinition of the problem which initiates a whole new round of investigation.

The design process is not linear but dialectical, taking the form of an argument between problem and solution. 'It is clear from our analysis of the nature of design problems that the designer must inevitably expend considerable energy in identifying problems confronting him. It is central to modern thinking that problems and solutions are seen as emerging together rather than one following logically upon the other.'[28] Following this view of design by Lawson it is clear that the nature of the problem becomes clear only as the process develops. Lawson also goes on to state that: 'Since neither finding problems nor producing solutions can be seen as logical activities we must expect the design process to demand the highest levels of creative thinking'.[29] Urban design, like any other design activity, involves creative thinking. It would, however, be misleading to assume that this does not apply equally in the field of scientific investigation. It would also be misleading to think that design solutions cannot be generated through logical deduction from theory or indeed that problem exploration is not an outcome of standard design procedures. It is, however, reasonable to suggest that an important feature of the design process is the exploration of problem definition through the examination of solutions or partial solutions.

Fundamental to the urban design process is the generation of ideas and design concepts. Theory may be a productive source of ideas but it is by no means the only one. Ideas can be generated in ways which fall outside the scope of inductive or deductive reasoning. Artists and creative designers make

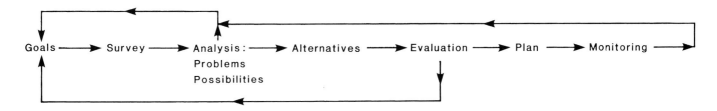

Goals → Survey → Analysis: → Alternatives → Evaluation → Plan → Monitoring →
Problems
Possibilities

Figure 1.5 The planning process.

use of analogy in their work. Analogy is a most useful tool for the creative designer. The use of analogy can be used to circumvent a mental block; a way of short-circuiting the design process. The alternative of waiting for inspiration to find new ways of seeing an old problem may be unproductive or at best time-consuming. De Bono suggests that: 'The usefulness of analogies is as vehicles for functions, processes and relationships which can then be transferred to the problem under consideration'.[30] Analogy is not the only technique available to the designer seeking ways of seeing problems and their solutions in a new light: ideas may be generated by a process of lateral thinking with its own range of standardized techniques. These techniques, along with the uses of analogy for concept formation, will be discussed in Chapter 5.

Urban design method is an iterative process, cyclical in nature. It has much in common with general planning method which was for some time based on Sir Patrick Geddes's dictum: 'Survey, Analysis and Plan'.[31] Others have since amplified the method outlined by Geddes inserting additional intermediate steps. Figure 1.5 illustrates one such interpretation of the essentially Geddesian method. As with design method the planning process is seen as cyclical having intermediate loops. For example, after an evaluation of alternative plans it may be necessary to redefine goals, or collect additional data, or to analyse the data in a different way. The urban design method suggested here mirrors the planning process with which it has so much in common. A book, however, is a linear presentation of material. Urban design method is therefore presented here as a simple progression starting with

goal formation and ending with techniques of implementation. This ordered and orderly presentation cannot do justice to the richness and complexity of urban design. The linear presentation of the material is adopted for clarity and convenience.

Urban design method like planning method is related to the main theoretical schools of thought which explain the procedures of public action in planning, development and design. According to Hudson there are five major schools of thought within normative planning theory.[32] The five categories are: the synoptic, incremental, transactive, advocacy-orientated and radical traditions. The method advocated here for urban design is very much in the synoptic traditions of planning. It is appropriate at this point to discuss the suitability of this method for the delivery of sustainable development and environmentally sound procedures in urban design.

Synoptic planning has its roots in rationalism and utilitarian philosophy. As the method described in this chapter outlines, synoptic planning method proceeds from analysis to target definition followed by a search for alternatives and their comparison. Synoptic planning method in some cases, and followed here, includes the process of implementation with its techniques for the feedback of information. This text adopts a compromise position, following a course described as 'limited rationality' since common sense suggests the impossibility of elucidating all possible alternative actions in any given situation. It may also be appropriate to follow Lawson's ideas, testing partial answers to the problem in dialectical fashion by confronting problem and answer.

Incremental planning has its roots in liberalism and theories about social learning. According to this theory it is not possible to define clear goals based on commonly accepted values. Only a limited number of alternative actions are considered in any development context and these differ little from the *status quo*. A good solution in incremental planning is not defined by the degree of goal achievement, but by how feasible implementation is with the means available and the degree of agreement among key decision makers.

Transactive planning places great emphasis on mutual learning and dialogue between those affected by planning. It seeks to build decentralized planning bodies which can give the population more control over the social processes that are affecting their welfare. According to Hudson, transactive planning is just as concerned with planning's effect on people's self esteem, values, behaviour and capacity for growth through co-operation, as with the instrumental consequences of the plan.[33]

Advocacy planning, as the name suggests, implies that planners become spokesmen and spokeswomen for various groups. The planner contributes to the development process by creating a situation with many competing plan proposals. The theory postulates that this model of planning provides for minority groups to be heard more clearly and that, as a consequence, the general public receives better information about alternative options.[34]

Radical planning has two main trends. The first is an anarchist-inspired approach emphasizing decentralized control and the experimentation with alternative societal organizations. The second main school of radical planning is more structurally orientated. It takes a Marxist direction focusing on the impacts of the economic system on class conditions and the role of planning in the class struggle. The first group of radicalist planning theorists includes the environmentalist movements. The Marxist radical version proposes government control of the means of production and that production, instead of being governed by profit motives, should be directed towards meeting societal needs as defined through the political process.

Naess analysed these five main alternative planning theories with a view to determining their ability to deliver sustainable development.[35] The criteria Naess used to evaluate these theoretical positions were:

(a) To what extent will the planning form be able to contribute to long-term preservation of global and national environmental qualities ... and management of natural resources in a way that does not reduce the abilities for future generations to meet their needs?
(b) To what extent will the planning form be able to contribute to the preservation of local environmental qualities?
(c) To what extent will the planning form be able to contribute to a distribution of goods which ensures basic rights to welfare for everybody, regardless of nationality or social group?
(d) To what extent will the planning form be able to advance, or be in conflict with civil and political rights, especially minority rights?
(e) To what extent will the planning form be able to contribute to the improvement of the conditions for planning in accordance with the criteria for a sustainable development?[36]

Table 1.1 shows the results of the evaluation conducted by Naess. It indicates that each planning model has certain strengths with regard to achieving sustainable development. Assuming that society has the political will and the power to promote sustainable development, then synoptic planning, which forms the basic philosophical underpinning of the method outlined in this text, is appropriate for the task. It is particularly well suited to the promotion of global and national environmental concerns and also to the promotion of justice in the distribution of goods. Its weakness lies in the practise of the theory where there is a tendency to neglect local knowledge particularly in the field of conservation.

Table 1.1 Benefits and drawbacks of various planning theories, in relation to different aspects of a strategy for promoting a sustainable development.

	Global/national environmental and resource concerns	Local environmental concerns	Fair distribution	Civil and political human rights	Potential for change of societal frame conditions
Synoptic	(+)	(−)	(+)	(−)	?
Incremental	−	−	−	(+)	−
Transactive	(−)	(+)	(+)	+	+
Advocacy	?	+	(−)	+	+
Radical	+	?	+	−	+

+, Usually well suited; (+), may be suited under certain conditions; ?, vague or ambiguous function; (−), may have a negative effect; −, usually has a negative effect.

This is evidenced in Britain, where the synoptic model of planning is predominant, by the total disregard for local protests at road and airport development sites. The views of the community activist appear to carry little weight.

Incremental planning appears to be poorly suited to the promotion of collective objectives which address major issues such as global, national or even local environmental concerns. A more just distribution of resources is also not a priority for the incremental planning process and this, of course, is a fundamental requirement of sustainable development. The transactive planning model implies the sacrifice of the important controls needed to attain targets for global environmental protection and the equitable distribution of goods on which such environmental protection are predicated. Both transactive planning and advocacy planning do appear well suited to addressing local environmental problems. Advocacy planning is particularly supportive of civil and political rights together with community involvement in development which is so important in the theory of sustainable development. Having strong parochial concerns to the fore, advocacy planning is a little ambiguous in relation to global concerns and a more just distribution of resources. The attempts to execute Marxist planning theories have revealed serious shortcomings with regard to securing civil and political rights while socialist states of a communist leaning have poor records in achieving environmental quality. The critical perspective of radical planning does, however, form a basis for outlining strategies to overcoming obstacles towards achieving global environmental concerns.[37] In the hands of the radical environmentalists the ideas about a global system of self-sufficient villages is a refreshing contribution to the debate about sustainable development.

It seems that the normative planning theories, to some extent, are complementary and that common sense suggests an eclectic approach where planning style is dictated by the needs of a particular situation. There seems no good reason to believe that compatible features from different planning styles cannot be combined within the same planning or urban design task. Naess seems to be speaking for a wider audience than his Norwegian colleagues when he suggests that: 'Synoptic planning should be used to the greatest possible extent'.[38] He suggests, however, that implementation of plans should take place, where possible, in small steps so that experience can be incorporated in later phases. It seems wise also to include within the framework and objectives of synoptic planning method adequate provision for active public participation. It is not sufficient simply to pay 'lip service' to participation, such tokenism can be counterproductive by raising false expectations or by feeding a public cynicism towards all development. Public participation is a procedure which can illuminate genuine alternative development strategies suggested by people with a specialist local knowledge. With these caveats it appears that the synoptic method of design advocated in this book is an appropriate tool for delivering sustainable development.

Chapter 2 will outline the ways in which problems in urban design are defined, writing design briefs, developing or negotiating the programme, regeneration initiatives, land assembly, the costing of development and problems associated with development control. Chapter 3 deals with the survey; in particular, it covers techniques of site investigation including site history, townscape analysis, urban legibility, permeability studies, and visual analysis. Chapter 4 covers techniques of problem analysis, including SWOT analysis, constraints and possibility mapping, the use of computers in urban design, in particular Geographic Information Systems and Space Syntax, trends, forecasts and scenario writing. The concern of Chapter 5 is methods of generating alternatives, including a discussion of the nature of design concepts, synectics and the use of analogy, brain storming, lateral thinking and history as a source of ideas. The chapter is particularly concerned with those ideas which are compatible with sustainable development. Chapter 6 covers the techniques used in evaluating alternative proposals. Project evaluation for major urban design projects which aim at delivering sustainable development and therefore at the promotion of equity should include a consideration of the distribution of costs and benefits: the gainers and losers should be clearly identified. This chapter therefore covers social and economic evaluation

such as cost-benefit analysis, financial appraisals of projects, in addition to environmental analysis. Chapter 7 is concerned with communication of ideas; it includes techniques of report presentation and case studies in visual presentation of urban design projects. Chapter 8 discusses the process of implementation, summarizing the whole process of design using project management as a means of relating the construction phase, monitoring and feedback to the earlier phases of design method. Chapter 9 is a short conclusion summarizing the contents of the chapters and raising a number of questions left unanswered in the text.

REFERENCES

1 Little, W. *et al.* (revised by C.T. Onions) (1952 reprint) *The Shorter Oxford English Dictionary,* Vol. 1, Oxford: Clarendon Press (first published in 1933) p. 1243.

2 Morris, W. (ed.) (1973) *The American Heritage Dictionary,* New York: Houghton Mifflin, p. 826.

3 Little, W. *et al., op. cit.,* Vol. 2, p. 2140.

4 Morris, W. (ed.) *op. cit.,* p. 1321.

5 Little, W. *et al., op. cit.,* Vol. 1, p. 1243.

6 Little, W. *et al., op cit.,* Vol. 2, p. 2140.

7 Morris, W. (ed.) *op. cit.,* p. 1321.

8 Howard, E. (1965) *Garden Cities of Tomorrow,* London: Faber and Faber.

9 Wotton, H. (1969) *The Elements of Architecture,* London: Gregg.

10 Moughtin, J.C. (1992) *Urban Design: Street and Square,* Oxford: Butterworth-Heinemann, and Moughtin, J.C., Oc, T. and Tiesdell, S. (1995) *Urban Design: Ornament and Decoration,* Oxford: Butterworth-Heinemann.

11 Moughtin, J.C. (1996) *Urban Design: Green Dimensions,* Oxford: Butterworth-Heinemann.

12. Lomborg, B. (2001) *The Skeptical Environmentalist,* Cambridge: Cambridge University Press.

13. Scientific American, (2002) Science defends itself against the skeptical environmentalist, *Scientific American,* January.

14. Moughtin, J. C. (2003) *Urban Design: Street and Square,* Oxford: Architectural Press, 3rd edition, Chapter 7.

15. Department of Transport, Local Government and the Regions (2002) *Planning Green Paper, Planning: Delivering a Fundamental Change,* DTLR. See also Planning (2002) Sustainability to be at heart of new system, *Planning,* 22nd March.

16. World Commission on Environment and Development, (1987) *Our Common Future: The Brundtland Report,* Oxford: Oxford University Press.

17. Blowers, A. (ed.) (1993) *Planning for a Sustainable Future,* London: Earthscan.

18. World Commission on Environment and Development, *op. cit.*

19. Department of the Environment (1990) *This Common Inheritance, Britain's Environmental strategy,* CM 1200, London: HMSO.

20. United Nations (1972) *Conference on the Human Environment,* New York: UN.

21. Elkin, T. and McLaren, D. with Hillman, M. (1991) *Reviving the City,* London: Friends of the Earth.

22. *Ibid.*

23. Moughtin J.C. (1992) *op. cit.*

24. *Ibid.*

25. RIBA (1965) *Architectural Practice and Management Handbook,* London: RIBA.

26. Markus, T.A. (1969) The role of building performance measurement and appraisal in design method, in *Design Methods in Architecture,* eds G. Broadbent and A. Ward, London: Lund Humphries. See also: Maver, T.W. (1970) Appraisal in the building design process, in *Emerging Methods in Environmental Design and Planning,* ed. G.T. Moore, Cambridge, MA: MIT.

27. Wallace, W. (1980) An overview of elements in the scientific process, in *Social Research: Principles and Procedures,* eds J. Bynner and K.M. Stribley, Harlow: Longman.

28. Lawson, B. (1980) *How Designers Think,* London: Architectural Press.

29. *Ibid.*

30. de Bono, E. (1977) *Lateral Thinking,* Harmondsworth: Penguin.

31. Geddes, P. (1949) *Cities in Evolution,* London: Williams and Norgate.

32. Hudson, B.M. (1979) Comparison of current planning theories: Counterparts and contradictions, *Journal of the American Planning Association,* Vol. 45, pp. 387-398.

33. *Ibid.*

34. Davidoff, P. (1973) Advocacy and pluralism in planning, in *A Reader in Planning Theory,* ed. A. Faludi, Oxford: Pergamon Press, pp. 139-149.

35. Naess, P. (1994) Normative planning theory and sustainable development, *Scandinavian Housing and Planning Research,* Vol. 11, pp. 145-167.

36. *Ibid.*

37. *Ibid.*

38. *Ibid.*

NEGOTIATING THE PROGRAMME 2

The urban designer may be employed by a local authority or working in some capacity for a developer. There are other careers open to those with an interest in urban design in, for example, academia or the civil service. This chapter, however, is concerned with the contrasting roles of design normally associated with protecting the community's interest in the environment and with the role of maximizing a developer's profit. These contrasting and sometimes conflicting roles have been crudely described as working 'as gamekeeper or poacher'. In reality, both groups share much common ground and common interest. The chapter begins with a summary of the peculiar debilitating conflict which is often played out between architects and planners. The chapter emphasizes the benefits which ensue when good environmental design is the goal of both developer and local authority. The chapter goes on to discuss the identification of sites for development, making them available for regeneration by identifying any funding gaps and then securing planning gain for the community. Negotiated development, development guidance and design briefs make up the middle part of the chapter; all are important tools for the urban designer to understand, no matter which side of the design fence he

or she may straddle. This part of the development process is illuminated by a case study from Leicester. The aim of the chapter is to introduce the practical problems encountered when attempting to write the project programme or schedule of uses and building floor space. This process is intimately linked with implementation and ultimately with development control: it is argued here that the process of programme development is most efficiently and effectively achieved when it is the product of negotiation between developer and the local authority.

ARCHITECTS AND PLANNERS – THE STORMY AFFAIR

The past decades have seen a shift in attitude in relation to design. In the late 1980s the debate between architects and planners was furious; architects being concerned that planners were not trained in the areas of design, therefore they considered any design criticism from a planner invalid. Such a prejudice might be held by an architect steeped in design who, subjectively, had encountered a young development control planning officer who had dismissed the architect's design as unsatisfactory because it did not fit in, without explaining why exactly it did not 'fit in'. The British Government's view, with some reason, fifteen years ago was also that planners should not get involved in design issues.

There has, however, been a growing awareness that the relationship between development projects and adjacent areas has not been addressed. The schemes that were gaining planning permission hitherto were inward looking and did not take into account wider issues, such as the qualities of the environment which make it both enjoyable and safe to use throughout a twenty-four-hour day. Housing schemes, for example, were based on the home as a defended space. The cul-de-sac attained prime position as a desired residential layout, following closely many of the points identified in *The New Essex Design Guide*.[1] This led inevitably to layouts with high defensive walls around the perimeter. The entrance roads were often marked by rumble strips and sleeping policemen, while areas at the edge of the site were places in which no one felt safe when walking. This has been further exacerbated by the document from the police on crime prevention by design, which has taken a very defensive approach to residential layout.[2] However, these residential layouts have sold well in the past and still sell well. The house builders, therefore, are meeting certain needs of many prospective buyers. These unimaginative schemes by house developers have proved to be a tried and trusted recipe with which to circumvent obstructive planners. Such housing areas still litter the towns, cities and countryside. They have left a legacy of increasing car dependency, a massive use of valuable greenfield sites, an increased fear of crime and a lack of vitality in our towns and cities.

Prince Charles initiated discussion about design with his open criticism of architects and planners and their unimaginative approach to design in the city. He made the obvious point that since we have managed to create lovely places in the past we can, therefore, produce a better environment with

greater vision now. His support led to the development of the Urban Villages Forum in 1992 which is working to create mixed-use urban developments on a sustainable scale and is making the case for a more people-friendly environment. There is also a growing awareness of the city as a work of art: 'Those who develop prime sites must not be allowed to focus on their own problem and we need to know how they will contribute to the City as a work of Art'.[3] The development of urban design has provided an intellectual bridge for architects and planners, permitting each profession to view development from a new and different perspective.

The attitude of the British Government has gradually changed: a greater emphasis is now being placed on urban design. Various planning policy guidance documents and circulars have been produced to encourage better urban design with less emphasis being given to the use of the car. These include Planning Policy Guidance (PPG) 6 and 13 and more recently 1. PPG1 now places the emphasis firmly on urban design, giving local authorities the power to ask for an assessment of surrounding areas and buildings.[4]

Lord Rogers and the Urban Task Force have, since 1998, intensified the debate around urban design, regeneration and sustainable densities for communities, culminating in the Urban White Paper, *Our Towns and Cities: the Future in 2000*.[5] The report examines mixed-use sustainable development, identifies a new vision of urban living with good quality services, and delivering an urban renaissance. It starts to address issues of density and improvements to the public realm. It has subsequently been recognized that the public realm has been a poor relation in funding allocation decisions, but its deterioration has a disproportionate effect on the perception and prospects of an area. This recognition led to the publication (by the then Department of Transport Local Government and the Regions, now the ODPM) of *Green Spaces, Better Places*,[6] an interim report by the Urban Green Spaces Taskforce in November 2001, and followed by *Living Places - Cleaner, Safer, Greener*[7] in 2002.

To support public spaces, and a better relationship between buildings and the street, emphasis has recently been placed on increasing density of development.

It is difficult to achieve innovative and sustainable designs where density of development is low. Average housing developments in England generally tend to be at around twenty-three dwellings per hectare.[8] At the Urban Summit held on 31 October, 2002, John Prescott announced that any proposal to build at a density of less than thirty dwellings per hectare had to be referred to and be approved or disapproved by the ODPM.[9]

Such measures were instigated to prevent the continued erosion of greenfield sites, and to continue to meet Government objectives of developing sustainable communities and bringing forward brownfield sites - a term used for previously developed sites which require redevelopment. An increase in housing densities would increase values through development and should reduce funding gaps. As a result, there would be more money for investment in urban design and a greater population to support facilities within walking distance and lessen dependency on the car, supporting the development of sustainable and lively communities. Barcelona, recognized as a model city in terms of urban regeneration, has developments which achieve residential densities of 300–400 dwellings per hectare, according to its Mayor, Joan Clos.

URBAN REGENERATION

Regeneration is a risky business for all those involved. Successful regeneration requires the input of local communities, developers, financiers, funding agencies, the public sector in all its guises (looking at the physical, social and economic well-being of an area) and the close collaboration of all the different professions associated with the built environment.

Successive governments have targeted the development of brownfield sites for the regeneration of cities by producing guidance, changes to legislation, and the creation of new agencies for their development. European initiatives have, in most instances, supported this type of approach. Government offices were first established in 1994 to provide a regional presence and to carry out functions for several government departments. Their key objectives include supporting and promoting a coherent regional approach to issues including regeneration and social inclusion, promoting and sustaining partnerships. The Regional Development Agencies (RDAs) were established in eight English regions in 1999, and in London a year later, with the remit to further economic development and regeneration, promote business efficiency, investment and competitiveness, generate employment, and encourage and enhance the skills of people in the region. Funding for the RDAs is expected to be £1.7 billion in 2003/4 and £2 billion by 2005/6.

English Partnerships was also set up as the key regeneration agency for England. Various initiatives have been developed by English Partnerships. In 1996 they focused attention on urban design by producing a booklet *Time for Design, Good Practice in Building, Landscape and Urban Design*.[10] English Partnerships subsequently teamed up with the Urban Villages to help fund various schemes throughout the country aimed at developing areas of mixed use on previously derelict land. As part of the Partnership Investment Programme (PIP), grants were made available to assist development. However, this scheme was discontinued in1999 because it was deemed to contravene European Commission directives as it gave assistance directly to developers. The Government has since negotiated several schemes that partially replace the old PIP regime and these can be accessed via the Regional Development Agencies.

English Partnerships, and its private-sector funding partners AMEC and Legal and General, developed the English Cities Fund in December

2001.[11] It is worth £100 million and deals with investments in large mixed-use schemes in English Assisted Areas. Igloo Regeneration has also been formed with Norwich Union, which is targeted at the top twenty city centres in the UK. Local authorities are also becoming involved in limited partnerships, allowing institutional investors to invest directly in joint ventures with councils and property developers. This structure has the benefit of removing liability from individual investors since liability is limited only to the amount invested. The Deputy prime minister (John Prescott) also announced at the Urban Summit that Housing Corporations would have to work directly with English Partnerships and vice versa to promote regeneration and deliver homes on previously developed sites.

Local authorities are now regularly working with the various agencies and the private sector to unlock redevelopment potential of sites. This has been required, as local authorities have not had funding available for land assembly or the finance to reclaim land and to put the infrastructure in place. By taking a long-term view, the local authority is able to contribute significantly by making sites available for development through partnership working. This can be achieved by correctly identifying the scale of regeneration required in an area, followed by the preparation of a planning policy framework for the project. Policies must be established that support proposals identified in guidance for development. Guidance and policies must be flexible enough to ensure that the private sector can ensure the viability of the project.

One of the best ways of making sites available for development is by contributing local authority land that may at times be at less than best consideration. 'Best consideration' is a term used in Section 123 of the Local Government Act (1972). This requires local authorities to achieve the best value they can for a piece of land. The reason for this section of the Act is to protect the public purse and to ensure a clear audit trail. This will usually involve active marketing of a site and an assessment of all submissions prior to any release of land. Special permission needs to be sought if it is proposed to sell land at less than 'best consideration' and a clear justification must be submitted to central government. Relaxation of this act will help make sites more easily available for regeneration purposes. In this way, the contribution of land shows commitment to the private sector.

Other areas of funding from the local authority can also be accessed. There may be funding available for education, housing, social services and economic regeneration initiatives. This requires local authorities to have a corporate approach and the breaking down of traditional barriers between departments. The Government is actively supporting this approach and promoting 'joined-up thinking' within its own Ministries. Infrastructure requirements can be identified and funded through the Local Transport Plan (LTP).[12] Regular assessments of the viability of projects need to be made to ensure realism about public sector works financed via Section 106 agreements. Most importantly, the local authority can coordinate with the various agencies focused on delivering regeneration.

IMPOVERISHED LOCAL AUTHORITIES AND DEVELOPMENT OPPORTUNITIES

Local authorities for a number of years have been trying to resist monotonous and bland development. However, to date there has been little support from the Government. Most authorities are desperately underfunded and therefore fear refusing permission for major developments which might bring resources to the area. Local authorities, in addition, cannot afford more than a limited number of Public Inquiries or Planning Appeals per year. Such Appeals and Inquiries can result in substantial costs being awarded against an authority. It is not surprising, therefore, that local authorities try wherever possible to avoid costly public hearings. In order to improve design advice and reduce the possibility of expensive conflict with developers some city authority planners form a close working alliance with architects and urban designers. This is also, in part, a response to the emphasis now placed on Urban Design. The expert advice received from qualified professionals in the fields of urban design and architecture lends more weight to negotiations with developers to improve the quality of urban design in preparing projects. The benefits of this imaginative approach to teamwork between the professions are beginning to emerge in the form of more sensitive development. This design team approach is appropriate for all types of development from a change of use application to major projects.

There has been little development and construction by local authorities in recent years since their finance has been depleted. It is still expected by landowners, developers and the general public that local government should continue to provide all the ancillary services for housing developments. This includes not only the maintenance of existing services but also the provision of new services such as new parks, schools, community facilities, leisure centres and any other requirements of the local community. This service expectation has a revenue implication for the local authority. When a local authority develops its own land it is assumed that all the capital realized from the sale is at the disposal of the local authority. However, at present the local authority will only be allowed to spend 50 per cent of any financial gain resulting from development. There is the expectation that the local authority will provide facilities in the neighbourhood where the land sale takes place, an assumption that is misplaced. All local government spending involves deciding priorities in the allocation of public money which is likely to involve a political decision based on need across the whole of the particular local authority.

These tighter financial constraints under which local government operates has led to the development of planning gain or betterment. Planning gain operates primarily through what has come to be

known as the Section 106 process. Local authorities can no longer provide many of the services required to make a community function and so it is incumbent upon planners to co-ordinate negotiations with developers in an attempt to get necessary services provided as part of the development. This makes the process of planning lengthier and enables developers to negotiate with a number of authorities in an effort to develop land where the planning requirements are less stringent.

There is in developers' negotiations an emerging view that development opportunities should be seized wherever they arise, provided the public is consulted at every stage. Opportunities may arise throughout the development process and may take a number of different forms; the submission of a planning application which may lead to negotiations for improvements both on and off the site in terms of uses, links, vitality, mix of uses; the development of written advice and guidance for sites; the application of funding from organizations and different funding regimes such as Regional Development Agencies, English Cities Fund, City Challenge, Single Regeneration Budget, Capital Challenge, New Deal, Lottery Funding, English Partnerships or Urban Villages Forum; or through Planning Gain, as already mentioned.

New proposals are currently being considered for changing the Section 106 planning gain process. The Government is concerned that the current system is unfair, works on an 'ad hoc' basis and is lacking in transparency. Agreements may take a long time to negotiate and involve unnecessarily high legal costs. This can frustrate or delay development and even cause it to be abandoned. In response, the Government proposed a 'standardized tariff system' whereby local authorities set tariffs for different development types through the plan-making process. Such an approach is considered to be more transparent and speedier, as it would be based on standard contractual terms. Local authorities would have the discretion to determine the type, size and location of development on which a tariff would be charged and how it would apply in different circumstances. Tariffs may be set on a cost per gross floorspace basis for both commercial and residential development; on a cost per dwelling basis for residential development and gross floor-space for commercial; or as a proportion of the development value. The Government also proposes to legislate to enable local authorities to pool contributions from tariffs for use towards the delivery of significant development infrastructure. In addition, local authorities who so wish could work within a sub-regional framework, to avoid undercutting each other in order to lure attractive investment.

CASE STUDY: FINANCING DEVELOPMENT THROUGH THE PRIVATE FINANCE INITIATIVE

For the past decade the Private Finance Initiative (PFI) has become one of the British Government's main instruments for developing higher quality and more effective public services. It aims to bring the private sector more directly into the provision of public services, with the public sector as an enabler and, where appropriate, guardian of the interests of the users of public services.[13] PFI is not simply about the financing of capital investment in services, but also about exploiting the full range of private sector management, commercial and creative skills. The idea, therefore, is to focus on service rather than on assets, diverting the focus from capital expenditure to long-term revenue expenditure. Ultimately, PFI is about generating greater value for money, by using private sector finance and expertise and by placing risk where it can be best controlled, managed and priced. The transfer of finance and management responsibilities to the private sector limits the liability of the public sector which then becomes the buyer of services.

As a procurement mechanism, PFI also means that the public sector is no longer responsible for the design of specifications, but for specifying

service requirements. It no longer determines the contract, but waits for its prescribed service through the PFI service contract. More importantly, it no longer invests capital over the construction period, but pays for the service on receipt, and only when it is available. The private sector provides the capital cost, which recoups through the payments by the local authority and operating profits. The private sector therefore operates the asset and the public sector monitors service delivery and performance. An example of a PFI scheme is the Nottingham Express Transit (NET) project. At an estimated cost of approximately £200 million, this project is the largest local authority-led PFI scheme to receive government support to date. The PFI route was selected as no other funding mechanism was available for the level of financing required. In the past, similar projects that were procured in more traditional ways left the risk of delays, overruns and cost increases on the public sector. Through the PFI route the NET project has transferred those risks, as well as most financial and contractual risks, to the private sector. This, in theory, protects the local authority from contractor insolvency, abandonment of works, material failure to operate the system in compliance with the output specification, and from failure to complete the project within the defined period after scheduled completion.[14] A further advantage to the promoters of the project is that they only start making payments once the project is available and demonstrates that it fully complies with the output specification. On the other hand, the private sector company operating the project has the incentive to run the project as efficiently as possible, to avoid reductions on the payments made by the local authority.

The main disadvantage of the PFI route is that the private sector can allocate very high costs to the risks involved, thereby increasing the total project cost by approximately 20-30 per cent. This can leave a funding gap between the required payments and the expected revenue support grant from Government, to be covered by the promoters of the scheme. For many public sector organizations, however, the funding gap is less onerous than the cost of maintaining old infrastructures. Other disadvantages of the PFI route is the complexity of the contractual documents which are immensely complicated, time-consuming and extremely expensive. It also has fixed revenue commitments for many years, which could have an impact on other services, if future cuts in expenditure are required.

Development projects for which PFI is likely to be suitable include the replacement or enhancement of schools, prisons, hospitals, leisure facilities and other developments that can be constructed, maintained and operated by finance from the private sector. Infrastructure projects such as roads, bridges, car parks and rail-based schemes currently have the highest profile and consist of 80 per cent of PFI allocations. Other schemes that could be suitable include: street lighting schemes, recycling plants, refuse incinerators, crematoriums, residential homes, community health centres, social service accommodation, housing schemes, regeneration schemes, libraries, police headquarters, and general office accommodation.

The PFI provides new means of procuring services by transferring the risks of construction, funding and operation to the private sector. The process is still in its early stages and will need further refinement. However, it provides opportunities for better value for money for local authorities in a wide range of regeneration projects.

IDENTIFYING SITES

All too often site development and its integration into the surrounding urban structure is limited by individual land holdings. Although local authorities have the power to compulsorily acquire land, this power is rarely used even if there is the prospect of beneficial development. This reluctance to use

Compulsory Purchase Order (CPO) powers arises for the following reasons: local authorities do not have the time to identify a vision for the future of the area and are involved in a great deal of reactive and abortive work; local authorities are under-resourced both in terms of staff for the work involved in processing a CPO and the finance required to actually acquire land; the process is not widely understood in local authorities nor is the legal expertise always available; and finally the process is time consuming.

The difficulties of using CPO procedures usually deter most local authorities. They are therefore encouraged to look at other ways of achieving site development. This may involve either entering into a partnership with developers or seeking planning gain from a development. A compromise may have to be negotiated with developers to make the scheme acceptable to both partners. The resulting compromise may be a development which, although better than may have originally been proposed, does not achieve the environmental quality originally desired by the local authority.

COMPULSORY PURCHASE FOR DEVELOPMENT PURPOSES

The use of compulsory purchase for the purpose of assembling land for development is a complicated process, as outlined above. This section, therefore, aims to assist practitioners in understanding the process required for securing the land where development, re-development or improvements can take place. In most cases, property can be acquired either by agreement or through compulsory acquisition. Compulsory acquisition is the expropriation of private property, usually by Central or Local Government, although in recent years other bodies have been given compulsory purchase powers, particularly following the privatization of statutory undertakers. In theory, compulsory purchase powers should be used only where there is some public benefit to be gained. It is also accepted that the dispossessed property owners should not suffer, since they would receive appropriate compensation.[15] There are some sixty-seven Parliamentary Acts that authorize compulsory purchase, usually by government departments, local authorities and public bodies of various sorts. Plenty of Private Acts authorize acquisition for particular purposes - for example, for light rapid transit projects or to develop local airports. The Transport and Works Act 1992 has provided a faster, alternative, means of acquiring land and reduced the need for Private Bills.[16]

In general, a four-stage process is followed to secure compulsory acquisition. First, there must be statutory authority for the purchase through a Private Act, a Public General Act or a Specific Act, which unequivocally states that land and/or rights may be acquired compulsorily. Second, land that is suitable for the intended purpose must be selected, in general or planning terms, and then clearly referenced parcel by parcel. The reasons for their acquisition should also be clearly and correctly identified. This process gives objectors the opportunity to have their say when a scheme or proposal comes forward for planning permission and before it reaches a public inquiry. Third, having chosen the land, steps must be taken to authorize its acquisition, by making and confirming a compulsory purchase order (CPO) following a public inquiry. In the case of a Public General Act, the confirmation of the order comes from the Secretary of State who notifies the decision to the acquiring authority, the objectors and any other persons who may have appeared at the inquiry. If the order is confirmed, the acquiring authority must publicize such, as soon as possible, in one or more local newspapers and notify all affected parties of the Secretary of State's decision. Assuming the Scheme is not abandoned, this will normally be followed by a 'notice to treat', which must be served on property owners within three years of the confirmation of the order. A 'notice of entry' is then issued to secure possession

of the land. Finally, the price must be agreed, or if disputed, the Lands Tribunal will determine the overall price, including compensation, within six years of entry on the land by the acquiring body.

Compensation in this context has three elements to it, namely the actual value of the land, disturbance compensation, and the reduction in value of the retained land. Such a reduction in value is termed 'injurious affection' due to severance. Compensation is payable to anyone who has had some property interest acquired under compulsion and is generally viewed as a sum of money which should adequately reimburse the affected person for all losses and expenses that have been incurred as a consequence. The person should, by receipt of this compensation, be left in a position after compulsory purchase which is no better or worse than the situation prior to the CPO. In some cases, sites that are strategically located can draw an enhanced 'ransom' value which reflects their role in unlocking development sites by providing access to it.

New proposals for improving Compulsory Purchase procedures were published in July 2002 and the Government announced its intention to replace the current CPO power with a 'wider and more clearly defined power' under which the authority could acquire land for wider purposes. This will apply where it is considered that land will be used for 'economic, social and/or environmental benefit of its area'. This has the inference that regeneration projects can be expected to have a much higher priority and a detailed scheme or financial/implementation plan may not need to be in place before the formal commencement of CPO procedures.

NEGOTIATING DEVELOPMENT

The ideal situation for the development control planner and the developer is where there is already design and planning guidance available for a given site. This advice appears in a number of different places: it can be found in the Local Plan or in the

Master Plan which may also include planning briefs, design briefs, planning frameworks, specific site guidance, city centre action plans, etc. Whatever the title of the document the objective is to give clear ideas about the design requirements for any given site. Such a document will also outline any considerations which the local authority thinks the developer should take into account. Design guidance should not be limited to those areas dictated by the boundaries of land ownership: wherever possible design guidance should cover areas with a cohesive structure and a planning rationale for the boundary. The stronger the guidance the better will be the chance of achieving the objectives outlined in the document. Where clear guidance incorporating good design practice is prescribed for a site, a developer would have to prepare a convincing project which addressed the issues raised by the guidance. When sound design guidance is outlined by a local authority it becomes more difficult for developers to produce mediocre development.

PREPARATION OF DESIGN GUIDANCE

The preparation of design guidance should be started as early as possible and preferably be produced in partnership with landowners and developers. The greatest advantage in adopting this approach to design guidance is that development costs are identified from the start of the development process. The guidance should have a realistic appreciation of land values and the viability of the development proposed. Consultation with developers enables assumptions to be challenged and current economic conditions to be taken into account. Timescales for development are, as a consequence, likely to be more robust. The land price where possible should already reflect the requirements of the local authority before it is put on the market. There is then less opportunity when the land is being sold to a developer for the developer to circumvent the implementation of design

guidance by appealing to the vested interests of either the local authority or the landowner.

The landowner knows the requirements of the local authority from the beginning of the process. This, in theory, enables the land to be marketed and planning permission obtained in a shorter period of time. The early knowledge of the local authority's requirements may also assist in determining the best way to phase the development of a site. For example, there may be expensive infrastructure costs which would suggest that the most lucrative developments be constructed first, perhaps prior to the provision of some other necessary community facilities, in order to finance these less profitable developments later in the process.

When site development guidance is drawn up in advance of serious development negotiations, there is more chance of achieving a strategic approach to regional development, thereby preventing development in a piecemeal and incoherent fashion. Such piecemeal development is often perceptually illegible. There may be the loss of existing landmarks; a blurring of features which distinguish the district from adjacent areas; the development of ill-defined routes without clearly structured node or centre. It is difficult to produce a strategic landscape plan for such featureless areas so that restoring identity and legibility is often a forlorn effort in remedial action.

DEVELOPMENT COSTS

When producing site development guidance (SDG) it is important to build into the guidance the overall idea or vision. A good quality environment will never result from a scheme without a central theme. The guidance should provide an imaginative framework which allows the developer the freedom to develop his own vision. However, this will need to be tempered with a realistic look at the costs of achieving development in accordance with SDG. Table 2.1 provides a list of some of the planning requirements which affect development costs.

Table 2.1 Planning requirements which affect development costs.

Infrastructure
Topography – drainage, sewage and engineering works
Cost of on-site road construction
Cost of off-site road construction
Landscape
Play areas
Contributions to public transport
Affordable housing
Access housing
Community facilities – schools, libraries, community halls, social services
Leisure facilities – sports centre, sports pitches
Sites reserved for places of worship
Building houses to higher energy specifications
Location of local shopping to benefit from passing trade
Retention of existing landscape and ecology
Incorporation of Public Art

It is equally important to understand the effect planning requirements may have on current land values and to appreciate the complex mechanisms for land finance. Clearly it is not in a landowner's interest to be benevolent and suggest anything which would detract from the value of their property. The landowner or developer would be working against their own self-interest if they did not try to reduce costs. Nevertheless, in certain areas land values may be low and compromise made in order to obtain viable site development guidance. There may be planning objectives to meet in accordance with local plan and structure plan development. These considerations, along with other desired planning gain, will have to be prioritized so that the local authority can achieve the most important of its objectives without destroying the viability of site development. When carrying out this type of assessment it is important to realize that

both the landowner and developer will have ongoing costs which increase as time passes and that development will not occur unless both have a reasonable opportunity to make a profit.

There is a tendency for local authorities to be over-optimistic about the potential of a site: some have even been known to seek to impose the same planning requirements on completely different sites. There are, of course, differences in the values of sites; therefore, it is an extremely worthwhile process to understand the factors which affect the commercial value of a site and to make a rough calculation as to the value of the land before starting any negotiation with developer or landowner. Only then is it possible to assess the level of planning gain that is possible on any given site and from that assessment to prioritize the local authority's main requirements.

Land value changes over time and is affected by government legislation and planning policies. At the moment, a greenfield site in a good area will be much easier to develop than a brownfield site. With a reduction in the availability of greenfield sites, brownfield sites could increase in value as the only land with development potential. However, if development requirements are wildly different in neighbouring authorities, investment may be lost to one authority when it becomes cheaper to build elsewhere. The following example illustrates this point: 100 acres of residential land may be worth £230 000 per acre, depending on where the land is located. The land is worth £23 000 000 to the landowner. If an average density of thirteen houses per acre is permitted on the land, and if each house is worth £50 000, this would equal a potential revenue of £650 000 per acre from house sales. Each house may cost £20 000 to construct, totalling £260 000 per acre. The total development cost equals £260 000 plus £230 000, or £490 000, leaving only a total of £160 000 per acre for the house developer (see Table 2.2). The house developer is therefore going to be extremely resistant to further burdens imposed by the local authority.

Table 2.2 Housebuilding on 100 acres of land.

Cost per acre	£230 000
Total cost of 100 acres	£23 000 000
Density thirteen houses per acre	
Construction cost per house	£20 000
Construction cost per acre	£260 000
Total construction cost	£26 000 000
Total cost to housebuilder	£49 000 000
Site value of house	£50 000
Value of 1300 houses	£65 000 000
Total profit for housebuilder	£16 000 000
Profit per acre	£160 000

Table 2.3 Landowner's profit, sale of 100 acres of land.

Sale 100 acres at £230 000	£23 000 000
Costs to landowner	
Tax at 40 per cent	£9 200 000
Ten acres open space	£2 300 000
Drainage and engineering works	£5 000 000
Affordable housing	£3 000 000
Primary school	£1 500 000
Contribution to public transport	£200 000
Leisure facilities	£1 000 000
Public art	£500 000
Total	£22 700 000
Net profit to landowner	£300 000 or £3000 per acre

Land values are readily affected by market forces and will reflect conditions in the neighbouring district. Land values will also reflect house prices which, in turn, are affected by the location of facilities, such as schools, in the area, together with the proximity of any existing or proposed affordable housing. It may, therefore, be more sensible for planning requirements to be negotiated before development is contemplated and at a time when the landowner is achieving high land values because of local plan proposals. It is at this stage that any betterment for the community can be realistically contemplated.

This demonstration can be taken a step further to show the effects of planning requirements on profit margins and ultimately on the viability of the project. For example, within the 100 acres of land the local authority may require ten acres of public open space and children's play areas as a matter of policy in the local plan. This will result in the reduction of £2 300 000 in the eventual profit for the landowner, as this land can no longer be used for house construction. Drainage and sewerage and engineering works may cost a further £5 million. The local authority may require up to 30 per cent of the whole development for affordable housing. This will reduce the value of the land for the affordable housing and also the adjacent land will be affected by the proximity of the affordable housing. This may affect the land value, in this case by £3 million. The cost of constructing a primary school may be £1.5 million and contributions to establish public transport may be approximately £200 000, depending on service provision in the area. Leisure and community facilities may cost a further £1 million, depending on requirements, while Public Art and improving the urban quality may add a further £500 000. Accepting the original figure of £23 000 000 for the cost of the land and deducting 40 per cent tax at £9 200 000 leaves a profit of £13 800 000 for the landowner. However, the rough planning requirements outlined above amount to £13 500 000 leaving the landowner with a net profit of £300 000. This is equivalent to the approximate value of the 100 acres of land for agricultural use. It is therefore unlikely that in the scenario outlined above the landowner would be interested in developing the land. If, however, the drainage and engineering works are only going to be £3 000 000 and the local authority requires only five acres of open space, the landowner may then achieve £3 450 000, or £34 500 per acre, which may make the scheme viable (see Table 2.3).

There are other costs and requirements associated with development but the above demonstration is used purely to show that the planning requirements for development can and do impact on whether a site is viable for development. If the local authority planning and urban design team is supported by professionals that will carry out land valuations and assessments of development costs the negotiating ability of the local authority will be much stronger. Formal valuation methods are outlined below. Developers should be aware of the constraints under which local authorities work and understand their role and obligation to secure betterment resulting from planning for the community. Negotiations carried out with a knowledge of the other's bargaining position are more likely to lead to a negotiated development programme which satisfies the objectives of all the actors in the process.

VALUATION TECHNIQUES

The Concise Oxford Dictionary defines valuation as the 'estimation of a thing's worth'. The worth estimate of major redevelopment depends on factors such as the balance of supply and demand, potential users, economic and social conditions of the area, infrastructure and accessibility, environmental quality, and land availability. These factors will have a significant impact on the price of major redevelopment.[17]

In the past, valuation has often been seen as a somewhat esoteric discipline. However, the Mallinson Report on commercial property valuations commissioned in 1994 by the Royal Institution of Chartered Surveyors[18] recommended greater 'transparency' in the use of methods and techniques in valuation practices. Methods of valuation differ significantly. Underlying each of them is the need to make comparisons, since this is the essential ingredient in arriving at a market value. In general, financial returns will be the dominant consideration in undertaking schemes. Developments will be promoted when and where the realizable value from the finished project exceeds total costs and leaves sufficient margin for profit on sale, or adequate income return when the investment is retained.

The simplest and most direct approach in arriving at a value is to compare the object to be valued with the prices obtained for other similar projects. This technique works best if the comparable objects are identical. The technique is limited to the simplest cases as development schemes can never be absolutely identical. Another simple and straightforward conventional technique is the residual valuation method. In this method, the total development costs are deducted from the estimated value of the completed development to establish the development potential of a project and whether it produces an adequate rate of return. The return is measured either in terms of trading profit (value over expenditure) or in terms of an investment yield.[19]

In the example in Table 2.4, the residual figure represents the value of the development in its unimproved state, reflecting the development potential. This simple residual valuation method is dependent on many variables such as land prices, building cost, accommodation costs, rent/prices, interest rates, investment yields and time. Numerous inaccu-

Table 2.4 Assessment of value by the residual method

1. Estimate the gross development value. This will be the value of the development after it has been undertaken.
2. Estimate the total cost of development.
3. Subtract the cost of development from the gross development value. This will leave a residual figure.

Gross development value:	£200 000
Less: Total cost of development:	£130 000
Residual figure of value:	£70 000

racies may occur during this process. Some of the weaknesses can be overcome by using other development appraisal techniques such as cashflow method; discounted cashflow methods (NTV/NPV)*; sensitivity analysis; scenario analysis; and probability and simulation. The cashflow method forecasts the amount of cash expected to flow into and out of a project over a prescribed period of time. The cashflow appraisal enables the flow of expenditure and revenue to be spread over the period of the development, presenting a more realistic and accurate assessment of development costs and income against time.

Alternatively, the NPV approach can be used. The NPV approach discounts all costs and income to present-day equivalents to establish the value of the profit today rather that at the end of the development.[20] The discount rate used is the cost of borrowing the money and the formula used to convert cost and values to the present day is the 'Present Value of £1', which is $1/(1+i)^n$. The advantages of this discounted cashflow technique is that it allows the calculation of the internal rate of return (IRR), which is the measure used by some developers to assess the profitability of a scheme opposed to a percentage return of cost, especially if the developer is to retain the development within their portfolio. The IRR can be defined as the percentage discounted rate used in capital investment appraisal which brings the cost of a project and its future cashflow into equity. To calculate the IRR, the discount rate is varied by trial and error to the rate, which will discount all the future costs and income back to a present value of 0.

The residual valuation, as well as the cashflow method, relies upon a set of fixed variables, which are presented as selected 'best estimates' without giving a true impression of the range from which they have been selected. These 'best estimates' can alter individually during the development, either in similar or different directions, and so a combination of these changes can cause large variations in the residual value. These variations can be assessed through a number of methods that vary in their sophistication. These are sensitivity analysis, scenarios, and probability/simulations.[21]

Sensitivity analysis is the procedure for testing the effect of variability. The most basic sensitivity analysis will show how different changes in each variable separately affect the residual value, indicating how sensitive the profit margin or site value bid is, and which changes can exert the greatest change on the scheme's viability. It also allows assessment of the likelihood of a break-even occurring. However, its main disadvantage is the failure to consider the rather more likely occurrence of combinations of variables changing simultaneously rather than in isolation, and the probability of these changes coming about.

The scenarios approach involves an examination of how a combination of changes in the variables of an appraisal affects the residual value. At least three scenarios would normally be examined – optimistic, realistic and pessimistic. Professional judgment is crucial in this approach in order to select reasonable estimates regarding variables and market conditions. Although this approach is more advanced than simple sensitivity testing, it is still a 'hypothecation' of the future and the problems of forecasting probability remain.

The final technique to be considered is probability/simulation analysis. This approach involves the construction of a full range of possible values for each variable, from extremely pessimistic to extremely optimistic and estimating the probability of each occurring. A Monte Carlo simulation, which, through its true randomness approach, can allow detailed comparison of different scenarios, can identify similar residual values for a combination of variables, allowing a pattern of returns and their chances of occurrence to build up. This simulation approach provides a lot of information about profitability and also enables alternative schemes to

---

*Net Terminal Value/Net Present Value.

be examined in greater detail, thereby encouraging an informed decision.

It is recognized above that the residual valuation technique can be a very crude and inaccurate method, especially if no comparative information exists. The inaccuracy in the calculation of interest costs can be overcome by using any of the cashflow techniques, including the NPV approach. However, all the methods discussed only produce a residual figure, based on best estimates at the date of the evaluation, which hides the true uncertainty of the outcome of the development. Sensitivity and probability analysis, including a thorough analysis of underlying market conditions, improves the assessment of uncertainty and risk. In the final analysis, all the above methods assist, but do not replace, a balanced and informed decision-making process. Hence, the selection of the best strategy is the responsibility of those participating in the process.

SECURING DEVELOPMENT

The main mechanisms for achieving planning gain are either by the use of a Section 106 agreement as outlined in the Town and Country Planning Act or by planning conditions attached to a planning approval.[22] A Section 106 agreement will always be required for planning gain related to off-site works such as road improvements. It is also possible to use negatively worded conditions to ensure a circumstance before development commences. This is known as a Grampian type condition. It has become known as this since it was given the approval of the House of Lords in the case of *Grampian* (1984).[23]

Grampian Regional Council applied for planning permission to carry out industrial development. As the City of Aberdeen failed to determine the application within the required period, the application was deemed to be refused. However, on appeal it was stated that the application would have been approved if the development had not resulted in unacceptable traffic danger at a road junction outside the site. A condition to require the closing of part of the road would have been invalid as it may have been beyond the powers of the applicant. The decision upholding the refusal of permission was challenged on the ground that while a condition requiring the road to be closed would have been invalid for unreasonableness, a condition could have been imposed to the effect that development was NOT to commence until the road in question had been closed. Compliance with a negative condition is within the control of an applicant and is therefore enforceable by a local authority.[24]

Optimistic assumptions are often made about the powers of the local authority to develop its own land. The public may assume that the planning authority will be able to achieve its main design criteria and all the facilities required to make the development work. However, those in charge of the city council's finance have a duty to make as much money for the local authority as possible, which may mean that one department ends up in very difficult negotiations with several other departments. The department responsible for planning and urban design will be seeking to obtain the best possible design and benefits for the local community and to be consistent with the approach taken with private landowners. This problem is becoming more apparent as local authority budgets are less able to respond to the full range of local community wishes.

DESIGN BRIEF CONTENT

Once basic planning requirements are established, planning negotiations enter a different level. A design concept should already have been established for the site, and the local authority should be developing and detailing the concept with the relevant parties. All new development is expected to provide variety and choice for people. 'A comprehensive urban design policy, spelling out the full range of design considerations that are important in a locality is important as the cornerstone of all design policies.'[25] The design brief should consider the following main subject areas: means of access by road and by other modes of transport; the relationship of the pedestrian, cyclist and the car; safety in the public realm; quality of design in street and public square including notes on achieving vitality and permeability; the identity and legibility of place; features of sustainable development; and open space and landscape strategy.

Until quite recently great emphasis has been placed on designing for the car. Highway engineers concerned to minimize road accidents have influenced site layout considerably, by their insistence on separating the movement of cars from that of people. As a result, it is not permitted for houses to front main highways because the drives to those houses would create too many potential accident spots, given the speed for which the highways are designed.

In certain authorities such as Leicester there are proposals to slow traffic throughout the road system. Preference is now being given to other modes of transport and the dominance of the car is being reduced in the design of urban areas. For example, Leicester City Council is trying to ensure that all new development is within 200 m of a public transport route, in response to Design Bulletin 32. In addition 20 mph traffic zones are being introduced in residential layouts. The process of negotiating new residential road standards with highway engineers however, is relatively new, and many highway engineers remain to be convinced of this new orthodoxy.

In the public domain it is essential to consider how a development can be made as safe as possible by ensuring that public places are overlooked and that users feel comfortable using the streets by any mode of transport. The police have, until recently, concentrated on the home as a defended place so that housing has often turned its back on public places, so making people feel that they are unwelcome unless they actually live in the neighbourhood.

Defining private and public spaces in design terms is essential in order to reduce the perceived fear of crime. This is possible by improving the quality of public spaces and by encouraging more people to use the streets, thus increasing natural surveillance. This should also be effective in creating a more vibrant atmosphere on city streets. Access considerations in urban areas need to emphasize the value of permeability and easy movement for the elderly, women, children and the disabled. Public Art policies also play a valuable role in creating a vibrant city and have their place in the design brief.

The Urban Design movement has been much influenced by the work of both Cullen and Lynch and a return to city legibility as an aim of design policy.[26] There is now a clear consensus amongst urban designers that development should aim to create a sense of place and community. A legible development can also be created by the emphasis given to paths, landmarks, nodes, edges and districts. There should be a clear design strategy for the use of materials, colours, and building heights to strengthen features which give identity to the quarter or district.[27]

Open space provision should be closely linked with conservation and should be designated before the housing layout is attempted. A greater emphasis is being placed on street trees and the greening of the street, all of which may have maintenance and management implications for the local authority; it may also have cost implications for developers. Nevertheless, these are important considerations for the design brief.

It is argued in this book that all development should be sustainable development. See Moughtin (1996)[28] for a fuller treatment of this subject but this section of the design brief would include the topics shown in Table 2.5.

The emphasis being placed on good design may take a variety of forms but all such supplementary planning guidance should be cross-referenced to establish policy and be in accordance with it. An area of concern for the design brief will be a desire

Table 2.5 Topics for sustainable development.

Mixed land uses
Local access to facilities
Transport choice opportunities, i.e. foot, cycle
routes, buses, light rapid transit
Water conservation
Energy conservation
Nature conservation
Long-life developments
Adaptable buildings for flexible land use
Building height restriction
Brownfield sites

---

to link new developments with existing urban structure. The ways of making these connections should form a major theme of the design brief. The structure and content of the design brief may take a variety of forms but its main aim should be to stimulate good urban design, not to restrict imaginative or innovative development.

CASE STUDY IN NORTHEAST LEICESTER

A planning brief was produced for a district centre site in 1990. This was in accordance with the Hamilton Local Plan[29] and the soon-to-be-adopted City of Leicester Local Plan.[30] The District Centre site provided for 9700 m² of retail floorspace to serve the community of Hamilton, which is a greenfield development of 4000 dwellings. Progress on this development, which was to meet the needs of the expanding Leicester population, had been constrained because of the development of a controversial road infrastructure.

The development was slow owing to the economic recession in the housing market. The developers started negotiations with a very basic scheme in 1995, claiming that the planning brief was out of date and that retailing had moved on since 1990. The developers stated the scheme was in accordance with the basic remit of the outline

planning permission. Analysis of the scheme suggested that little or no attention was given to the layout or to the planning of the development in relation to the adjacent residential areas. The outline planning application had been renewed on a number of occasions and permitted 10 200 m² of retail floorspace. This allowed for a superstore, four larger shop units, a public house, a doctor's surgery and a petrol station.

After several meetings and intense negotiations, it was clear the developer was unwilling at this point to amend the scheme in any substantial way. Further design guidance relating to the layout was also provided. Internally, officers debated the issues and came to the conclusion that the application should be resisted for a number of reasons, particularly because of the poor layout and poor design. There was the threat from the applicant of an appeal against the local authority. The decision was taken that the City Council should not be promoting or permitting a scheme which was of such poor design quality. This decision was relayed to the applicant who after consideration placed the application in abeyance rather than obtain a refusal. This approach reserved the applicant's right to reactivate the planning application and later to lodge an appeal.

A fresh application for full planning permission was then submitted in February 1997 by the developers and negotiations were restarted. This is known as twin tracking an application. It is a device often used by applicants to increase the pressure on the local authority. The applicant was also concerned about the length of time taken by the negotiation. Central Government places a great emphasis on encouraging local authorities to determine an application within eight weeks which, if the development is complicated, may lead on occasion to less than satisfactory schemes.

The scheme was developed in line with the further guidance already provided. The revised scheme included direct cycle-path links to continue already existing green routes through new residential development; internal bus stops to enable permeability and mobility for all users; land reserved for community facilities in the position easiest to reach by local residents; seven shops suggested to enclose an entrance square containing features of art by locally commissioned artists, so bringing life and vitality into the public realm. The applicant's modified scheme was supported. The car park was to be screened from the majority of residential properties by buildings which overlook the main road and provide natural surveillance. Links were provided to the District Centre via a pedestrian and cyclist bridge, together with footpaths related to pedestrian desire lines to promote ease of access. A doctor's surgery, petrol filling station and public house were also indicated on the plan. A concession was made to the applicant by permitting the inclusion of a non-food retail store. This was, however, in keeping with the Central Leicestershire Retail Strategy which had been adopted in February 1997. Even with the non-food retail store the total amount of retail floorspace did not exceed the agreed 10 200 m^2.

Over fifty planning conditions were attached to the document giving planning consent to ensure satisfactory development. Two negatively worded, or Grampian type, conditions were utilized to enable the development to obtain planning permission but also to ensure that the necessary road infrastructure was in place before the development was started. These conditions prevented the District Centre from being started until contracts for a link road had been agreed and signed, so preventing the main food store from opening until such time as the link road was open to traffic. This device enabled the conclusion of protracted negotiations between landowners in the area over the funding of this road.

This was the first stage of development and a robust approach was subsequently taken to withstand amendments to the scheme throughout the construction process. The scheme has now been implemented. The link road was constructed and the retail store has been functioning for a number of years. The public art and public realm have all been provided as agreed in the negotiations. There are still some remaining units to be developed and further community uses are still awaited.

CONCLUSIONS

There is a strong requirement for establishing development frameworks and site development guidance. A framework should encourage variety and be capable of accommodating a range of development interests. The intention of guidance is to encourage and guide development, not to stifle the creativity of the designer or to thwart the economic needs of the developer. The development framework should enable the developer and his designers to prepare the scheme's programme of land uses and floorspace requirements together with a concept for development.

Raising the quality of new development, however, also requires vision and innovation by local authorities. Local authorities need to be innovative in their use of development control powers to influence positively the design of the city, its quarters and places. Conventional approaches to development control may need to be reconsidered in the light of the need for discussion, negotiation and agreement between landowner, developer and the local authority. From such discussions, realistic project goals based on sound financial planning can be formulated as a basis for innovative urban design.

REFERENCES

1   Stone, A. (1997) The New Essex Design Guide, *Urban Design Quarterly*, No. 62, pp. 31-35.

2   Association of Chief Police Officers, Project and Design Group (1994) *Secured by Design*, Stafford: Embassey Press Ltd.

3 Turner, T. (1992) Wilderness and plenty: construction and deconstruction, *Urban Design Quarterly*, No. 44, pp. 20-23.

4 Department of the Environment, *Planning Policy Guidance, Transport, PPG13* (1994), *Planning Policy Guidance, PPG6, Town Centres and Retail Development* (1993) and *Planning Policy Guidance, PPG1, General Policies and Principles* (1997) London: HMSO.

5. DTLR (2000) Urban White Paper, *Our Town and Cities: The Future in 2000.*

6. DTLR (2001) *Green Spaces, Better Places.* Interim report of The Urban Green Spaces Taskforce.

7. ODPM (2002) *Living Places - Cleaner, Safer, Greener.*

8. ODPM (2002) Circular: *The Town and Country Planning (Residential Density) (London and South East England) Direction.*

9. John Prescott (2002), *Urban Summit*, 31 October.

10 English Partnerships (1996) *Time for Design, Good Practice in Building, Landscape and Urban Design*, London: English Partnerships.

11. *Regeneration and Renewal Magazine*, pp. 16-17, 14 June 2002.

12. CABE and ODPM (2002) *Breaking Down the Barriers.*

13. Rook, P. (1998) *Development Finance and Appraisal*, Reading: College of Estate Management.

14. Turner, R. (1997) *The Commercial Project Manager*, New York: McGraw-Hill.

15. Telling, A.E. *et al.* (1993) *Planning Law and Procedure*, London: Butterworths Law.

16. Roots, G. (Ed.) (1999) *Butterworths Compulsory Purchase and Compensation Service*, London: Butterworths Law.

17. Britton, W. *et al* .(1980) Modern methods of valuation, *The Estates Gazette.*

18. The Royal Institution of Chartered Surveyors (1994) *The Mallinson Report on Commercial Property Valuations.*

19. Darlow, C. and Morely, S. (1982) New views on development appraisal, *Estates Gazette*, Vol. 262.

20. D.J. Freeman Solicitors (1995) *The Language of Property Finance*, British Council for Offices.

21. Palmer, C. (1997) *Management Sciences*, Reading: College of Estate Management.

22 Department of the Environment (1990) *Town and Country Planning Act: 1990*, London: HMSO.

23 *Grampian Regional Council* v. *City of Aberdeen District Council* (1984).

24 Healey, P., Purdue, M. and Ennis, F. (1995) *Negotiating Development*, London: E. & F.N. Spon.

25 Punter, J., Carmona, M. and Platts, A. (1994) Design policies in development plans, *Urban Design Quarterly*, No. 51, pp. 1-15.

26 Lynch, K. (1960) *The Image of the City*, Cambridge, MA: MIT Press, and Cullen, G. (1961) *Townscape*, London: Architectural Press.

27 Moughtin, J.C. (1995) *Urban Design: Ornament and Decoration*, Oxford: Butterworth-Heinemann.

28 Moughtin, J.C. (1996) *Urban Design: Green Dimensions*, Oxford: Butterworth-Heinemann.

29 Leicester City Council, Planning Department (1990) *Hamilton District Planning Brief*, Leicester: Leicester City Council.

30 Leicester City Council, Planning Department (1994) *City of Leicester, Local Plan*, Leicester: Leicester City Council.

SURVEY TECHNIQUES

3

INTRODUCTION

The survey techniques used in site analysis depend upon the nature and scale of the project. The information which is necessary to complete the preparation of a design for a small infill site is quite different from that required for an investigation of inner city regeneration proposals. This chapter will outline survey techniques used in moderate- to large-scale projects; it will omit reference to small street improvements and projects for single buildings on individual sites. The techniques outlined here aim to build an analytical framework for the delivery of sustainable development which is the underlying theme of this book. A book of this size cannot cover survey techniques for all aspects of sustainable development but concentrates on the conservation of cultural identity and of the built environment. The first part of the chapter deals with historical analysis so important as a basis for conservation and for the promotion of ideas compatible with a developing culture. The second part of the chapter discusses townscape analysis including urban legibility, permeability and visual analysis.

HISTORICAL ANALYSIS

Understanding the *genius loci* is a good starting point when beginning study of the site. The sensitive perception of the spirit or nature of a place often provides the key to charting the direction for future development. Peeling back the layers of history which encrust the modern city reveals the reasons for its present form and function. Knowing 'how that which is came to be' is a sound basis for future action. The richness of the urban realm is the product of a long process of historical development. The drabness of much late twentieth-century development is, in part, the product of a rather childish attitude commonly held by city designers, which treated history as irrelevant for 'modern development'. In the recent past the ideal platform for city development was considered to be the uninterrupted site cleared of all former traces of occupation.

'Peeling back the layers of history' is one of those ringing expressions which can have many meanings. It can mean, simply, the examination of an early ordnance survey map in order to determine

Figure 3.1 Radford. A return to a street architecture after demolition of 1960s deck access flats.

the scale of urban grain prior to a faceless development in the 1960s. After the demolition of the unwanted development it is possible, using the information from the ordnance survey to restore the site to something resembling its former richness of street patterning (Figures 3.1 and 3.2). Even the most perfunctory site analysis would include an investigation of those structures of historic or architectural interest. If the site has an ancient history the study may include a detailed archaeological investigation. More simply, it may identify those buildings, trees and other structures which have been listed for protection, including sites of scientific or ecological interest. The analysis of the site and its history would conclude with a study of more recent pressures on the urban structure, which would include an analysis of recent planning

documents in order to determine those policies which currently affect development on the site. It may also be relevant to identify those ideas and suggestions for development which, for one reason or another, have not been implemented. An understanding of the reasons for inactivity in the area may provide the key for choosing a successful form of development in keeping with its history and function. As a part of this study of contemporary pressures on the site an analysis should be made of all recent planning applications which completes the picture of the site and its potential for development.

Great works of urban design develop over many generations. The Piazza del Popolo as a major entrance to Rome, dates from AD 272 when the Porta del Popolo, gateway to the square, was built

Figure 3.2 Radford. A
return to a street
architecture after demolition
of 1960s deck access flats.

into the Aurelian wall at this place in the city's
defence. The piazza was repeatedly reformed and
remodelled by succeeding generations, the role of
the Papacy being of particular importance in
maintaining a fine tradition of urban architecture in
Rome throughout Medieval times and into the
Renaissance. Valadier gave this great entrance to
Rome its final form as seen today, with its twin
churches by Rainaldi, central obelisk and hemicycles
or sweeping exedra to east and west.[1] Bacon
stresses the role of the second designer in the development of any great work of urban design.[2] It is the
second person involved in a project who, according
to Bacon, determines if the design forces set in
motion by the initiator are achieved, developed and
enhanced, or destroyed. It is the second designer
who has to forgo his or her own egotistical instincts

in order to develop the vision of another. Bacon
cites the development of the Piazza Annunziata in
Florence as a model for the selfless behaviour of the
second designer. Brunelleschi set in motion the
development of this great square, in the form we
know it, when he built the Ospedale degli
Innocenti. Sangallo the Elder, ninety years after the
death of Brunelleschi, completed the opposite side
of the square repeating in almost exact detail the
hospital arcade.[3]

The actions of the second designer involved in an
urban development are clearly critical in the evolution of a masterpiece of civic design: his or her role
is of great significance. In addition, however, the
supporting roles of all those concerned in urban
development, if quality is to be maintained, should
not be underestimated. Our cities are the product of

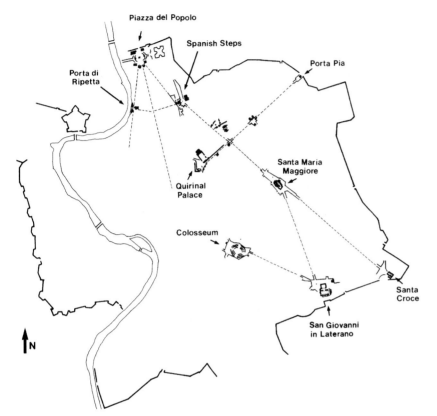

Figure 3.3 The planning of Rome by Sixtus V.

the actions of countless individuals and groups: it is, therefore incumbent on all engaged in this long communal process of urban design to appreciate and understand the forces which have formed the environment and to distinguish clearly those structures which give direction to future development. A basic survey of the history of the site is a standard procedure for any urban design project. These standard procedures have already been outlined; following them gives a sensitive designer much to stimulate the thought process. However, an understanding of the design forces, the almost natural and self-evident structuring components, requires greater effort than the automatic implementation of a set of standard survey procedures. It requires the understanding of the historic forces which continue to pattern development. Understanding these forces enables each designer to perform effectively the critical role of the 'second person'.

Completing the items on the basic check list of studies for site history outlined earlier is fundamental for any urban design project. A rational analysis should go further: it would include an examination of the main form-giving components of city development. These studies involve the examination of the

Figure 3.4 S. Maria Maggiore, Rome.

fundamental geographical reasons for settlement formation, including topography, geology, soils and drainage; the dominant axes of development, including lay lines and vistas of symbolic importance; dominant buildings of historic significance; focal points of activity; movement patterns of ancient origin, including processional routes; changing seats of power and influence; changing economic patterns as evidenced by the ebb and flow of land values, the density of development, building conditions and their occupation; the patterns of population intrusion, invasion and succession; and finally, the developing patterns of functional areas in relation to changing modes of transport.

An example of urban development structured by ancient lines of movement is the transformation of Rome by Pope Sixtus V and his architect Fontana

Figure 3.5 The Spanish Steps, Rome.

Figure 3.6 Chester.

Figure 3.7 Chester.

Figure 3.8 Chester.

3.7

3.8

between 1585 and 1590. The technique used to create the framework of the city plan from the chaos of Medieval Rome was the long vista. Using wide, straight roads he connected the seven main churches, the holy shrines which had to be visited by pilgrims in the course of a day. The lines of the traffic web of a modern city were first formulated here in Rome by Sixtus V, based upon a long-established set of pilgrim pathways.[4] Each great axial street terminated at one of the centres of pilgrimage and at these points of enhanced activity were raised obelisks originally brought from Egypt during Ancient Roman times when the city rulers

dominated the Mediterranean world. It was these ancient lines of pilgrimage which structured Rome for succeeding centuries, providing the base for real estate development along their lengths. They still act as a patterning device for the tourist, the modern pilgrim to Rome (Figures 3.3 to 3.5).

City street patterns continue to govern urban form long after their original *raison d'etre* has ceased to exist. Many fine European city centres owe their foundation and current grid pattern to a Roman origin dating from the early centuries of the first millennium AD. Chester is a particularly fine example of such a city centre. Chester retained its

Figure 3.9 Isle of Dogs, The Greenwich Axis.

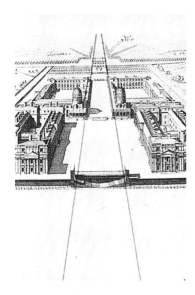

Figure 3.10 Greenwich.

Figure 3.11 St Ann's Church, Limehouse.

Roman grid structure through the period of urban decline in the Dark Ages to be reborn in Medieval times and given its delightful half-timbered two-storey shopping arcade built largely upon its Roman street lines. Chester is a particularly good example of a city which owes its existence and current economic well-being to a living tradition of conserving the best from the past and building intelligently upon this fine legacy (Figures 3.6 to 3.8). Gosling attempted to structure development in the Isle of Dogs, London, using the lay line or axis connecting The Queen's House by Inigo Jones in Greenwich to St Ann's Church by Hawksmoor in Limehouse. The axis so formed was intended to be a structuring line, giving definition to this section of the Dockland's regeneration. Unfortunately, this proposal was never implemented and the opportunity to stamp the area with a discipline generated by a sensitive appreciation of this magnificent location and its history was lost (Figures 3.9 to 3.12).[5]

Development in Nottingham during the 1960s and 1970s illustrates a misdirection of urban structure which resulted in part from an application of principles of architectural and planning design associated with 'modernism'. The almost total disregard for Nottingham's urban form which had developed over a long history has resulted in areas of the city in need of attention and repair, or as Alexander says, 'in need of healing' (Figures 3.13 to 3.16).[6] The fate of Nottingham mirrors developments of the time in other British and European cities. The main geographical and historic structuring elements of Nottingham remain evident today. Two main factors determined the siting of Nottingham. The River Trent on which the city is sited was navigable and easily fordable. Bunter sandstone coinciding broadly

Figure 3.12 St Ann's Church, Limehouse.

with Sherwood Forest terminates abruptly in a river-cut cliff, about two miles long and overlooking the Trent flood plain. The earliest settlement stood on the highest point of this cliff, a sandstone spur with good defence on three sides. The city has the physical remains of two ancient settlements which were sited on the defensive sandstone spur. The former Saxon settlement, or Anglian Burh, centred on the area now known as the Lace Market is to the east of the city centre and the former Norman Borough to the west of the centre was planted on Castle Rock, the most impregnable site in the area (Figures 3.17 and 3.18).[7] The two settlements were unified administratively probably from the twelfth century, symbolized by the development of Market Square, known locally as 'Slab Square'. Around the large triangular square has grown the nucleus of the town centre. The Norman and Saxon centres were, and to some extent are still, connected to each other and to Market Square by a series of narrow Medieval streets such as Castle Gate, Hounds Gate and Bridle Smith Gate (Figures 3.19 to 3.21). Nottingham, unlike many other British cities, is physically separated from its main river. The much smaller River Leen was diverted in the thirteenth century to run beneath the Castle Rock but never became a major trade carrier. It was not until the opening of the canal in the 1790s and the building of a series of warehouses along its length that there was pressure for the centre to move southwards. The early rail network ran round the outside of the built-up area of the town (Figure 3.22).[8] The easiest route into Nottingham at the time of railway expansion was on the south side of the town across the Meadows; the entry point being south of Carrington Street on the edge of the built-up area. Nottingham's Victoria Station to the north of the city was opened in 1901. It served The Great Central and The Great Northern routes. The Great Central Line through the heart of Nottingham connecting The Victoria Station and The Midland Station, which was rebuilt on a grander scale in 1903/1904, was finally and short-sightedly closed by Beeching in 1967. Despite the

Figure 3.13 Maid Marion Way, Nottingham.

Figure 3.14 Entrance to The Victoria Shopping Centre, Nottingham.

Figure 3.15 Entrance to
The Victoria Shopping
Centre, Nottingham.

Figure 3.16 Entrance to
The Victoria Shopping
Centre, Nottingham.

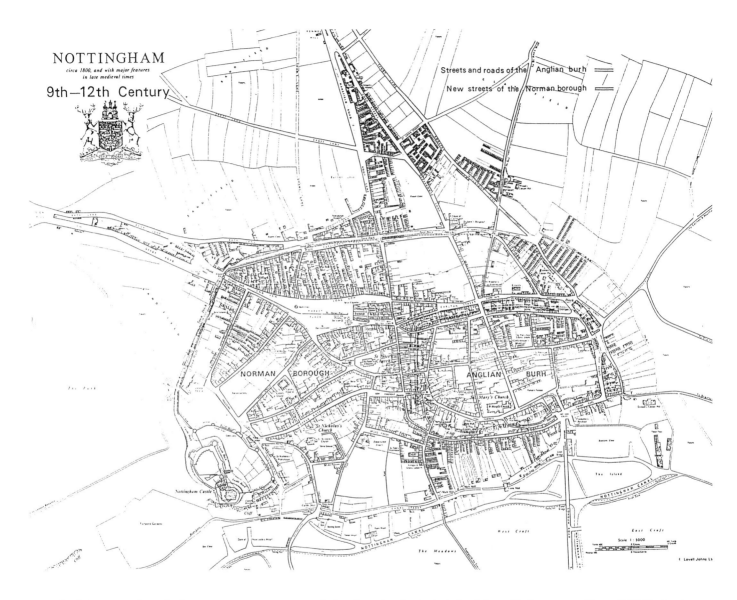

NOTTINGHAM
circa 1800, and with major features in late medieval times

9th–12th Century

Streets and roads of the Anglian burh
New streets of the Norman borough

NORMAN BOROUGH

ANGLIAN BURH

St Peter's Church

St Mary's Church

St Nicholas's Church

Nottingham Castle

NOTTINGHAM CANAL

The Meadows

Scale 1 : 5000

© Lovell Johns Ltd

Figure 3.17 Medieval Nottingham.

growth of the city early in the last century, Nottingham remained focused on Market Square until the more recent post-World War Two developments.[9]

Maid Marian Way, begun in 1959 and completed in the late 1960s, was built to accommodate the motor car. It cuts across the Medieval street pattern radiating from the Castle, isolating it from Market Square and the Lace Market area. Two major commercial developments, Victoria Centre in the north and the Broadmarsh in the south, were built to provide additional shopping floorspace. Both encourage shopping by car, providing multi-storey

43

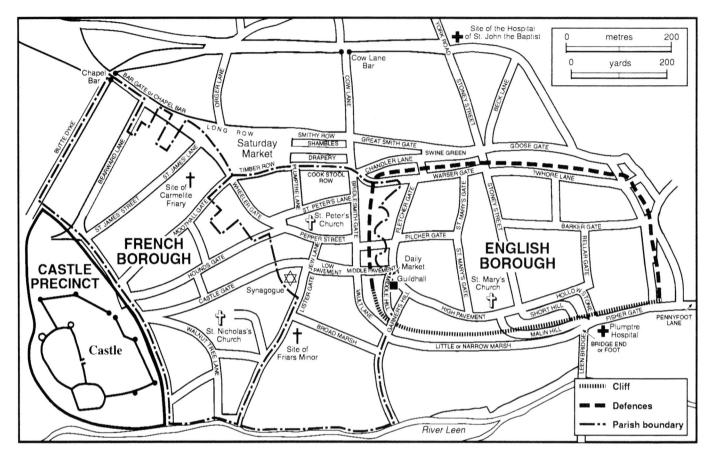

Figure 3.18 Medieval Nottingham.

car parking facilities. The developments extended the centre along a north–south axis reducing the viability of shopping in the vicinity of Market Square and the Lace Market. The massive gyratory road system associated with the southern shopping pole, Broadmarsh, virtually cut off the direct pedestrian connection between the city's main rail entry point and its heart at Market Square. (Figures 3.23 and 3.24). These three developments of the 1960s and 1970s, Maid Marian Way, Victoria Centre and Broadmarsh, together with the accompanying facilities for the motor car, are totally out of scale with the grain of the city and must be classed amongst the ugliest urban developments in Europe. The

commercial and symbolic heart of the city was further damaged by moving the market to the Victoria Centre and by the building of 'edge of town' developments such as Castle Marina, about a mile from Market Square, together with a number of large commercial and retail 'out of town' developments (Figures 3.25 to 3.27).

An interesting transport planning experiment was carried out in Nottingham during the 1970s. A restraining collar was placed round the city centre, the purpose of which was to control the numbers of private cars entering the city centre while giving bus movements priority. Influenced by the change to a Conservative-controlled local authority in

Figure 3.19 Castle Gate, Nottingham.

Figure 3.20 Castle Gate, Nottingham.

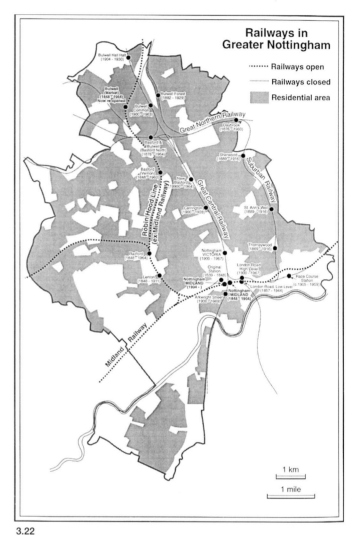

3.21

3.22

Figure 3.21 Bridle Smith Gate, Nottingham.

Figure 3.22 The Nottingham rail network prior to Beeching.

Nottingham and the later Thatcher years in Central Government, forward-looking experiments, such as that at Nottingham and the Greater London Council's policies for subsidized transport fares, were abandoned. Until very recently, making provision for the motor car has dominated transport planning driven by the philosophy that the market knows best. The simple belief was that de-control of buses together with the building of more roads would solve urban transport problems. There is now a growing awareness of the need to reduce the consumption of the finite stock of fossil fuel and to reduce the levels of pollution, including greenhouse gas production, caused in part by the use of this

Figure 3.23 The Broadmarsh Centre, Nottingham.

Figure 3.24 The Broadmarsh Centre, Nottingham.

Figure 3.25 Suburban centres, Nottingham.

Figure 3.26 Suburban centres, Nottingham.

Figure 3.27 Suburban centres, Nottingham.

fuel for road transport. Fundamental changes at Government level have given a fresh impetus to the search for more effective public transport systems for cities. There is also a new drive to find means of reinvigorating the city centre, serving it with effective public transport, and making it the location for those land uses which generate traffic. The city centre will then, once again, become the prime location for important commercial, office and residential developments served by public transport. Nottingham is experimenting with the development of public transport, securing funding for a light rail rapid transit system (LRT) while implementing an extension to its system of 'park and ride'. The city centre is being redeveloped along the length of the canal with some fine buildings including the Inland Revenue Building, Law Courts and other public, commercial and residential developments. This is a natural location for the city-centre extension bringing back into use the canal and connecting the main railway centre with the new extended city centre. The redevelopment of the Midland Railway Station will create an impressive gateway to the city, connected to the centre with landscaped pedestrian, cycle and public transport links.

Where does Nottingham go from here? A broad strategy for healing the wounds caused by the developments of the 1960s and 1970s is in process. Methods of controlling the use of the private car remain to be discovered while new uses may have to be found for the inner-city multi-storey car parks. In addition, at a time when sustainable development is so important in guiding urban design strategies, ways of encouraging a vibrant residential population to reoccupy the city centre have to be devised. Following on from the example of continental cities, Nottingham has yet to define a large central zone where pedestrian needs are considered paramount. Finally, probably the most demanding problem facing Nottingham is devising strategies for dealing with the two large 1960s shopping centres, The Victoria Centre and Broadmarsh, and the out-of-scale inner ring road, Maid Marian Way, again dating from the 1960s. Each of these major developments, characteristic of similar developments of the period in other British cities, continue to be destructive in terms of the urban fabric of central Nottingham.

TOWNSCAPE ANALYSIS

There are three main aspects of townscape analysis. The first concerns the legibility of the urban structure, that is, the ways in which people perceive, understand and react to the environment. It concerns those qualities of a place which give it an immediate identity, one which is quickly perceived or grasped by its users. The second aspect of townscape analysis concerns the permeability of the environment, that is, the choice it presents to the user. The third aspect of the analysis, a visual study, conforms more closely to the more traditional meaning of townscape, as used by Cullen following on from Sitte and his disciples.[10] The visual analysis includes studies of urban space, the treatment of façades, pavement, roofline, street sculpture and an analysis of the complexity of visual detail which distinguishes one place from another.

PERCEPTUAL STRUCTURE

The small traditional city and those parts of the traditional city which survive twentieth-century development have qualities admired by people, many of whom feel psychologically alienated by the impact of a visually bland and overpowering city governed, not by local burgers, but by the power of international commerce. Legibility is one of the qualities of the traditional city. The traditional city is 'easy to read'. The important public and religious buildings were the tallest and most imposing in the city; the main public squares and streets for parade were embellished with decoration, fountains, sculpture and ornamental lighting. Districts within the city were clearly apparent, defined and given distinct names such as The Lace Market in Nottingham or The Jewellery Quarter in Birmingham. Places had a beginning, an end, a defining boundary and, above all else, a centre for meeting and commercial display. Kevin Lynch illustrated a method for analysing legibility and suggested ways in which the concept can be used to structure new developments and strengthen the legibility of existing areas where this quality of the environment has been impaired by modern developments.[11]

Lynch demonstrated with his studies of mental mapping that a legible environment is one that is capable of being structured by people into accurate images. With this clear perceptual image of the city, the user can react to the environment more effectively. Lynch also found evidence that groups of city users share features of a common image. Mapping this common image is fundamental for an urban design study. There are five key physical features by which the user structures city image; they are paths, nodes, districts, edges and landmarks.[12]

The path is probably the most significant structuring element in image building. Most people relate other imaging features to their main network of paths. Paths are the main channels of movement,

Figure 3.28 Castle Rock, Nottingham.

whether by foot, bicycle, bus or car. Paths are the routes we take to move about in the city. The need to reduce the use of the private motor car will inevitably increase the importance of the network of pedestrian routes. It is these networks of pedestrian paths which form the distinctive images of districts and quarters in the city. Memorable paths, or those paths which evoke a strong image in the user, are often of a distinctive form and clearly modulated. The memorable path has important places and landmarks along its length.

Nodes are focal points of activity, such as the junction of paths, meeting places, market squares or places of transport interchange. According to Alexander, interesting and lively paths have nodes of activity at a maximum distance of 300 m along their length.[13] A city, town or village usually has a centre

which is probably the most important node, if not in terms of activity then as a symbol for that place. A good example of a symbolic city centre is Market Square in Nottingham which is no longer the main shopping focus for the city and its region as a result of a decision to move the market away from the Square in the 1960s. But it is here in Market Square that Nottingham Forest, recently the most successful city football team, returned victorious to present its trophy to adoring fans. It is here, too, beside the sculpted lions which flank the steps beneath the Council House Dome, that young people arrange to meet. Market Square with its fountains, formal paved garden and seating, is the focus for celebrations such as those which occur on New Year's Eve when throngs gather in front of the Council House, the headquarters of the City Council. Other impor-

Figure 3.29 Castle Rock, Nottingham.

tant nodes occur on routes as they enter the city or one of its main quarters. The gateway to the city is traditionally the place where travellers rest, where markets develop and where controlled entry to the city is maintained. Piazza del Popolo has been, as we have seen earlier, Rome's northern gateway for nearly 2000 years and is a model for such entry points to city or quarter. The perceptual study of place should aim to establish the distribution and location of nodes. Equally important for the study, however, is a classification of nodes by type, function and relative importance.

Landmarks are points of reference which are experienced at a distance. They are three-dimensional sculptural objects in contrast to nodes which are places to be entered and experienced from within. Landmarks can be natural phenomena such as Castle Rock in Nottingham or important buildings or monuments such as the dome of Nottingham's City Council House. Nelson's Column in Trafalgar Square, London, is a typical city landmark. The landmark is often a feature used in giving directions to a stranger. The landmark may, therefore, not always be the great monument but be something much more commonplace, such as an oddly shaped shop window or a small but highly visible street fountain. Discovering the wealth of small-scale landmarks is one of the functions of the perceptual study. It is the intricate nature and complexity of these perceptual clues which give to a place its interest and vitality (Figures 3.28 to 3.31).

The city is organized into quarters or districts each having some identifying characteristic. The district is a medium- to large-scale section of the

3.30

3.31

Figure 3.30 Nelson's Column, Trafalgar Square, London.

Figure 3.31 Wren's Column, London.

city. Soho and Mayfair are well known districts of London while Nottingham, like many other medium-sized cities, is divided into areas such as Lenton, The Park, Forest Fields and The Meadows. Districts have known names: they have a resident and/or a working population who contrast themselves with 'outsiders'. Each district has a boundary where it ends and the next place begins. Determining the position of boundaries, however fluid they may be, is an important step in deciding the nature and extent of the study area.

The final major element by which the city image is structured is the edge. Edges are two-dimensional linear elements where the function of pathway is of less importance than the role of boundary. Examples of boundaries are railway lines, canals, rivers, sea fronts and the vertical cliff face of a natural escarpment. Alexander suggests that boundaries should be 'fleshy' and permit movement.[14] Such 'fleshy' boundaries, he believes, reflect the complexity of city life,

where activities overlap in endless combinations. This is most true of the boundary between districts but less apparent for the major perceptual structural barriers such as the river or sea front. It would, however, be a very dull city if all boundaries were similar to the prison wall where entry is through one or two controlled gateways: a concept, incidentally, which security-conscious North American-style housing developments closely follow. Even the boundary of the shore line is not a complete barrier and is used as a connection between land and sea by fishermen, swimmers and pleasure boats. The subtle change of architectural style from one district to another is a common feature of the civilized city and so different from the 'peace line' in Belfast with its high security fence which is the ultimate expression of exclusion.

Paths, nodes, landmarks, districts and edges all have a significant role in determining the legibility of the city, but even at the smaller scale of the

Figure 3.32 Entrance to The Lace Market, Nottingham, from Middle Pavement.

district or city quarter they have similar functions of giving identity to place. Districts, too, have minor paths, nodes, landmarks, identifiable sub-areas with distinctive boundaries. These structuring ideas help the designer to focus on the kinds of physical components which, if used sensitively, can make a district or city memorable and rich in perceptual detail for both the citizen and visitor.

PERMEABILITY STUDY: PRIVACY AND ACCESSIBILITY

We all live both public and private lives. One measure of a civilized society is the freedom with which citizens can walk the streets in safety. A function of urban government is to ensure the safe use of the public realm. Another, apparently contradictory, role of urban government is to guarantee to its citizens the levels of privacy demanded by its culture or cultures. Securing safety and privacy in the home and delivering easy access to public space are two functions of urban government. The contrary demands for privacy in the home and easy access to the streets, squares and parks of the city are resolved at the interface between the public realm and the private domain. The design of the interface between the public realm and the more private areas of individual properties is a legitimate concern of urban design. This section outlines techniques for studying and understanding the relationship between privacy and accessibility in a given location. The technique highlights points of conflict in the environment, indicates those places

where improvements are possible and provides a basis for discussing the topic with members of the public.

According to Bentley *et al.*, 'Both physical and visual permeability depend on how the network of public space divides the environment into blocks: areas of land entirely surrounded by public routes'.[15] Clearly, an area divided into small blocks gives greater choice of routes than one divided into large street blocks. Contrast The Lace Market and The Victoria Centre, both in Nottingham (Figures 3.14 to 3.16 with Figures 3.32 to 3.34). The Victoria Centre, being in private ownership, has a system of internal streets which remain open to the public largely at the discretion of the owners. Access to these internal streets for pedestrians and therefore through the development is limited to four main entrances. The entrances to shopping malls like The Victoria Centre in Nottingham clearly indicate that the citizen is entering private property: these areas are not public streets. One of the problems facing future generations of designers is how to break down the scale of development such as in The Victoria Centre and so increase accessibility in the public realm. A rough guide for an acceptable level of permeability is a street layout with street blocks somewhere between one acre and one hectare in area.[16] Such a layout would mean that street junctions would occur at centres of 70 to 100 m. The pattern of street blocks is therefore one measure of permeability and accessibility; it is also an indication of the degree of flexibility which the user has in moving round the area.

Figure 3.33 Entrance to The Lace Market, Nottingham, past Weekday Cross.

Examining the street layout to determine the level of choice and variety of route for moving from place to place will indicate the degree of permeability in the neighbourhood. Hierarchical layouts, based on cul-de-sac development as opposed to the traditional layout of small street blocks surrounded by public roads, have a tendency to reduce choice of route. 'Hierarchical layouts reduce permeability: in the example below (Figure 3.35) there is only one way from A to D, and you *have* to go along B and C: never A–D directly, or ADCABCD but always ABCD. Hierarchical layouts generate a world of culs-de-sac, dead ends and little choice of routes.'[17] It should be noted, however, that the cul-de-sac development in traditional Muslim cities serves well the cultural norms of privacy and family seclusion which are of paramount importance for that society. Now that there are many Muslim people settling in Western cities this is not a problem peculiar only to distant lands. Cul-de-sac development also provides great security for residents. With cul-de-sac development there are fewer escape routes, that is, less choice for the mugger, rapist or burglar. Designing an environment with a high level of permeability for the law-abiding citizen has to be weighed carefully against the possibility of establishing areas which give freedom of action and a greater sense of security for those breaking the law.

Public safety on streets depends primarily on the intensity of use which, for this purpose, is probably more important than the physical form of the street. Streets are safer if heavily used and if overlooked by

Figure 3.34 The Lace Hall marking the entrance to The Lace Market, Nottingham. Since the writing of the manuscript for this book The Lace Hall has been converted into a fashionable bar and restaurant (Pitcher & Piano), and a visitor centre established near the weekday cross. See also page 87, Figure 4.11.

Figure 3.35
Hierarchical layouts reduce permeability: here there is only one way from A to D and you *have* to go along B and C, never A–D directly, or ADCABCD, but *always* ABCD. Hierarchical layouts generate a world of cul-de-sacs, dead ends and little choice of routes.

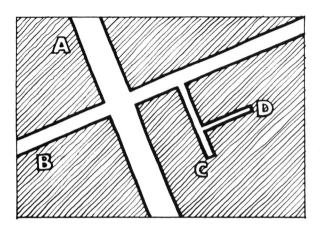

occupants of surrounding buildings. Such streets in the terms used by Jacobs are 'self-policing'.[18] Complete segregation of pedestrians and motor vehicles, when carried to extremes, can in some circumstances dramatically reduce the activity on streets and, by default, can place control of the environment in the hands of the unlawful. Some streets which are heavily trafficked by pedestrians throughout the day are clearly a sound proposition for pedestrianization. At the other extreme are the urban motorways which are not the place for pedestrians. There are, however, a whole range of city streets which fall into neither of these categories. The tree-lined boulevard is an elegant way in which road planners in the past have arranged for pedestrians and vehicles to use the same street. The *woonerf* pioneered in Holland aims to combine pedestrian and vehicular movements in the same neighbourhood street. In the case of the *woonerf*, vehicles move at speeds which are compatible with walking and cycling. A permeability study includes some estimate of current pedestrian, cycling and vehicular movements, noting blind or dead spots with little activity and points of pedestrian–vehicular conflict. Residents can provide invaluable information about trouble spots and 'no-go' areas where violence is likely to erupt.

The frontage between public and private space is the mechanism for ensuring privacy while maintaining a friendly and safe environment on the public street. The building frontage performs this function using both visual and physical means. In most places in the city there is a gradation between public, semi-public, semi-private and private space. The interface between the privacy of the inner home and the public space of the street is the building frontage which contains the semi-public and semi-private spaces. Security along the street is maintained by views from the front garden, balcony, lace-covered bay window and porch. Many access points along the street frontage increases activity and, together with the visual links, enrich the public scene. The permeability study concludes with an analysis of street frontage, noting those areas where there is little or no visual or physical contact across the building frontage and also noting places where it may be possible to enrich the street scene and increase levels of permeability between the private domain and public realm.

VISUAL ANALYSIS

The visual analysis has three main parts: a study of three-dimensional public space, a study of the two-dimensional surfaces which enclose public space and a study of the architectural details which give to an area much of its special character.

There are many books dealing with the delights and composition of public space, the classic being the seminal work of Sitte.[19] It is not the intention to repeat this well-worked subject matter but to outline the main techniques used in the survey and analysis of external public space. Urban space is appreciated in serial vision as the observer moves around the city.[20] The most common tools for recording spatial composition are the camera and the three-dimensional perspective drawn from normal eye level (Figures 3.36 and 3.37). For this form of analysis to be useful, the viewpoints must

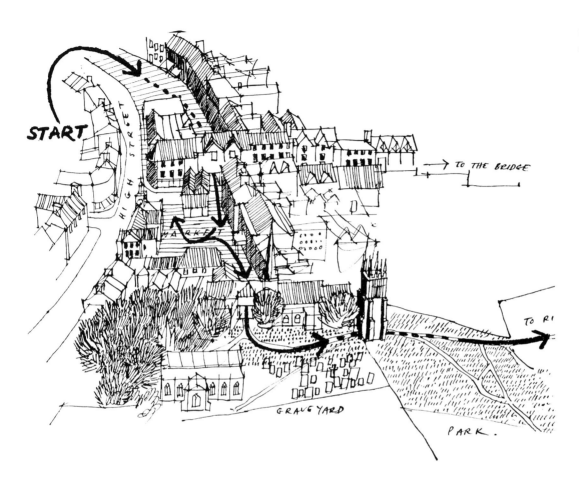

START

HIGH STREET

MARKET

TO THE BRIDGE

TO RI

GRAVEYARD

PARK.

Figure 3.36 Townscape sketch by Cullen.

be carefully chosen along pathways through the area. Particular views are chosen to illustrate dramatic changes in composition, such as the point of emergence from a narrow passage into a bright and expansive public square. It is argued that it is a series of such dramatic pictures as they register on the mind which makes a pathway memorable. This technique because of the compositional nature of each view which is chosen for the record is, of necessity, picturesque, exaggerating the charming aspects of the study area.

The two-dimensional map has long been used to show the form and distribution of public space. Of particular interest for urban design is the map of Rome by Nolli in 1748 (Figure 3.38). On this map the streets and squares are voids and the buildings solid black, with the exception of the main public spaces or semi-public spaces within buildings which are also depicted as voids. Nolli's map, therefore, shows the external public spaces and their connection with the main internal spaces of churches and other buildings used by the public. This is a most useful technique for recording public space in the city then analysing its distribution and connection. When reading maps the eye is accustomed to seeing the spaces between buildings as voids and the

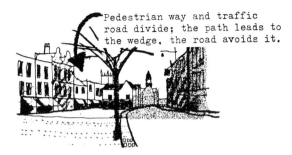

Pedestrian way and traffic road divide; the path leads to the wedge, the road avoids it.

The exit is spied at the end of the narrows............

...and reveals a further development across the road

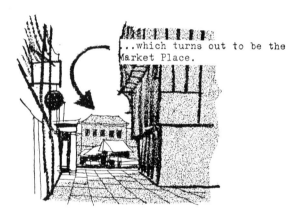

..which turns out to be the Market Place.

Figure 3.37 Townscape sketch by Cullen.

Turning round in the Place the expected view back along the High Street is screened off. The transition is complete.

buildings as solids. Gibberd suggested an alternative form of mapping.[21] He suggested alternating the way the form and ground are represented: in this type of map the buildings remain white and the public spaces, the streets and squares are represented as black. This change of perspective concentrates the mind not on the buildings and their forms, but on the spaces between the buildings, the anti-form (Figure 3.39). A basic visual analysis of the city should include these two figure ground studies. From these studies it should be possible to highlight weaknesses in the enclosure of public space, points of weak connection and the general characteristics of spatial composition.

Useful techniques for spatial analysis are the aerial photograph, aerial perspective and the aerial axonometric (Figures 7.6 to 7.10). The aerial photograph shows the relationship of the building forms to the surrounding public and private open space at a given time. Unfortunately, the choice of viewpoint is often not under the control of the designer. A time series of aerial photographs can give valuable insights into recent developments. Both the aerial perspective and aerial axonometric have the advantage of greater control and choice of vantage point. The aerial axonometric is a little easier to construct than the perspective, particularly if it is simplified to show buildings in block form. For this reason it is used more often than the perspective during the analytical stages of the design process. It is a particularly simple procedure for use with the computer which can translate a two-dimensional map together with spot heights, into a series of axonometric drawings from a multitude of viewpoints. When used in this way, the aerial axonometric becomes a powerful design tool. The aerial perspective is usually reserved for the presentation of the completed proposal either to the client or at public exhibition.

The distorted bird's eye perspective used by J.H. Aronson to illustrate the form of a public square and show its relationship to the city is a remarkable tool for the analysis of urban form.[22] The technique

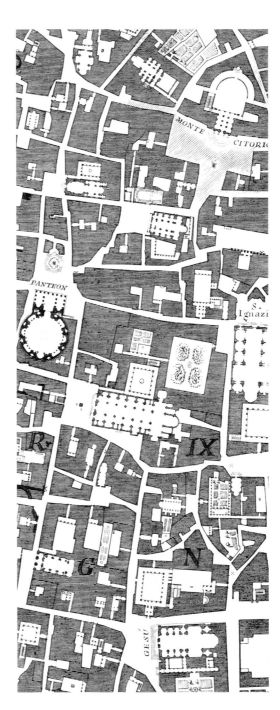

Figure 3.38 Fragment of the map of Rome by Giambattista Nolli.

Figure 3.39 Figure ground study of Piazza Annunziata, Florence by Gibberd.

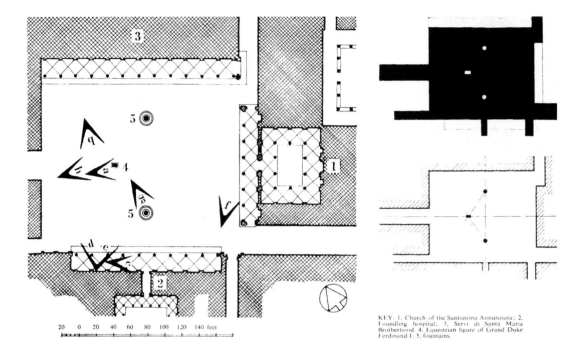

20 0 20 40 60 80 100 120 140 feet

KEY. 1. Church of the Santissima Annunziata; 2. Foundling hospital; 3. Servi di Santa Maria Brotherhood. 4. Equestrian figure of Grand Duke Ferdinand I; 5. fountains.

is based upon multiple vanishing points and is widely distorted; by revolving the drawing it elegantly reveals the dynamic relationship of the façades of the buildings and the space they enclose (Figure 7.9). The three-dimensional model is a useful technique for the analysis of urban form. There are many types of model used in urban design, the most highly sophisticated and beautifully finished normally being reserved for presentation purposes (Figures 7.11 to 7.14). The more usual model type for analysis and for testing alternative ideas is often robust and cheap to construct. Gibson makes a virtue of the need for cheap modelling techniques. He suggests that when the public are involved in the design process nothing is more destructive of participation than a beautifully finished three-dimensional model.[23] If such a model is presented it suggests that there is nothing more to say on the subject, the design is complete. Gibson suggests the use of cheap paper models which participants can

change, move about, destroy and recreate. It seems clear that the flimsy paper model of the type advocated by Gibson does, in fact, assist in the process of engaging the public in design and is a most useful tool for this purpose (Figures 3.40 and 3.41).

A study of the existing surfaces enclosing public space presents the opportunity to develop strategies for dealing with colour, materials, roofline, major junctions between elements and architectural detailing. Most traditional cities exhibit a distinctive use of colour and a set of building materials which form the bulk of the urban fabric.[24] Lenclos has developed a technique for studying colour in the city from which study he develops strategies for colour use in keeping with the traditions of the region.[25] Lenclos collects swatches of materials from the area. Using these swatches of predominant colours, he prepares a colour range for use in future developments. The technique can be

Figure 3.40 'Planning for real' model.

Figure 3.41 'Planning for real' model.

Figure 3.42 Holford's
analysis of roof profiles for
St Paul's London.

Outline of existing
building remaining

Outline of new building

Outline of existing
building to be demolished

Outline of
Block H.

Faraday House

College of Arms

Looking north up Godliman Street.

extended to include the preparation of lists of
predominant building materials, noting the parts of
the façade or street pavement where each material
is used. This particular study should analyse the
subtle changes of colour, material and detail from
district to district, noting any characteristic features
of path, node and landmark. One function of implementing a colour and material strategy is to
enhance the clarity and distinction of the five
perceptual components by which the image of the
city is constructed.

The roofline is a distinctive feature of the city,
reflecting power structures of former times in
addition to current patterns of wealth, prestige and
influence. A visual study of the existing roofline is
the first stage in determining the parameters for
building heights in future developments. If sustainable development and energy efficiency are to have

any meaning for built form, then, probably, the
general roofline and height of buildings in urban
areas may be close to that of the three- and four-
storey traditional city.[26] Certainly, the skyscraper as
the symbol of the wasteful competition for height
and commercial prestige in the city may be nearing
the end of its lifespan as an idea for development.

Two techniques for the analysis of building
heights in the city are the studies by Holford in the
area around St Paul's, London and the strategy for
high buildings in San Francisco.[27] The Dome of St
Paul's is one of the most imposing landmarks of
London; Holford in his plans for the precinct
around St Paul's was determined that it should
retain this form. He made careful perspective
studies of the Dome from critical viewpoints. In his
plans for the precinct, Holford interposed between
these critical viewpoints and the Dome only buildings of a height and bulk which did not damage the
view of the Dome (Figures 3.42 to 3.44). The result
was the imposition of a height strategy around St
Paul's Cathedral. In San Francisco, a careful study of
the landform and its topography was the basis for
determining building height or roofline strategy.
Building forms were used to enhance the landform
and a 'hill and bowl' effect was created; tall buildings being restricted to the hill tops and lower
buildings sited in the valleys.

Two features of the city which, to some extent,
determine its character, are the treatment of street
corners and the design of the pavement. Most
traditional cities have a wealth of ornate street
corners. The street corner has been classified into
a simple typology.[28] The typology is a useful tool
for the analysis of street junctions in a particular
study area but this part of the city fabric lends
itself to an imaginative and exuberant decorative
display: the typology should therefore be used to
stimulate, not restrict, ideas. The treatment of the
ground floor and its junction with the pavement is
the part of the city street which receives the most
detailed attention from the pedestrian. It is the
area of exchange between the public and the

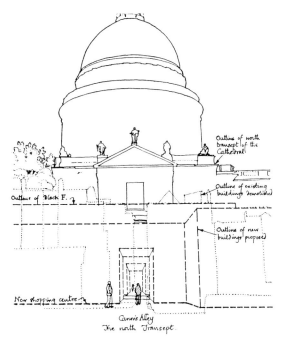

3.43

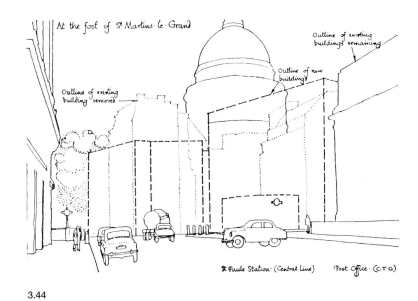

3.44

private parts of the street. A lively and active city ground floor with many entrances, shop windows, alleyways to internal courts, is the essence of a vibrant city. A visual study of the ground floor, consisting of elevational drawings or a photographic series can indicate those areas of the city which are popular with users and which work well. It will also show those 'dead' areas without a frontage which generates activity. Such areas are shunned by pedestrians and are in need of remedial action.

The three-dimensional computer model of the urban environment is a wonderful tool which can be used at many stages in the design process. The most obvious use for the three-dimensional computer model is to assist in visualizing changes to individual buildings and public spaces. This technique is no more than an extension of the traditional process of visual analysis which relies

upon various types of perspective, physical models and photographic records. The three-dimensional models of Edinburgh Old Town, designed in Strathclyde University, and the Georgian city of Bath, designed in Bath University, enable the examination of the impacts of proposed developments on the existing urban structures in those cities (Figure 7.17). Using the computer model, alternative arrangements can be assessed rapidly, opening the design process to informed public debate. All too often in the past public debate has been confused by the submission of projects slickly drawn, illustrated by perspectives carefully contrived to obscure the truth from a planning committee. It is only when the building is completed, that it is found to intrude on its surroundings in ways that were never anticipated. The three-dimensional computer model has the potential to overcome this particular problem by its ability to generate accurate perspectives from many different viewpoints and by the computer's power to analyse the visual effect of proposed development on any part of the immediate surroundings.[29]

Figure 3.43 Holford's analysis of roof profiles for St Paul's London.

Figure 3.44 Holford's analysis of roof profiles for St Paul's London.

Figure 3.45 Haverfordwest, town gateway.

CASE STUDY: HAVERFORDWEST

In the summer of 1995 Pembrokeshire County Council were preparing a bid for development finance. As part of that bid a townscape analysis was prepared by CITYFORM 21, an urban design consultancy. The townscape analysis was structured around a perceptual study using the technique developed by Lynch, followed by a visual study. The aim of the project was to make suggestions to consolidate and stimulate existing regeneration initiatives and opportunities.

Haverfordwest is a small Pembrokeshire town sitting astride a river. It has an appealing setting, a Medieval street pattern, an attractive street architecture, a rich urban fabric with many picturesque views and dominant landmarks (Figures 3.45 to 3.48). The vision for the town was to build on its Medieval character and to restore it to regional importance, so that a rather run down Haverfordwest would be transformed into a Welsh County Town of distinction.

In order to obtain a coherent view of Haverfordwest townscape, the physical form of the town was studied in terms of the main visual elements which make up the structure of the town. The five types of perceptual structuring elements described by Lynch were identified. From this analysis of town structure it was possible to distinguish quite clear town quarters. Each quarter had a distinct character, a clearly defined boundary, at least one important node connected by major paths to adjacent areas. These main quarters, listed in

Figure 3.46 Haverfordwest, the river.

Figure 3.47 Haverfordwest, the High Street.

Figure 3.48 Haverfordwest, The George.

Figure 3.49 Haverfordwest environmental areas.

Figure 3.49 and shown in diagrammatic form in Figure 3.50 became the environmental areas where co-ordinated action or interventions were proposed.

The visual study of Haverfordwest identified the main spaces, the modifying elements and the details. It is the size, shape and arrangement of the main public spaces, the streets and squares which give the town its Medieval character. The frontages, trees, fences, walls, and even the projecting advertisement signs, enclose and form the shape of the public space. For the purpose of this analysis they were defined as the modifying elements. Details are the finer points of the architectural composition, materials, mouldings and colour which enliven public space. These features of the townscape were categorized as having a positive, negative or neutral role in the townscape. From this detailed analysis it was possible to propose detailed interventions for each space.

The Central Environmental Area is one of the most important quarters in the town. It is formed by the High Street and the adjacent commercial areas: it is the centre of commercial activity in Haverfordwest. The High Street is the central spine of the town, containing the most important public spaces. The High Street provides the first impression of the town for most visitors. The area has a number of attractive links with the river which, when upgraded, should prove to be an attraction to tourists. There is an urgent need for landscaping and general upgrading of this, the central core of the town. Some of the proposed improvements suggested by CITYFORM 21 are shown on Figure 3.51. Figure 3.52 shows a

1 Central environmental area (EA)
2 Castle EA
3 Market Street/Goat Street EA
4 Saint Thomas Green EA
5 The Parade EA
6 Dew Street EA
7 Riverside EA
8 The Administrative Centre (EA)

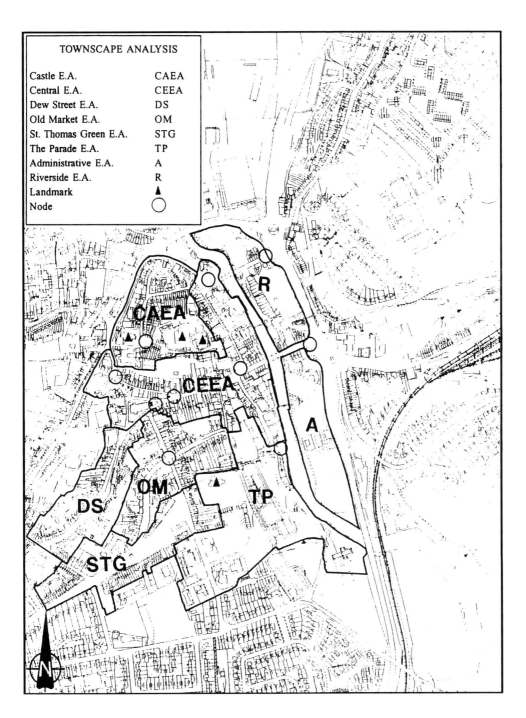

Figure 3.50 Haverfordwest environmental areas.

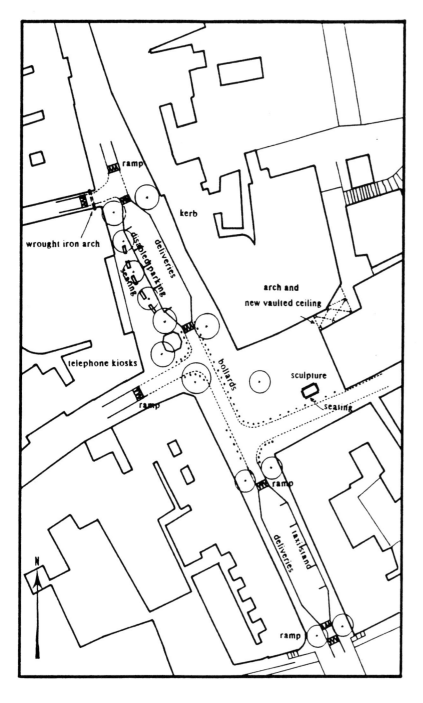

similar treatment for the main town gateway which is the entrance across the river to the High Street. The proposals for all eight environmental areas are linked with a plan for Town Trails where environmental upgrading is suggested for all the main paths in the town (Figure 3.53).

Unfortunately, in the case of Haverfordwest there was neither time nor finance for the inclusion of residents in the perceptual study. A perceptual study is a useful technique for site analysis but it is given greater authority when members of the public are involved in the survey. For a public exercise of this nature to be useful, it should be part of a wider project in participation where people can freely express views about the problems in their neighbourhood, suggest ideas for its development, and become involved in the management of their environment. The perceptual study should be advertised as part of this more far-reaching exercise of public engagement in planning. For the perceptual study, the views of a wide range of users is most useful. Participants should include residents, people who work in the area and visitors. It is good practice to identify particular groups of user for inclusion in the exercise. Such groups may include school children, youths, young mothers, working people, the aged and those with disabilities. Using Lynch's techniques participants are asked to make a sketch map of the study area.[30] The resulting sketches are analysed to discover those elements common to all users. The common perceptual image should be checked against the designer's own mental map of the area (Figures 3.54 and 3.55).

Figure 3.51 Haverfordwest, proposals for the Central Environmental Area.

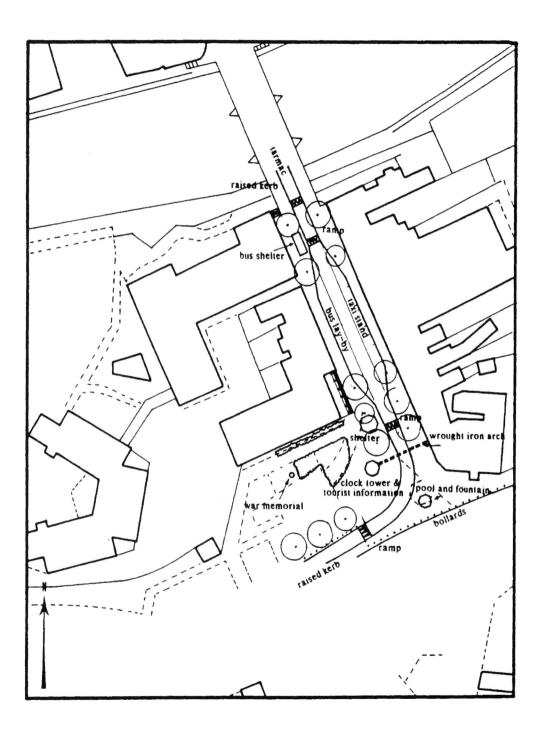

Figure 3.52 Haverfordwest, proposals for the main town gateway.

Figure 3.53 Haverfordwest, proposed town trails.

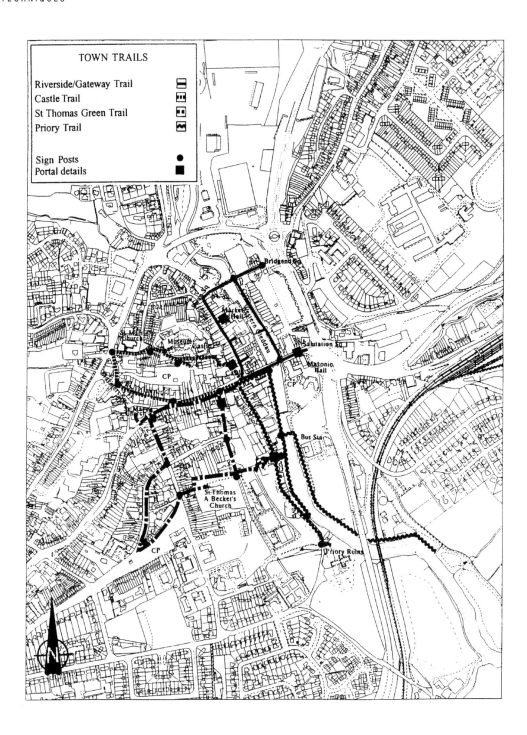

CONCLUSION

This chapter has introduced techniques for historical and townscape analysis. It is emphasized that the survey strategy adopted will depend on the nature and scope of the project and upon the time allocated for project preparation. There is always a great danger of collecting too much information, much of which, while of academic interest, may have little influence on the final design outcome. The main purpose of the survey and its analysis is to form an understanding of the problem being investigated and to provide a framework for the development of innovative ideas for solving that problem. The use of an extensive survey should not be used as an alternative to thought nor should it be permitted to stifle imagination. The purpose of the survey is not to provide instant recipes for action or catalogues of ready made design details. However, an understanding of the environment and its history is the foundation from which innovative development springs. This understanding of a particular city or town begins with an analysis of past developments in the area, followed by a perceptual study to define the structure which determines the image and identity of that city or town. Detailed studies of the city or town, in terms of its permeability and visual qualities, complete the townscape analysis.

REFERENCES

1 Ashby, T. and Pierce Rowlan, S. (1924) The Piazza del Popolo: its history and development, *Town Planning Review*, Vol. xxi, No. 2, pp. 74-99.

2 Bacon, E.N. (1975) *Design of Cities*, London: Thames and Hudson, Revised Edition.

3 *Ibid.*, and Moughtin, J.C. (1992) *Urban Design: Street and Square*, Oxford: Butterworth-Heinemann.

4 Giedion, S. (1956) *Space, Time and Architecture*, Cambridge, MA: Harvard University Press, 3rd edn, Enlarged.

5 Gosling, D. and Maitland, B. (1984) *Concepts of Urban Design*, London: Academy Editions.

6 Alexander, C., Neis, H., Anninou, A. and King, I. (1987) *A New Theory of Urban Design*, Oxford: Oxford University Press.

7 Barley, M.W. and Straw, I.F. (undated) Nottingham, in *Historic Towns*, ed. M.D. Lobel, London: Lovell Johns-Cook Hammond & Kell Organization.

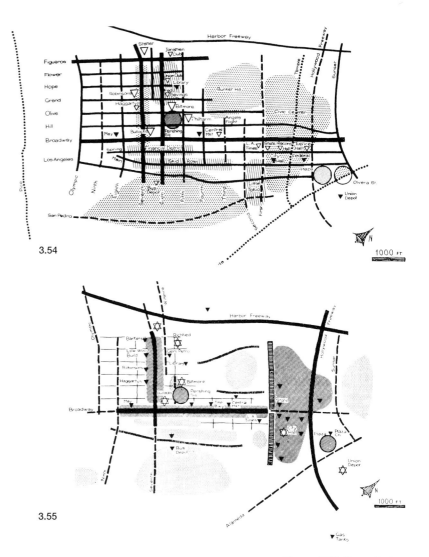

3.54

3.55

Figure 3.54 Perceptual image: the Los Angeles image derived from sketch maps.

Figure 3.55 Perceptual image: the visual form of Los Angeles as seen in the field.

8 Beckett, J. and Brand, K. (1997) *Nottingham, An Illustrated History*, Manchester: Manchester University Press.

9 Straw, F.I. (1967) *An Analysis of the Town Plan of Nottingham: A Study in Historical Geography*, Unpublished Thesis, University of Nottingham, Nottingham.

10 Cullen, G. (1961) *Townscape*, London: Architectural Press, and Sitte, C. (1901) *Der Stadt-Bau*, Wien: Carl Graeser and Co.

11 Lynch, K. (1971) *The Image of the City*, Cambridge, MA: MIT Press, 2nd edn.

12 *Ibid.*

13 Alexander, C. *et al.*, *op. cit.*

14 *Ibid.*

15 Bentley, I., Alcock, A., Murrain, P., McGlynn, S. and Smith, G. (1985) *Responsive Environments: A Manual for Designers*, London: Architectural Press.

16 Moughtin, J.C. (1992), *op. cit.*

17 Bentley, I. *et al.*, *op. cit.*

18 Jacobs, J. (1965) *The Death and Life of Great American Cities*, Harmondsworth: Penguin.

19 Sitte, C., *op. cit.*

20 Cullen, G., *op. cit.*

21 Gibberd, F. (1955) *Town Design*, London: Architectural Press, 2nd edn.

22 Bacon, E.N., *op. cit.*

23 Gibson, T. (1979) *People Power*, Harmondsworth: Penguin.

24 Moughtin, J.C., Oc, T. and Tiesdell, S. (1995) *Urban Design: Ornament and Decoration*, Oxford: Butterworth-Heinemann.

25 Urbame, M. (1977) France: how to paint industry, *Domus*, No. 568, March, pp. 14-18.

26 Moughtin, J.C. *Urban Design: Green Dimensions*, Oxford: Butterworth-Heinemann.

27 Attoe, W. (1981) *Skylines: Understanding and Molding Urban Silhouettes*, New York: John Wiley and Sons, and Holford, W. (1950) St Paul's Cathedral in the City of London, *Town Planning Review*, Vol. xxvii, No. 2, July, pp. 58-98.

28 Moughtin, J.C. *et al.* (1995) *op. cit.*

29 Day, A. (1994) New tools for urban design, *Urban Design Quarterly*, No. 51, July, pp. 20-23.

30 Lynch, C., *op. cit.*

ANALYSIS

4

INTRODUCTION

It is unproductive to try to define a rigid dividing line between survey and analysis. The collection of *particular* pieces of information implies the use of a preconceived analytical framework. The accumulation of facts without purpose is wasteful and can only confuse the outcome. Even the drawing of a simple sketch presupposes that a particular view has a relevance for the problem under investigation. Furthermore, it presupposes that the elements in that view which are emphasized in the drawing also have some bearing on the task. If this is not the case, then why make that particular sketch? Similarly, the collection of social or economic data cannot be all-inclusive. Only those sets of information of immediate use should be stored ready for analysis. A useful principle to follow in survey design is to keep it brief, at least initially. It is always possible to extend the search as the analysis illuminates the problem definition. In reality there may be no clear distinction between survey and analysis. But, for the sake of convenience, the analytical stage of the design process can be deemed to begin when thought is given to the strengths and weaknesses of the project site, the opportunities presented by the project and the potential threats to the area which any intervention may have to counter. This chapter begins with an outline of the considerations involved in making a forecast of the future and the use of such a forecast as a design tool. The chapter then examines the techniques for assessing the constraints on development and for assessing the possibilities of intervention. The central part of the chapter is focused on **SWOT** analysis; applying to urban design the techniques for discovering the **S**trengths and **W**eaknesses of a project; the **O**pportunities for development; and the **T**hreats which may disrupt implementation. The chapter ends with two case studies. The first is The Lace Market in Nottingham and the second is the New Campus for the University of Nottingham.

TREND, FORECAST AND SCENARIO

Planning in Britain after the 1947 Town and Country Planning Act, to some extent depended for its method on the analysis of trends and from those trends, making predictions about the future. The plan was then based upon those predictions. It was found from experience that predictions and forecasts about the future can be wildly out when based on such calculations. The story of the changing forecasts of national population in Britain during the post-1947 period is a salutary lesson for those in the business of forecasting the future and also for those relying on those predictions for plan making. The other major difficulty with the forecast is that it can become a self-fulfilling prophecy. For example, the prediction of fast-rising car ownership and usage in the 1960s provided the rationale for Government policies. These policies gave priority to road-building programmes to the detriment of pursuing vigorous investment in public transport. The extra road miles built on the strength of Government policy stimulated demand for the use of those same roads. With that stimulus in demand, came the inevitable increase in car ownership and the use of the car, even for short journeys. The forecast for the growth in car ownership was therefore shown to be true, or to some extent to be a 'self-fulfilling prophecy'. This analysis of the growth in car ownership in Britain over the last forty years may have been overstated, nevertheless there is some truth in the belief that this prediction, particularly about car usage, has some of the characteristics of a circular argument where the forecast reinforces the trend. Trends in the changing patterns of lifestyle are evident, even under the most superficial of examinations. An analysis of these trends may stimulate ideas about the nature of the problem being investigated and also actions which may be necessary to modify a trend leading to an undesirable outcome. The apparent trends in changing lifestyles, however, are no more than an indication of what might happen in the future. And only if the conditions governing these trends remain the same. If trends are viewed in this light, then there is little danger that they may evolve into a forecast leading to an authoritative prediction of future conditions. The only certainty about a prediction is that it is more likely to be misleading than to give an accurate picture of the future.

The ways in which some factors governing everyday activity and current lifestyle are changing may critically affect development, or the designer's view of development, potential in the project area. It may, therefore, be appropriate to analyse such economic, social and cultural factors. For most

development projects, forming an understanding of the dynamics of population change is standard procedure. A knowledge of what might happen to the target population is fundamental for many urban design projects. This study may be a simple attempt to gauge the rate of growth or decline of population, or it may aim to discover which sections of the population, in terms of age, sex, race or socio-economic group, are growing or declining and at what rate.

Population studies are the starting point for determining the land requirements and for the allocation of space for competing activities or land uses. A knowledge of present population is necessary in order to make some prediction for the future. The most basic information is the size of the present population. This may not be as straightforward as it sounds. The resident population may be supplemented by tourists and a daily commuting population. For some projects this visiting population may be extremely important. It is often essential to have some knowledge of the breakdown of the population in terms of age, sex, race and socio-economic group. From this information the specific needs of the community for services and facilities can be gauged. It may, if the project area is large enough, be necessary to examine the physical distribution of the various groups which comprise the population. The physical distribution of the population gives some indication of the location of facilities. An assessment of the population can be made by conducting a specially designed survey. This is both expensive and time consuming. It is more usual to use the Registrar General's Census of Population, adjusted to allow for assumed changes between census dates.

Predicting future population is based upon an examination of existing trends. It is important to know if there are any signs of change in the factors governing population size. For example, it is useful to know the birth, death, marriage, and fertility rates, together with the levels of migration. The underlying tendencies in the population should be examined to see if there is a trend in the population towards ageing, or a trend towards a greater number of working females, or towards more but smaller households. The designer would want to know the tendency towards the physical distribution of changes. Knowledge of the existing population, together with any trends and tendencies which can be discovered, together form the basis of forecasting future population.

Forecasting population is a speculative business. Demographers are extremely guarded about attempting to forecast the future particularly of small districts of the city. The smaller the area of study, the less reliable are the forecasts. If it is decided to engage in this hazardous enterprise then there are a number of techniques for making population forecasts. The most basic is a continuation of the recent past into the future by extending a straight line graph based on the assumption that current trends will persist. A popular technique for forecasting future population is the Cohort Survival Method.[1] This technique adjusts census figures in forward steps, by age and sex groups, year on year, until the date of the project completion. Adjustments are made to the figures for changes in birth, death, fertility, in- and out-migration: 'In essence what it does is to trace a particular age group, for example 0–4 years through their estimated life cycle making deductions for projected deaths based upon life tables, and amendments for net migration. The next 0–4 age group is calculated by reference to the fertility rate of the number of 'survivors' remaining in preceding groups or cohorts'.[2]

There may be other areas, as well as population, for which projection may prove useful. For example, further information about population and its changing patterns of employment, income and expenditure may throw light on possible demand for housing or other goods. The rates at which the housing stock is declining in numbers and quality of maintenance or the changes in patterns of owner-ship, or, indeed the general changes in land-use patterns may be of significance to the project. The nature of the project and its goals will determine the factors to be investigated and which particular trends, when analysed, will prove useful for the development of the project.

The analysis of trends becomes a more useful design tool when comparisons can be made between the study area and the city, its region, or the nation as a whole. A knowledge of population trends in the study area may be essential for design purposes but when those local trends are compared with those in the larger community the significance of local change may be highlighted. This comparative element in trend analysis applies equally to employment, housing conditions or car ownership patterns. All trend analyses should embody a comparative element.

A more imaginative technique than trend analysis for assessing future possibilities is scenario design. Using this technique the designer constructs possible futures imagining the major factors which may affect the way people live. Major events such as a sea change in political attitudes; an oil crisis; a stock market crash; joining or not joining the EURO; and many other possible future events can be built into a series of different scenarios. These scenarios can be fed back into the forecasts, which in turn result in a set of different trends for any topic analysed. The trends can then be presented graphically. It is usual to present three trends and their resulting forecast for each topic; one where the assumptions are favourable, one where they are unfavourable and the third somewhere between the extremes. Scenario building is, above all else, a tool of the imagination and therefore most useful for the designer seeking ideas.

CONSTRAINTS AND POSSIBILITIES

Two useful analytical tools are constraints and possibilities mapping. The constraints and possibilities maps focus mainly upon the physical factors which affect development. The constraints map contains information, for example, on the location and design of any approved projects such as road widening, sites with planning approvals, land use or building height restrictions, buildings designated as of historic interest, together with any important features of the land or its servicing. The constraints map can have a debilitating effect upon design if each constraint is not challenged in terms of its current importance and also examined in the light of any possible waivers or methods of circumventing the effects of the constraint. The possibilities map includes items such as areas ripe for development, possible linkages with adjacent areas in the city, features which are special to the area, groups of buildings of outstanding architectural significance which, with a change of use, would bring distinction to the quarter, positions where development would enhance the appearance of the built environment and areas where landscape intervention would be advantageous.

SIEVE MAPPING AND GEOGRAPHIC INFORMATION SYSTEMS

Analysing constraints and possibilities can be expressed graphically as a series of sieve maps. Mapping a number of constraints as transparent overlays to an ordnance survey map of the project area eliminates those areas which, for one reason or another, present difficulties for development. The technique, when combined with the power of the computer using Geographic Information Systems (GIS) technology, can bring together many layers of physical and socio-economic data, so affording complex analyses which relate population studies to the environment occupied by the community. The use of large-scale three-dimensional computer models is becoming more common in urban planning and design. In addition to the use of the computer model for design, it is being developed to act as the core of an urban information system. Systems are being developed for linking objects in a three-dimensional model with other kinds of information, including text and photographs, records of a building's history, social statistics, data about energy use and digital material for sound and video. Computer models are beginning to appear in which 'The visualization capacities of the computer aided design (CAD) model and the analytical power of the geographic information system can be brought together to provide new kinds of tools for urban design'.[3]

However, to date, urban design has been largely unaffected by developments in GIS, yet the possibilities are immense. This potential has encouraged recent research that explores the prospective use of GIS as an urban design support system. 'Urban design sits astride the world of two- and three-dimensions and, as yet, there are only the most tentative links between desktop GIS and CAD'.[4] The main links between GIS and CAD have taken place in the area of visualization, especially in the area of three-dimensional models of cities. However, their potential rests in the ability to perform spatial analysis using a wide range of data. Some of the most important developments in the use of GIS for urban design derive from the work of MIT where tools for sketch planning, visualization and local urban analysis have been developed.[5] The release of detailed information at the local scale of street block and street segment such as the Ordinance Survey's Land-Line.Plus data is an incentive for the development of GIS tools for urban design. This Ordinance Survey data, for some areas includes large-scale data (1:1,2500,1:2,500, 1:10,000), depicting artificial and natural elements.[6] Additional comprehensive data include socio-economic datasets,[7] and aerial photography.[8]

Batty et al. explore built-in functions of desktop GIS as supporting tools for different stages in the urban design process.[9] They endeavour to adapt the proprietary ArcView GIS to support some of the most common urban design activities. A straight-

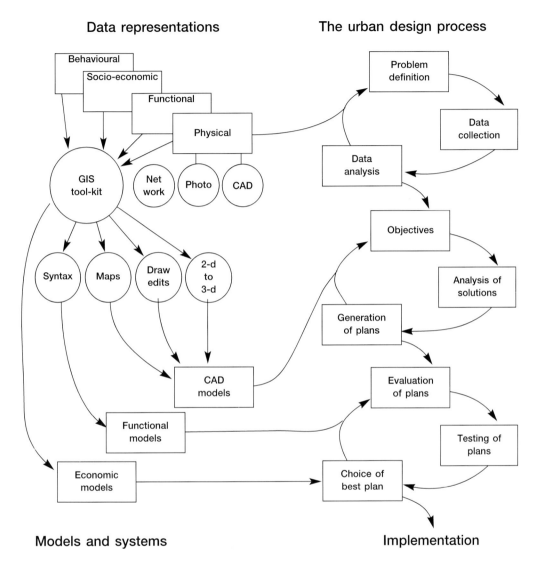

Data representations

The urban design process

Behavioural

Socio-economic

Functional

Physical

GIS tool-kit

Net work

Photo

CAD

Syntax

Maps

Draw edits

2-d to 3-d

CAD models

Functional models

Economic models

Problem definition

Data collection

Data analysis

Objectives

Analysis of solutions

Generation of plans

Evaluation of plans

Testing of plans

Choice of best plan

Models and systems

Implementation

forward support system in which various computer technologies are identified to support the different stages of urban design has been devised. In Figure 4.1 the right-hand side shows the main stages of the process, while the left-hand side exemplifies the range of descriptive issues to be taken into account

when generating plans. The description of the urban environment is based on different types of information that can be handled devising a range of toolkits. Four main information groups are identified: (1) *socio-economic information* that at a macro level can be represented using administrative areas such as wards and enumeration districts; (2) *functional information* which represents relationships between parts of the urban system; (3) *behavioural infor*mation on a local scale about individuals and their use of space; and (4) *physical informatio*n about streets and building blocks. All of this information can be handled, in varying degrees, in a GIS while other appropriate technologies are computer mapping, formal models and CAD.[10] Existing GIS functionalities, which can be used at different stages of the urban design process, include thematic mapping, overlay analysis and structured queries. One of the most important developments, however, is the exploitation of GIS analytical capabilities to solve urban design questions. The next section will illustrate an example of the use of this technology.

SPACE SYNTAX

In terms of capability, Batty *et al.* show how a technique called 'space syntax', which Hillier and Hanson[11] developed to explain how space influences human behaviour and social activities, has been transposed in a GIS environment. According to Jiang *et al.* 'Space syntax is a set of theories and tools for spatial morphological analysis with a particular application in urban science'.[12] This theory is based on the notion that the urban environment is composed of spatial obstacles such as buildings and free space between them, where human beings can move freely. It is this element of free space that forms the basis of this theory. Again, according to Jiang *et al.* 'Space syntax focuses on free space and decomposes an entire area of free space into small pieces of space, each of which can be perceived from a single vantage point. As such, this representation constitutes the cognitive fundamental modelling reference of the space syntax approach'.[13]

Space syntax representations of a neighbourhood are based on the linearity of free spaces; that is, a free space is recognized as an axial line or 'vista'.

'According to how each line intersects every other line, a connectivity graph, taking axial lines as nodes and line intersection as links, can be derived'.[14] The technique is based on three parameters derived from the connectivity graph. The first is *connectivity* defined as the number of nodes directly linked to each other. The second is the *control value* which corresponds to the level of variety each node represents for nodes diametrically linked to it. The third is *integration* which indicates the degree to which a node is integrated or separated from the system as a whole. Each of these parameters can be represented mathematically: for further information the interested reader should refer to Jiang *et al.*[14] These parameters are used to describe an urban space in terms of integration or segregation. 'A space (that is, smallscale) is said to be more integrated if all other spaces can be reached after traversing a small number of intervening spaces; it is less integrated if the necessary number of intermediate spaces increases. This concept is measured by *global integration.* Similarly, *connectivity* and *local integration* measure the degree of integration or segregation at the local level. Basically there is a correlation between these local and global parameters'.[15] A relevant application of space syntax's concept of local integration in the urban environment is the analysis of pedestrian movement. The advocates of this technique attest that people's movements can be predicted from the analysis of the morphological structure of a design plan. From such an analysis adjustments can be made to the structure of the plan in order to generate the desired pedestrian flows in locations where, for example, shops will be located. Urban designers place great stress upon improving connections between places: for this purpose space syntax is an essential tool.

While proprietary GIS such as ARC-INFO and ArcView have tools for the calculation of accessibility at a large scale they lack a tool that can deal with the geometry of the urban scale. Accessibility is a very common spatial measure that computes the relative 'distance' of one place to another place. However, geographic accessibility measures based on a gravitational equation presume that accessibility is uniform from any place to any other place within the system, thus reducing its use for computing the accessibility for streets and routes:[16] for this reason, a software that incorporates the graphic components of the space syntax approach was developed as an extension to the proprietary ArcView GIS. This is called Axwoman and is based on a vector data structure.[17] This means that each spatial unit is geographically referenced. The functions used are drawing, computation and analysis: for more details of the implementation of the software see Jiang *et al.*[18] The innovation of this software rests on the new measures of accessibility developed in space syntax. An example of the analytical capabilities of Axwoman is provided by a case study based on the Gamston Development Plan designated by Rushcliffe Borough Council's Central Local Plan in 1986. Axwoman was used to explore the relationship between the layout of housing in Gamston and the pattern of burglaries.

At the time that the Development Plan was being devised, the Borough Council recognized the need to give developers a high degree of freedom in preparing housing layouts. It also regarded certain design aspects of development as being appropriate for the area: these included the type of vehicle and road networks. The requirements for these networks were detailed in the development brief.[19] This brief suggested that the basic element of development should be based on 'neighbourhood groups', of varied street scene, composed of 'staggered' blocks of housing, distinguished from adjacent groups by its architecture and by its own loop road or cul-de-sac. Furthermore, the brief required that the road network be based on a hierarchical system of distributor, feeder and collector roads, and that the new road network should not link with the existing roads of West Bridgeford except from the designated primary access junctions (see Figure 4.2). The brief also required that all

Figure 4.2 Gamston, road network and crime locations.

internal roads be arranged to secure the maximum privacy for each dwelling while avoiding a corridor effect, normally associated with long straight lines.

At the time of drawing up the development brief there was little awareness on the ways in which these layouts would impact upon residential crime. Gamston has become one of Rushcliffe's hot spots of daytime residential burglaries and car crimes. The

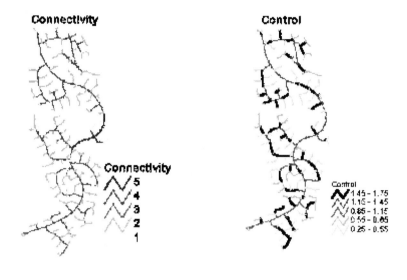

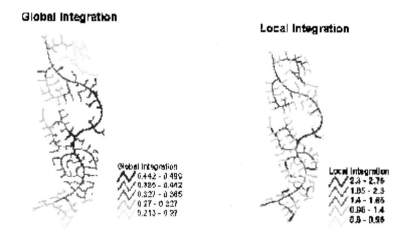

Figure 4.3 Gamston Development, space syntax parameters.

Gamston;[20] in addition to connectivity, it shows the remaining morphological parameters, *control, global integration* and *local integration*. The parameter *control* reflects how each street controls its neighbours: the results show that the roads with best control - that is, those that are most overlooked and most used - are those one step above the lower end of the hierarchical system. Finally, integration is split into *global integration*, which measures the extent to which any street is linked to every other street, and *local integration*, which measures the extent to which any given street is linked to every street three steps or connections away.[21] The Gamston development shows a clear correlation between areas of low *connectivity*, low *control*, low *global* and *local integration* on one side, and the location of crime on the other. While it is not possible to draw firm conclusions about cause and effect in the case of patterns of crime and urban layout, a study such as this at Gamston does question the advisability of a blanket use of the cul-de-sac for housing developments. The case study also underlines the use of this tool for analysing the relationship between an urban form and the way it is used and misused.

STRENGTHS, WEAKNESSES, OPPORTUNITIES AND THREATS

SWOT (strengths, weaknesses, opportunities, threats) analysis is a useful technique for the collection and structuring of data. SWOT analysis has its origins in business management where strengths and weaknesses refer to the internal workings of the organization while opportunities and threats are external to it.[22] This clear distinction between internal and external conditions is more difficult to apply when assessing the potential of a part of the physical world such a city district. The analysis in strict management terms could be applied to an organization contemplating a particular intervention in the world of real estate but not necessarily in quite the

trend is for these crimes to occur at the lower end of the hierarchical system of roads, the culs-de sac, where there are few or no people passing during the daytime; that is, in the least well-connected streets using the *connectivity* parameter of space syntax. Figure 4.3 shows a space syntax analysis for

Figure 4.4 SWOT analysis.

	Strengths	Weaknesses	Opportunities	Threats
Built Environment physical and aesthetic properties				
Natural Environment fauna, flora, air and water				
Socio-economic Environment including political and administrative conditions				

same way for the potential of the real estate itself. Many of the threats facing an inner city area or the opportunities it presents could be considered to be internal to the physical structure being investigated. For example, a continued loss of population in the inner city could be seen as a threat to regeneration but in many ways it is inherent to the inner city. Clearly there is overlap between all four analytical categories. A weakness, for example, can be viewed in a more positive light as an opportunity, while in some instances a strength in one area when viewed from a different perspective can appear as the source of a weakness. Nevertheless, the structure imposed by the listing and categorizing of aspects and qualities of the project site under these four broad headings does assist in formulating possible strategies for intervention. The completion of the analysis can also form the basis for questioning the assumptions underlying project goals and objectives. The SWOT analysis can, therefore, assist in the clearer definition of the design brief and point the way to design solutions.

SWOT analysis, when used in matrix form, is a powerful tool for dissecting the properties and potential of an urban area. If the examination of the data is structured, as shown in Figure 4.4, then the strengths and weaknesses of a number of the main aspects of life in a study area can be addressed and analysed. The properties and potential of the study

site or city district can be examined under a number of broad headings or factors. In Figure 4.4 the factors considered are the physical properties of the built environment of the area and its aesthetic quality, the natural environment which would include pollution, and finally the social and economic conditions in the area. Using this or a similar matrix, it is possible to examine, for example, the strength or weakness of the study area in terms of the factors listed in the matrix, which may be of more use to the designer than a simple aggregate statement about the area which may obscure more than it reveals. It is also possible, working horizontally along a line of the matrix, to examine any particular factor for its strength, its weakness, opportunities for its development and the potential threat it faces. The use of the matrix is simply an aid to analysis. The result of that analysis will be a statement which summarizes the potential of the site for achieving sustainable development, outlining the interventions or actions necessary to arrive at such an outcome.

CASE STUDY: THE LACE MARKET, NOTTINGHAM

A SWOT analysis is not possible without an understanding of the history of the study area and a

4.5

4.6

Figure 4.5 Stoney Street,
The Lace Market,
Nottingham.

Figure 4.6 Stoney Street,
The Lace Market,
Nottingham.

knowledge of its present function within the city.
Plans for the regeneration of The Lace Market in
Nottingham, for example, expressly emphasize the
quarter's history and the development of its special
character: it occupies the site of the former English
Borough (Figure 3.18). The Lace Market, as its name
implies, was the centre of the large and flourishing
nineteenth-century lace industry. Grand warehouses
and factories were built in pleasantly scaled streets,
which makes The Lace Market in Nottingham one
of the finest collections of nineteenth-century commercial architecture possibly in Europe (Figures 4.5

4.7

4.8

Figure 4.7 Broadway, The Lace Market, Nottingham.

Figure 4.8 Broadway, The Lace Market, Nottingham.

to 4.8). In the twentieth century, the lace industry went into decline. Many of the fine buildings were not properly maintained, became run down and were subdivided as workrooms for small clothing and textile firms. The rents such properties could command were low, so exacerbating the problems of maintenance. Following the destruction of some buildings during the Second World War, further buildings were demolished in the 1950s and 1960s. The road schemes in The Lace Market and its proposed comprehensive redevelopment in the 1960s were never completed, fortunately. The area was probably saved when it was declared a Conservation Area in 1969. In 1974 the City Council adopted a renovation strategy in the hope of reviving what had become a badly run down area with thirty derelict sites and many more decaying buildings. This strategy for renovation adopted by the City Council in conjunction with the Department of the Environment and English Heritage was remarkably successful, improving over 150 buildings, landscaping derelict sites, redeveloping other sites for housing, converting the Unitarian Chapel on High Pavement to a Lace Hall as a focus for tourists in the area and generally changing the fortunes of the area.

The former Lace Hall, now the Lace Centre, has since moved premises to a converted terrace house in High Pavement. The Unitarian Chapel has been converted once more, this time to a fashionable bar and restaurant: fortunately the very fine Pre-Raphaelite stained glass windows are still available for public viewing.

In 1988 the City Council, the Department of the Environment and Nottingham Development Enterprise appointed Conran Roche to carry out a study of The Lace Market which led to the adoption by the City Council of a new approach to the planning of the area. The unique history of the site, with its roots in Saxon times and a wealth of fine urban architecture, formed the backcloth to the study. Of particular importance was its long association with the lace industry. This led to a key proposal in the planning strategy to develop the quarter as 'a centre for fashion, clothing and textile industry, particularly for small and medium-sized companies who need a City Centre location'.[23] The textile industry, while giving to the quarter its special character, in terms of large-scale manufacture is a function in decline. In 1989, 5500 people were working in The Lace Market in 250 firms. In addition to the clothing and textile firms there were other light manufacturing industries with associated offices and warehousing; retailing along Carlton Street, Goose Gate and Hockley; together with

offices which at that time occupied 18 per cent of the total floorspace. A small but significant population of 500 people lived in the area, some in a design award-winning group of town apartments. In the area there was also the beginnings of a leisure industry with a small live theatre, cinema and a number of restaurants. Based on his understanding of the situation in Lace Market in 1989, Roche suggested six key principles for the regeneration of this city quarter.[24]

The first principle of the regeneration strategy was to ensure the survival of small textile companies in their present location within The Lace Market. For this purpose Roche suggested that Plumptre Street should be the focus of a programme of property acquisition and refurbishment for use as workshops. Two hundred square feet of floorspace was to be let at affordable rents. In addition, it was proposed that a Grade Two-listed school house should be developed as a Textile Experience Centre. The second strand in the strategy was to revive the Adams Building and create a new focus for a New Lace Market. The Adams Building is the most grand of the industrial buildings in the area. It was designed by T.C. Hine in the Italianate Style and built in 1885. It is the focal point of The Lace Market. It was to be rehabilitated and converted for retail use on the ground floor. There was to be a 120-room hotel and 30 000 square feet of residential apartments on the upper floors. A small public square was to be sited next to the Adams building on a dilapidated car park. The public square was to be enclosed on the west, with the new four-storey Lace Market Building acting as a gateway into the quarter. The third strand in the regeneration strategy was to create a major extension to the Broadmarsh Centre with direct links with The Lace Market, along a retail route through Weekday Cross. The remaining principles of the strategy were to maintain the present mix of land uses; to meet essential car parking requirements within each site and to build multi-storey car parks adjacent to the Ring Road; and finally to create The

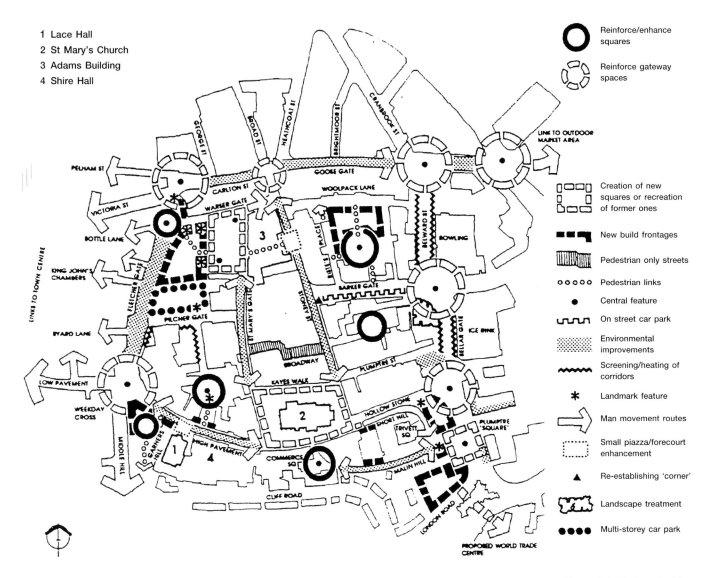

1 Lace Hall
2 St Mary's Church
3 Adams Building
4 Shire Hall

Reinforce/enhance squares

Reinforce gateway spaces

LINK TO OUTDOOR MARKET AREA

Creation of new squares or recreation of former ones

New build frontages

Pedestrian only streets

○○○○○ Pedestrian links

● Central feature

On street car park

Environmental improvements

Screening/heating of corridors

✳ Landmark feature

Man movement routes

Small piazza/forecourt enhancement

▲ Re-establishing 'corner'

Landscape treatment

●●●● Multi-storey car park

Figure 4.9 Strategy for The Lace Market by Tibbalds and colleagues.

Lace Market as an Historic Urban Park.

The Lace Market Development Company was launched in 1989 to stimulate the regeneration of The Lace Market. The Lace Market Development Company, together with Nottingham City Council and Nottingham Tourism Development Action Programme, commissioned a further report by consultants Tibbalds, Karski, Colbourne and Williams. The report by Tibbalds and his colleagues recommended the declaration of The Lace Market as a National Heritage Area.[25] Figure 4.9 illustrates the design strategy proposed in the report which is

Figure 4.10 SWOT
analysis (part).

Opportunities

1 Potential of Shire Hall
2 Boots first shop
3 Vacant/underused warehouse buildings and sites
4 Better pedestrian links to city centre
5 LRT
6 Improved traffic management
7 Bringing together of various activities associated with the area (e.g. lace)
8 Creating a mixed-use people's place
9 Environmental improvement
10 Events (e.g. Warser Gate Square)
11 Potential to link Broadmarsh caves and other caves
12 Possible relocation of English Heritage to Lace Market
13 Development of industrial tourism
14 Possible development of national (international) lace centre
15 Education
16 Interpret heritage in depth
17 Potential to provide Nottingham with a richer, more integrated national tourism product
18 Packaging of Lace Market as part of city centre
19 Pedestrian tourist trail from castle
20 Retailing (speciality/independent)
21 Factory shops
22 Thematic interpretation of Goose Gate
23 Opportunity to improve car parking
24 Opportunity for hotel development
25 Gateway treatment of Weekday Cross
26 Adams Building – focal point
27 Craft Festival Market
28 European aid
29 Cultural events
30 Media industry
31 Fashion Centre

Threats

1 Speculative increase in land values
2 Unecomonic costs of refurbishment
3 Constraints on local authority spending
4 Increased rents may displace independent shops
5 Ownership – single ownership/fragmented and private
6 Current economic circumstances – investment limited to north/south of centre/out-of-town retailing
7 Loss of traditional crafts in building industry (need for supervision by grant-aiding authorities)

based in part on a SWOT analysis. The summary of the SWOT analysis identified twenty-six items under the headings **Strengths**, thirty-two **Weaknesses**, thirty-one **Opportunities** and seven **Threats.** Figure 4.10 shows the opportunities and threats listed in the report. Such lists, resulting from brainstorming sessions with members of the public, are a useful starting point for an urban design study. Analysis of such long lists takes on greater significance if structured as shown in Figure 4.4 and arranged in some order of importance.

The onset of the recession in the late 1980s made it difficult to achieve a property-based regeneration. It was particularly difficult to achieve a development control strategy which prevented the loss of clothing, textile and other manufacturing floorspace to offices.[26] The Lace Market Heritage Trust was set up in 1993 as a private-/public-sector partnership to reflect the need for development not solely based on property regeneration.[27] Since then there have been significant improvements in conditions in Nottingham Lace Market. In terms of tourism, the Lace Centre is linked to Shire Hall and to the former County Gaol, which opened as a museum (Figures 4.11 and 4.12). In addition, Broadmarsh Caves, of great significance for Nottingham's history, have been opened to the public. While there has been a loss of textile and clothing manufacture, the Fashion Centre has expanded its activities and a new programme of

4.11

4.12

training courses involving local employees was developed, centred on Clarendon College, now part of New College Nottingham.[28] Several buildings have been, or are being, refurbished, including the Adams Building, which is being used by New College Nottingham, a highly significant event for The Lace Market. A further development which will affect The Lace Market is the building of Line 1 of the Nottingham Express Transit (NET). This light rapid transit system will, by the end of 2003, connect The Lace Market to the railway station and bus terminals.[29]

A SWOT analysis of The Lace Market carried out today would have to take into account the quarter's current function, the state of its social, economic and physical environment; recent developments;

Figure 4.11 Lace Hall, High Pavement, The Lace Market.

Figure 4.12 Shire Hall, High Pavement, The Lace Market.

and the commitment to new administrative structures. The Lace Market is in a considerably stronger position than it was even twenty years ago. There is now the Lace Market Heritage Trust with the ability to marshal public and private finance. The area has already received major private-sector investment. Other strengths include a growing list of refurbished properties of distinction, resulting in higher property values, a nascent tourism industry and media industry. The location of The Lace Market close to the city centre makes it an attractive proposition for real estate developments. When all of the proposed NET lines are complete there is the prospect of linking this quarter to many parts of the city by supertram, which will improve the centrality of its location. Despite the tremendous improvements, the main weakness remains the quarter's appearance in some places, of dilapidation and neglect. The location of New College Nottingham in the area - with its student body - together with the building of a number of new flats and apartments, has increased the numbers of people using The Lace Market. Nevertheless, at many times of the day large parts of the quarter are deserted giving the impression, which is not the case, that the Lace Market has been abandoned and left to decay like a deserted town. This isolation gives the area a bad reputation and attracts few pedestrians, particularly in the evenings. There seems little connection between The Lace Market and the city centre across Fletcher Gate from Weekday Cross to Carlton Street. Buildings under construction along Fletcher Gate have the potential to improve connections with the city centre. Service access into the area for industry is weak and conflicts with the need to pedestrianize more of the area. There are few land uses in the heart of The Lace Market - other than New College - which attract heavy flows of pedestrian traffic, and which would help to make the quarter a safer place. Since the relocation of New College in the area, the number of bars and cafés has increased but in some parts of the quarter there are still few ground floor uses which generate activities opening out onto the street. Service access into the area for industry is weak and conflicts with the need to pedestrianize more of the area. There are few land uses in the heart of The Lace Market which attract heavy flows of pedestrian traffic which would help to make the quarter a safer place. Despite recent developments, there are few visitor attractions and no inviting public squares. For pedestrian street traffic to increase significantly these deficiencies in urban structure will need to be addressed. Many of the weaknesses of a place, however, may present other opportunities if they are seen in a more positive light. Seeing only the problems faced by a city quarter can be so negative that it may inhibit the search for innovative solutions.

The Lace Market has the opportunity to build upon the successes of the last twenty years. There is a great opportunity to develop further the tourist potential of this part of Nottingham. It is the site of many nationally important archaeological, historic and townscape elements. These elements must be fully developed and linked if the area is to attract significant numbers of visitors. The area does have the potential to form an Historic Urban Theme Park (Figures 4.11 to 4.14). In addition to its long history and the area's association with the lace industry, The Lace Market also could be developed as a media centre because of its two existing theatres. It already has a street which attracts a fashionable clientele because of the specialized character of its ethnic shops, chic boutiques and restaurants. These attractions need very little to weld them into a viable all-year-round centre for visitors: it does mean establishing a critical mass in terms of the density and numbers of activities associated with tourism. New College, centred on the Adams Building through its expanding staff and student population, is introducing renewed interest into the area. In time, the additional college population will generate pressures for further development and presents an opportunity to bring back life and vitality to The Lace Market. The 'threats' facing The Lace Market should not be used as an excuse to

4.13

4.14

inhibit development. They too can be seen as an opportunity to make arrangements and develop strategies which avoid the effects of economic forces which may prove detrimental to the developmental goals. In the case of The Lace Market there is a danger that the very success of the scheme and the increase in property prices and rentals could damage the fragile basis of the textile industry. The improvement to the environment and the rehabilitation of the many fine buildings in The Lace Market will increase the pressure for floorspace for offices, restaurants, clubs and possibly

Figure 4.13 St Mary's Church, High Pavement, The Lace Market.

Figure 4.14 St Mary's Church, High Pavement, The Lace Market: detail.

Figure 4.15 Canalside development, Nottingham: The Inland Revenue Building by Michael Hopkins and Partners.

Figure 4.16 Canalside development, Nottingham: The Inland Revenue Building by Michael Hopkins and Partners.

residential accommodation. New users moving into the area will generate higher rents which will place additional pressures upon textile companies which presently enjoy low rents. Such companies may be displaced and unable to find alternative accommodation in The Lace Market. Because of the loss of jobs the area would lose its character. The very heart of The Lace Market could be torn out of the quarter as this process of gentrification proceeds. Other 'threats' which are faced by The Lace Market include stagnation caused by the area's incapacity to compete with large-scale developments in the city to the north and south of the site. Prestigious developments are being pursued on the sites of the old warehouses along the canal to the southeast of the city centre. These sites are unencumbered by existing buildings, having been largely cleared and the ground prepared for modern purpose-designed developments, more suited to the needs of the twenty-first century than the fine, but constrained, envelopes of the nineteenth-century buildings of The Lace Market (Figures 4.15 to 4.20). To the north of the city centre the large 1960s Victoria Shopping Centre is being expanded with some up-market shopping which offers strong competition to any possible retail developments in The Lace Market. There is evidence that The Lace Market will survive the challenges it faces; many existing buildings are being converted into residential use; new prestigious buildings for mixed residential and other uses are under construction; plans are being prepared for the complete redevelopment of The Broadmarsh Centre, which will have links with The Lace Market; finally, there are proposals by the City Council to acquire land for a public square in The Lace Market.

NEW CAMPUS FOR THE UNIVERSITY OF NOTTINGHAM

Extensive survey and imaginative analysis do not necessarily result, of themselves, in fine urban design. Without a broad concept or unifying idea the result can only be pedestrian. The University of Nottingham is engaged in building an extension on a new campus much of which is now built and occupied. After an architectural competition, the University of Nottingham engaged Michael Hopkins and Partners to design a new university of remarkable quality. This particular case study is used as a reminder that great city building results from inspiration and imagination and not from method alone. Method is to facilitate and stimulate the imagination. The case study is also used to illustrate how small components of the total problem can be analysed.

The project goal for the new campus is to regenerate a redundant site in Nottingham and to transform it into a distinctive, attractive and environmentally friendly setting for the University's much needed expansion of teaching, research and living accommodation (Figures 4.21 and 4.22). There were a number of reasons for this £40 plus million development. The University of Nottingham is the most sought-after university by prospective undergraduate students. It is also a leading UK university with an international reputation in top quality research as well as teaching. It is therefore anticipated that future expansion of research, teaching and 'technology transfer activities' will lead to pressure on the University Estate and the need for additional space. Perhaps the most interesting reason given for the development of the new campus was the desire to protect 'the treasured environment of the University Park Campus renowned and popular for the beauty and space of its landscape'. Fundamental to the project was the realization that an environment can only support or sustain a limited development before its quality is diminished. Environmental carrying capacity, here linked to the attraction of the main campus for prospective students, is a concept central to sustainable development.

The development of the new campus fully achieves the expectations of the master plan, reflecting some of the most distinctive qualities of University Park, the main university campus (Figures

4.28 to 4.31). The central idea for the regeneration of the site was the creation of a green lung, making it one of the many parks for which Nottingham is known and of which the city is justly proud. The site at Wollaton Road is small when compared with the existing campus. It is located between industrial landscape and suburbia. The concept is linear development following the main lines of the site. Efficiency is derived by segregating the movement of cars and pedestrians. Vehicular traffic, including buses, use one spine route running the length of the site and pedestrians the other main route. There are two main entry points into the site: both roads are lined with trees and are modelled on the Nottingham boulevards which are such a distinctive feature of the road system developed in the city during the nineteenth century and the early parts of the twentieth century. The design for the new campus places great emphasis on the quality of the environment. Existing woodland on the western edge of the site is retained and enhanced as a conservation area for plants and wildlife. A man-made lake is a feature of

Figure 4.17 Canalside development, Nottingham: The Inland Revenue Building by Michael Hopkins and Partners.

Figure 4.18 Canalside
development, Nottingham:
The Courts.

Figure 4.19 Canalside
development, Nottingham:
refurbished warehouse.

Figure 4.20 Canalside development, Nottingham: offices and restaurants.

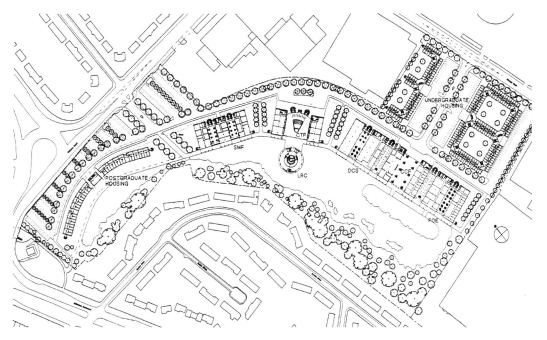

Figure 4.21 The New Campus for the University of Nottingham, by Michael Hopkins and Partners.

Figure 4.22 The New
Campus for the University
of Nottingham, by Michael
Hopkins and Partners:
axonometric.

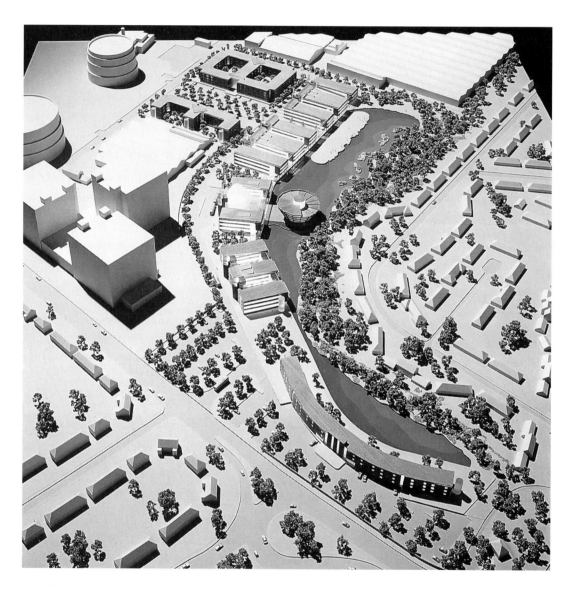

the proposed development.[30] On one side of the lake
is the existing woodland which serves as a buffer
between the university and the residential area. On
the other side, to the east of the lake, is the main
walkway linking all the new buildings. The width
and depth of the lake will vary, which will encourage the establishment of a variety of wildlife. There is
an environmental strategy for the buildings, the aim
of which is to deliver the optimum sustainable
construction and energy performance. The buildings
are designed with climate-modifying façades, an
efficient ventilation system and atria with extensive

Spaces between buldings

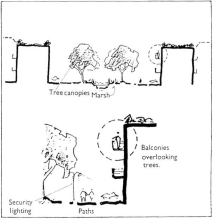

4.23

.........Pedestrians arcades & covered walkways

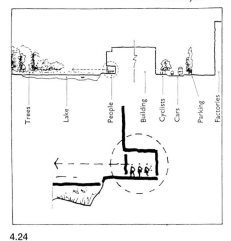

4.24

Glass covered walkways

4.25

Figures 4.23–4.27 The New Campus for the University of Nottingham, by Michael Hopkins and Partners: detail.

Fast running water....

4.26

....and calm water at open expanses.

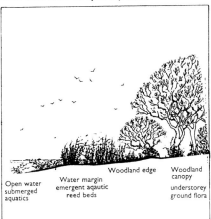

4.27

planting. The various departments are arranged in distinct buildings along the spine. The buildings are set in parkland following the landscape tradition of the main university campus. Visual and physical links are established by the sharing of common spaces which form internal piazzas where people can meet and socialize.

The illustrations for the new campus include a series of informative thumb nail sketches. They illustrate the solution to a number of the design problems in the new campus (Figures 4.23 to 4.31). This method of analysing and expressing ideas for solving key parts of the total problem is a most useful analytical technique during problem explor-

4.28

4.29

Figure 4.28 Nottingham
University, New Campus:
Postgraduate Residential
Accommodation.
Figure 4.29 Nottingham
University, New Campus:
Teaching Area.
Figure 4.30 Nottingham
University, New Campus:
Resource Centre.

4.30

Figure 4.31 Nottingham University, New Campus: Centre for School Leadership.

ation: thumb nail sketches are also worth many thousand words of explanation.

CONCLUSION

The New Campus for the University of Nottingham is the result of an International Competition won by Michael Hopkins and Partners. The new campus, having won awards for its environmental design, is proving to be a benchmark for architectural quality and a stimulus for the regeneration of a run-down area in Nottingham. It is, above all else, a fine example of urban design which should serve as a model both of method and of ideas for city development during the twenty-first century. Its inclusion in this particular place in the book is to emphasize that the design idea is as important as the method. Good design does not necessarily follow the application of sound method. Ideas may result from a

flash of inspiration and when it does, the idea should be grasped, developed and accepted with gratitude. The designer, however, cannot wait for inspiration. He or she follows a method which is likely to stimulate the generation of ideas. This chapter has examined the role of forecasting, constraints and possibilities mapping and SWOT analysis, while the next chapter will explore some of the techniques for generating alternative design concepts.

REFERENCES

1   More complex matrix techniques of forecasting for use in modelling can be found in McLoughlin, J.B. (1969) *Urban and Regional Planning: A Systems Approach*, London: Faber and Faber, and in Field, B. and MacGregor, B. (1987) *Forecasting Techniques for Urban and Regional Planning*, London: Hutchinson.

2   Ratcliffe, J. (1974) *An Introduction to Town and Country Planning*, London: Hutchinson.

3   Day, A. (1994) New tools for urban design, *Urban Design Quarterly*, No. 51, pp. 20-23.

4   Batty, M., Dodge, M. *et al.* (1998) *GIS and Urban Design*, Centre for Advanced Spatial Analysis (CASA), London, UCL.

5   Batty, M. *et al.* (1998) *op cit.*

6   Available to the academic community via EDINA Digmap, a national datacentre financed by the Joint Information Systems Committee based at Edinburgh University Data Library.

7   Available for academic purposes at Manchester Information & Associated Services (MIMAS).

8   Available via CHEST the Combined Higher Education Software Team.

9   Batty, M. *et al.* (1998) *op cit.*

10 Batty, M. *et al.* (1998) *op cit.*

11 Hillier, B. and Hanson, J. (1984) *The Social Logic of Space*, Cambridge: Cambridge University Press.

12 Jiang, B. *et al.* (2000) Integration of space syntax into Gis for modelling urban spaces, *International Journal of Applied Earth Observation and Geoinformation*, 2 (2/3).

13 *Ibid*, p. 162.

14 *Ibid*, p. 163.

15 *Ibid*.

16 Jiang, B., Claramount, C. and Batty, M. (1998) Geometric accessibility and geographic information: extending desktop GIS to space syntax, *Computing Environment and Urban Systems*, 23(2).

17 Axwoman is available at http://www.hig.se/~bjg/Axwoman.htm

18 Jiang, B. *et al.* (2000) *op cit.*

19 Rushcliffe Borough Council (1986) *Gamston Development Plan*, Nottingham, December.

20 Source: Rushcliffe Crime and Disorder Reduction Partnership.

21 Jiang, B. *et al.* (2000) *op cit.*

22 Bevan, O.A. (1991) *Marketing and Property People*, London: Macmillan.

23 Nottingham City Planning Department (1989) *Nottingham Lace Market, Development Strategy*, Nottingham: Nottingham City Council.

24 Roche, Conran (1989) *Nottingham Lace Market: The Vision, Report One*, and *Detailed Proposals and Impacts, Report Two*, Nottingham: Conran Roche.

25 Tibbalds, F., Karski, Colbourne, Williams in association with Touchstone (1991) *National Heritage Area Study: Nottingham Lace Market*, Nottingham: Nottingham City Council.

26 *Nottingham Evening Post*, 8 August 1991.

27 *Nottingham Evening Post*, 3 July 1996.

28 *Nottingham Evening Post*, 30 December 1996.

29 The University of Nottingham (12 November 1996) *New Campus Fact Sheet*, Nottingham: The University of Nottingham.

30 Fawcett, P. (12 November 1996) *The New Campus: An Architectural Appreciation*, Nottingham: The University of Nottingham.

GENERATING ALTERNATIVES

5

INTRODUCTION

Central to the urban design process is the exploration of problems through an examination and testing of solutions. Many of the problems in urban design could be described as 'wicked', in the sense that they are difficult to define and they are without an obvious and generally agreed solution. The nature of the process, therefore, by which these problems are approached is dialectical, taking the form of a dialogue between problem and solution. Inevitably the designer expends considerable energy understanding the problems with which he or she is confronted. Clearly the designer, by engaging in this dialectic between problem and solution, clarifies the definition of the problem and the direction of the investigation necessary to seek the solution, as the process itself evolves. The nature of the problem only becomes clear as the iterative process develops. The solutions or ideas used in solving urban design problems for the purpose of this text will be termed concepts. Generating design ideas for solving problems of urban structure is fundamental to urban design. Design concepts are the basis of the creative process: without them the process of urban design degenerates into a sterile activity. Generating concepts is an act of the imagi-

nation. Concepts, or the ideas which inform alternative ways of perceiving the problem, can be generated using a number of techniques. Ideas can be gleaned from an analysis of the site, from a study of historical precedent, from theoretical propositions, by using synectical techniques or the art of analogy, by techniques of lateral thinking including brainstorming and by seeking ideas directly from the public. This chapter explores the use of analogy for the generation of ideas; being particularly concerned with concepts drawn from nature. Case studies from Surrey, Derby and Norway illustrate the use of some of these concepts in practice. The chapter also explores techniques used when working with the public on the process of concept formation. The process of public participation in design is illustrated with a case study from Newark in Nottinghamshire.

According to Lynch there are three main metaphors which attempt to explain city form.[1] The magical metaphor for the earliest ceremonial centres attempted to link the city to the cosmos and to the environment. The second metaphor uses the machine as an analogy for the city. The concept of the city as a machine is quite different from conceptualizing it as a microcosm of the universe, a perfect unity modelled on the universe and anchored by orienta-

Figure 5.1 Linear city by Soria y Mata.

Figure 5.2 Cité Industrielle by Garnier.

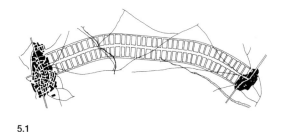

5.1

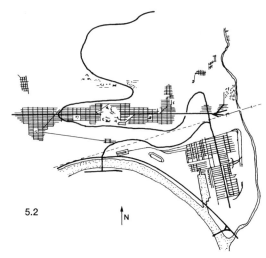

5.2 ↑N

Figure 5.3 The linear city of Miliutin.

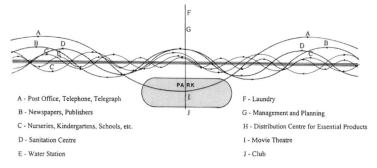

A - Post Office, Telephone, Telegraph
B - Newspapers, Publishers
C - Nurseries, Kindergartens, Schools, etc.
D - Sanitation Centre
E - Water Station

F - Laundry
G - Management and Planning
H - Distribution Centre for Essential Products
I - Movie Theatre
J - Club

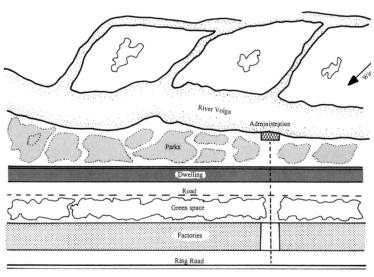

tion to the magical path of the sun. The idea of the city as a machine is not purely a twentieth-century phenomenon - its roots lie much deeper. In the last century, however, the idea was developed and elevated to a predominant position by movements such as Futurism and the writings of Le Corbusier, particularly his project for the Radiant City.[2] Other landmarks in the development of this idea of the city as a machine are the linear suburbs for Madrid by Arturo Soria y Mata in 1894 and the *Cité Industrielle* by Tony Garnier (Figures 5.1 and 5.2).[3] In contrast, followers of Geddes and Mumford describe the city in organic terms. For them the city is an organism which is born, grows and dies: it can be healthy or diseased.[4] Concepts of the city, in part, have their origins in one of these generic ideas and can only be understood when seen against this larger picture.

The city, when thought of as a machine, is composed of small parts linked like cogs in a wheel; all the parts having clear functions and separate motions. In its most expressive form it can have the clarity of a crystal or it can be a daring exposition of rationality. The early work of Le Corbusier exhibits these heroic qualities. It can also appear coldly functional with undertones of social engineering and state control. Miliutin develops the machine theme in his ideas for Sotsograd.[5] He uses the analogy of the power station or the assembly line for his city, separating it into autonomous parts of separate land uses connected by a rationally designed transport network (Figure 5.3).

The idea of the city as a machine is as old as civilization itself, pre-dating the nineteenth century and the industrial revolution: it is not based only on recent ideas, such as the complex assembly line made famous by Chaplin in *Hard Times*, but also parallels the use and development of simple ancient machines such as the lever, the pulley and that great invention, the wheel. The concept of the city as machine can be found taking a most inhuman form in the workers' villages in Pharaonic Egypt (Figure 5.4). The plan is based on the use of the regular grid; all the parts being repeated in a regular pattern.

The third metaphor, and the most relevant for the sustainable city, is the analogy of an organism. Using this metaphor the city is seen as being composed of cells which can grow, decline and die. This city metaphor is associated with developments in the biological sciences during the last 200 years. It can be regarded as a reaction to the worst features associated with the industrial revolution and the growth of cities. As an idea for city development the organic model is associated with Howard, Geddes, Mumford and Olmstead. In this country Unwin and Perry gave architectural form to these ideas. In North America Frank Lloyd Wright's work during the early part of this century set a pattern for an organic architecture wedded to the landscape.[6] Alexander in his writing also emphasizes the organic nature of environmental design: '... natural or organic order emerges when there is a perfect balance between the individual parts of the environment and the needs of the whole'.[7]

The main principle of organic planning is the structuring of the city into communities, each of which is a self-contained unit for the immediate necessities of life. The sustainable city would also be self-contained for much of its energy needs and would recycle day-to-day waste products, reducing

Figure 5.4 Workers' village, Amarna, Egypt.

the export of pollution to a minimum. Co-operation rather than competition is emphasized in the organic model of the city. Community members are interdependent within a unit of collaboration and offer mutual support. A community, when healthy, is a group of diverse individuals tending towards some optimum balance necessary for the smooth working of the community. The organic city is organized into a hierarchy of units within which are sub-units, which in turn are composed of smaller sub-sub-units.

The organic city has an optimum size: the city is born and, like organisms, comes to maturity, persists if healthy, or declines and dies if diseased. The aim of sustainable development is to prolong the life of healthy cities, that is, those cities which provide the basis of a good quality of life for their citizens without, at the same time, destroying the global environment. City health is maintained only while the balance within and between its components are maintained. Excess growth is managed and maintained by the birth or propagation of new settlements or colonies. How much growth, or indeed any growth, can be maintained at the global scale is debatable. Some scholars see population growth as a major cause of the problems which endanger the world. They advocate a steady state or preferably a decline in population and an economic slowdown.

The organic model of the city is most in tune with the concept of sustainable development, particularly when it takes on the attributes of the ecosystem. The analogy for the optimum stage in city development is the ecological climax, that is, where there is a sufficient diversity in its components to maintain a balance between the energy inputs and outputs. The optimum or balanced stage of city development reduces pollution and waste production through processes of recycling. In simplistic terms the city deals with its own dirty washing. Decay, according to the organic model of the city, is apparent in settlements where the delicate balance of its components breaks down, excessive growth occurs and where self-healing ceases. The result can be likened to cancer or uncontrolled growth. Sustainable development and organic city theory both conceptualize the settlement as a whole, and both develop within a holistic paradigm where the elements or parts of the city are not strictly separate but supportive. The organic city as an idea has the delight, diversity and subtlety of the natural world. It is, indeed, a part of nature.

An understanding of man's settlement pattern and its relationship with the larger world of nature is illuminated by the work of Lovelock and his Gaian theory.[8] Gaian theory has, as its premise, the idea that the Earth is a superorganism which is actively self-regulating. Lovelock rejects the notion that the Earth seen as a self-regulating organism is necessarily a teleological concept. He maintains that a self-regulating superorganism, such as his concept of Gaia, does not require a biota with both foresight and skills in planning. To investigate and dismiss this particular criticism of his Gaia hypothesis as teleological, Lovelock invented Daisyworld. Daisyworld is a simplified model of our planet consisting only of a flora of different coloured daisies. Lovelock showed mathematically how the living plants could adjust the proportions of the various coloured varieties, so

changing the planet's conditions, to maintain a life-supporting environment suited to the plants' requirements. Life on this planet is a paradoxical contradiction to the second law of thermodynamics which states that everything has been, is, and always will be, running down to equilibrium and death. It is rather like a wound clock spring, which slowly unwinds until the clock stops. Natural processes always move towards an increase of disorder, measured by entropy, a quantity that inexorably increases. The normal expectancy for a planet like Earth is an inert, lifeless mass such as Venus or Mars. Lovelock illustrates the paradox of life on Earth in this way: 'Yet life is characterised by an omnipresence of improbability that would make winning a sweepstake every day for a year seem trivial by comparison. Even more remarkable this unstable, this apparently illegal, state of life has persisted on Earth for a sizeable fraction of the age of the Universe. In no way does life violate the second law, it has evolved with the Earth as a tightly coupled system so as to favour survival'.[9]

Permaculture, a theory developed by Mollinson, like Gaia theory, has for its starting point life and the world of nature: like Gaia theory it, too, is a useful tool for the design of sustainable urban forms.[10] Both theories are essential reading for the Urban Designer in the new millennium. They provide the core of the ethics and philosophy of sustainable development. Permaculture, which is short for permanent agriculture, is 'the conscious design and maintenance of agriculturally productive ecosystems which have diversity, stability and resilience of natural ecosystems. It is the harmonious integration of landscape and people providing their food, energy, shelter, and other material and non material needs in a sustainable way'.[11] Permaculture parallels Lovelock's notion that the Earth is an information process which is self-regulating, self-constructed and reactive system, creating and preserving the conditions that make life possible. This system actively adjusts to regulate disturbances. Mollinson attempts to build a theory which will prevent humanity, in its present mindlessness, from developing into the final disturbance which the Earth cannot tolerate.

Permaculture has a strong ethical basis which lies at the root of its discipline. The ethical dimension of permaculture can be summarized by three guiding principles:

1   Care of the Earth by providing conditions for all life systems to continue and multiply.
2   Care of people by providing access for them to those resources necessary for human existence.
3   Setting limits to population and consumption in order to be in a position to set aside resources to further the above principles (paraphrased from Mollinson, 1992).

Permaculture is about adopting the mechanisms of a mature ethical behaviour for ensuring the survival of the Earth as a life-sustaining planet. Central to this ethical position is the conservation of energy and resources, the re-use of waste and the consequent reduction of pollution. The chief characteristic of permaculture is the design of a system where its energy needs are provided by the system itself. While modern crop agriculture is totally dependent on external inputs of energy, the Tropical Rain Forest, in contrast, creates its own energy. Consequently it is the model, par excellence, for a system of permaculture. It is self-sufficient and self-sustaining; it is, therefore, a powerful model also for the sustainable city (Figures 5.5 and 5.6).

Energy can be transferred from one form to another but it cannot disappear, or be created, or be destroyed. While the total energy in the Universe is constant the total entropy is increasing. Entropy is that energy which has been dissipated and is unavailable for work: it is no longer useful energy. When we put petrol into the car it has potential but when the potential is realized as movement the energy is dissipated as heat, noise and exhaust fumes. The question for the urban designer is: how best can the available energy be used before it

passes from the site or from the city? The aim for urban design then becomes to trap, store and re-use as much energy as possible on its path to increasing entropy.

Permaculture has a number of broad implications for urban design and settlement planning. Primarily, it means creating regions with stable populations where cities, homes and gardens feed and shelter the population. It is a question of getting our 'own house in order' so that it supports us and our daily needs. For Mollinson (1992) this is a process empowering the powerless to create 'a million villages' to replace the nation state: he sees this as the only safe route to ensuring the preservation of the biosphere.[12] While not wishing to be drawn into this large geo-political debate, it does seem sensible to organize city regions so that they are capable of both feeding the population and dealing with organic waste. The cities of today return little energy to the systems which supply them. They pass on wastes as pollutants to the sea and to the land, having developed a one-way trade with respect to their food supplies. For this to change, the city has to be planned as a self-governing and self-managing garden. One important objective for each development project within such a garden city is to maximize its food-producing capacity and have clear links with a local system for recycling organic waste.

The use of energy in city construction has been explained in *Urban Design: Green Dimensions*.[13] In summary, the practical design considerations are to construct systems which last as long as possible; to repair and renew systems rather than replace them; to construct buildings fuelled where possible by the sun; to design transport regions where the need for mobility is minimized and, where necessary, movements are largely by foot, bicycle and public transport. It requires that urban governance be conducted in a manner which emphasizes public participation in planning, design, system construction and environmental management. The basic components of such a sustainable city region are the

Figure 5.5 Ecological garden design.

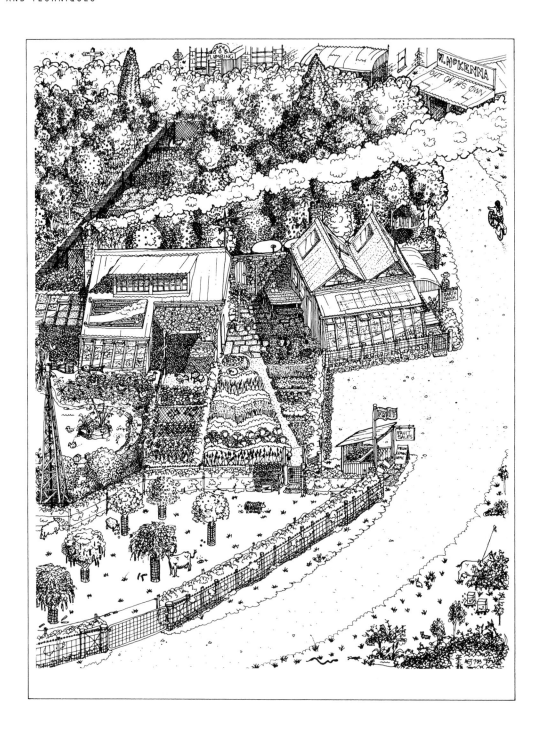

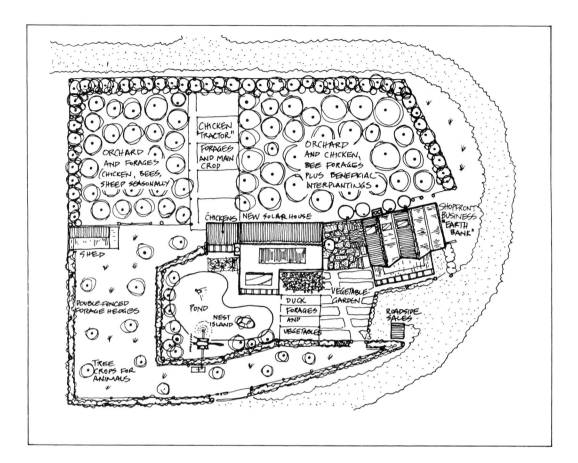

Figure 5.6 Ecological garden design.

quarter, or in Mollinson's terms, the village; the street block surrounding its own green space; the individual home with its own supporting garden; and the green wedge connecting the city centre to the surrounding countryside.

A technique used in permaculture and appropriate for urban design is systems analysis. A clear distinction exists between the 'closed system' of thermodynamics and the 'open system' of living organisms. Two quotes taken from Mollinson make this point graphically:[14]

> All living organisms ... are 'open systems'; that is to say, they maintain their complex forms and functions through continuous exchanges of energies and materials with their environment. Instead of 'running down' like a clock that dissipates its energy through friction, the living organism is constantly 'building up' more complex substances from the substance it feeds on, more complex forms of energies from the energies it absorbs, and more complex patterns of information ... perceptions, feelings, thoughts ... from the input of its receptor organs.

Most thermodynamic problems concern 'closed' systems, where the reactions take place in confinement, and can be reversed; an example is the expansion and compression of gas in a cylinder. But in an open system, energy is gained or lost irreversibly, and the system, its environment, or both are changed by the interaction ... the second law of thermodynamics (states that) energy tends to dissipate towards entropy, or chaos. In seeming violation of that law, biological systems tend to become increasingly more complex and efficient.

The aim of urban design is the development of the city and its parts as open systems, constantly building up more complex forms of energies from the energy absorbed. This view of the city is in contrast to the city visualized as a mechanism with its parts functioning like clockwork. The result of working to this philosophy of the city as machine is the parasitic metropolis feeding off its host, giving little in return and leading ultimately, if not checked, to the demise of itself and its host.

A design concept strongly associated with sustainable development is the idea of mixed land uses. As a concept it has its origin in the rejection of rigid and inhuman land-use zoning associated with the mechanistic model of city planning as practised earlier in the last century. For those espousing sustainable development, localities of mixed land use present the prospect of self-sufficient communities, while at the same time reducing the need to commute great distances from home to work, from home to school or from home to shopping centre. As a concept it is a tentative step towards an 'open systems' view of settlement. Such a systemic analysis of settlement concentrates on the relationship and linkages between design components. Any design for a human settlement involves concepts or ideas about the problem and its solution, techniques for performing essential design tasks, strategies for achieving a future goal and the materials of construction. Urban design is the method used to assemble the components of city design, whether they are concepts, ethical propositions, social imperatives or the physical structures of design such as buildings, infrastructure, land and vegetation: the purpose of the process being sustainable development and security of man and all living beings. Central, therefore, to urban design is an analysis of the linkages between the various components, even

if that analysis is no more than the simple listing of each component's characteristics. The ultimate aim of the analysis is the location at close proximity of those activities which are mutually supportive. Design policies which support mixed land uses at the local level of the quarter or residential neighbourhood are compatible with this aim. While the use of a regime of mixed land uses is not an alternative to a more detailed analysis of major linkages, it is a sound basis for such a more definitive study.

Each urban activity has outputs, yields or products which become resources only when they are used productively. They become pollutants if they are not used constructively by the system being designed. Each activity also has inputs, needs or demands on resources. If these inputs are not being supplied by the design system, then energy has to be found to satisfy those demands from without the system. In terms of permaculture theory, 'A POLLUTANT is an output of any system component that is not being used productively by any other component of the system. EXTRA WORK is the result of an input not automatically provided by another component of the system'.[15] The aim, therefore, of urban design is to develop systems where the outputs from activities become the inputs for adjacent activities. In the sustainable city the location of activities is not only or necessarily a function of economics, but more importantly it is location strategies which attempt to minimize the export of pollution and the importation of additional inputs of resources, or EXTRA WORK, from beyond the boundary of the system.

The concept of the self-sufficient, neighbourhood, quarter or urban village is a useful tool for structuring the sustainable city region.[16] The early new towns built in Britain after the Second World War, to some extent, achieved this aim. In many ways the early post-war new towns in Britain adopted an organic structure with components organized like living cells. New towns such as Harlow by Gibberd are structured on an hierarchical basis: the city comprising four main districts, each with its own district centre. Districts are sub-divided into neigh-bourhoods with a neighbourhood centre. The neigh-bourhoods further divide into distinct housing areas, which in turn sub-divide into housing clusters, each composed of the basic unit or cell - the home of the nuclear family (Figure 5.7).

McKie's concept for 'cellular renewal' is a partic-ularly good example of organic planning.[17] He devised a model for restructuring streets and run-down neighbourhoods in inner-city areas. His suggestion was to replace comprehensive redevelop-ment, then the favoured tool for city restructuring, with a more sympathetic small-scale process of rehabilitation and regeneration. There was evidence, at the time McKie was working, to show that comprehensive redevelopment destroyed many vital communities in the process of renewing the physi-cal structure. Cellular renewal depends for its success on a detailed survey of individual properties

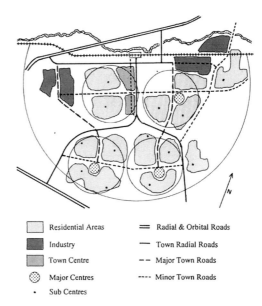

Figure 5.7 Harlow new town, structure diagram.

	Residential Areas		Radial & Orbital Roads
	Industry		Town Radial Roads
	Town Centre		Major Town Roads
	Major Centres		Minor Town Roads
	Sub Centres		

Figure 5.8 Cellular renewal.

Cells	1 Standard of amenities	2 Structural deficiency	3 Internal arrangement	4 Internal maintenance	5 Externalities/ social costs	6 Tenure	7 Household type/mobility	8 Household's perception of environmental deficiency	9 Social/kinship ties	10 Workplace ties	11 External amenity	12 Deficiency of effective demand for improved housing	Rating	Special notes
1	d	d	c	c	c	b	c	c	c	b	b	b	c	Small families in private lets
2	a	b	a	b	b	a	c	c	b	c	b	b	b	Small adult families, first time owner occupiers
3	c	c	c	d	c	d	d	c	d	a	b	c	c d	Mainly students
4	b	b	b	c	b	c	a	a	a	d	a	a	a b	Old people renting from local authority, improve?
5	a	a	a	b	b	c	c	d	c	c	b	b	a/c	Families anxious to move. Possible source of houses for internal relocation
6	c	b	b	c	c	b	a	a/b	a	d	a	a	a b	Older people in private lets. Improvement potential?
7														

Figure 5.9 Duomo, S. Maria del Fiore, Florence.

Figure 5.10 Rialto Bridge, Venice.

5.9

5.10

to determine the precise state of each structure and the stage of development of the social unit or family occupying that particular structure. Each unit or home was described as a cell. A soft cell, one ripe for immediate renewal, was one which was in poor physical condition and where the family was in great need of rehousing. A hard cell, one which could take low priority for redevelopment or rehabilitation, was a property in reasonable condition and was perhaps occupied by an elderly person owning the property and unwilling to move. Such a property could be left until the owner died or moved willingly to sheltered accommodation. This organic concept of the neighbourhood proposed a slow renewal process refurbishing some properties, replacing others, but carried out in a piecemeal fashion which did not disturb the community and which was in tune with the natural growth and decay of families (Figure 5.8).

Alexander, in *The Oregon Experiment*, developed a technique aimed at reproducing the organic order of the much admired, traditional European city[18] (Figures 5.9 and 5.10). Cities such as Florence or Venice seem to owe their great qualities to natural growth without recourse to formal planning. In the organic theory of urban design developed by Alexander *et al.*, process and form are one.[19] While the process of city structuring results in the form,

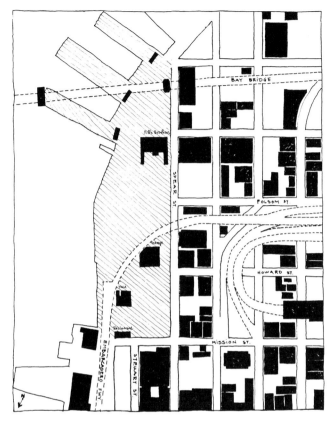

5.11

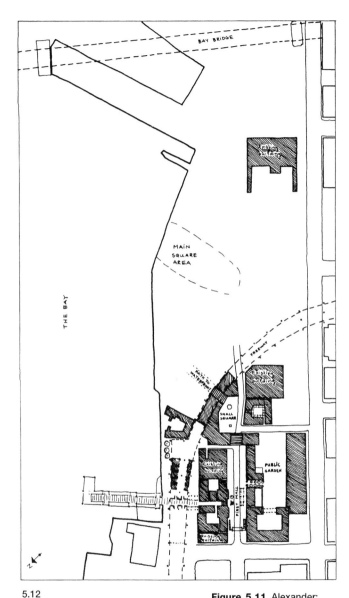

5.12

the form is apparent from the beginning: the pattern is in the seed, that is, at the point of origin. For example, while the growth of any acorn results in an oak tree, no two trees are identical even though each tree is composed of similar elements. So, too, with the organic or sustainable city, its pattern is established by the principles used for the design and linkage of the parts.

Alexander developed a number of key principles for the design of organic cities. One of these principles of organic development states that growth should be piecemeal with a guaranteed mixed flow of various size projects. In detail he specifies that no single increment should be too large and that

Figure 5.11 Alexander: organic design process, the site.

Figure 5.12 Alexander: organic design process, early stage in the process.

Figure 5.13 Alexander: organic design process, midway through the process.

Figure 5.14 Alexander: organic design process, towards the end of the process.

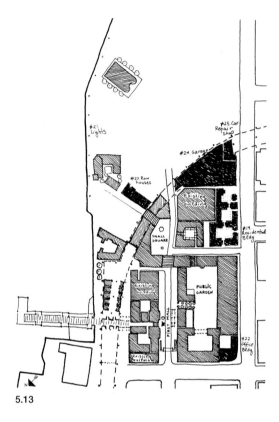

5.13

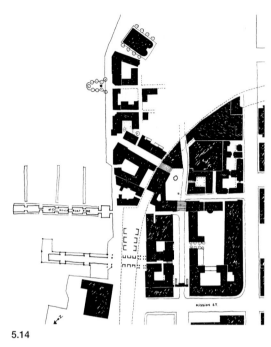

5.14

'There are equal numbers of large, medium and small projects'.[20] There is an argument in favour of reducing Alexander's figure of 100 000 for the largest single city development so that even the largest developments would be in keeping with the small scale of sustainable settlements.[21] The idea of developing the city as a series of incremental experimental steps without the guide of a comprehensive blueprint which defines in detail the form of the end product does seem to fit closely with the principles of permaculture.

Alexander's second rule for the organic urban design process is 'The Growth of Larger Wholes'. For the purpose of this particular rule every increment to the city should help to form one larger whole in the fabric of the settlement: 'In the

process of growth, certain larger structures, or centres, emerge. These larger centres are distinct and recognizable entities, larger than any individual building'. These centres are normally public spaces, the creation of which is detailed in Alexander's Rule 4 'Every building should create coherent and well-shaped public space next to it'. The essence of Alexander's theory is the aim to heal the city or to make it whole by the creation of a field of overlapping centres or wholes. Rules 5 and 6 deal with the detailed design of buildings and structures, which is not the main concern of this particular book. However, it is interesting to note that even in the case of building structure Alexander is still analysing the elements, such as windows, floors or columns in terms of the creation of centres and wholes. This is how Alexander defines the centre: 'A centre is not merely, as the word suggests, a point that happens to be a centre of some larger field. A centre is an entity; if you like, a "thing." It may be a building, an outdoor space, a garden, a wall, a road, a window, a complex of several of these at the same time ... In general, a centre has some kind of elementary symmetry, especially bilateral symmetry ... This does not mean that all centres are perfectly symmetrical. But when an asymmetrical situation occurs, the centring process will generally try to construct the asymmetrical thing, or centre, as a product of simpler centres which are themselves locally symmetrical. It does not permit random asymmetrical arrangements'.[22] Figures 5.11 to 5.15 illustrate the result of Alexander's organic urban design process. For this experiment he used groups of students to design an incremental series of individual projects. Without a master plan and armed only with the principles for the healing or centring process, the design groups prepared ground plans for a new city district which would exhibit some of the qualities associated with a Medieval town in Europe and therefore would fulfil the aim of the process.

CASE STUDIES

This section of the chapter illustrates, with case studies, the use of analogy in the generation of ideas for urban design in the pursuit of sustainable development. The first case study is from Surrey. It explores the theme of permaculture. It is a project which develops from ecological analogy. The second case study is from Derby and outlines the rehabilitation of railway cottages, developing the idea of the urban village. The third case study takes further this idea of the small urban community and shows how such a community can become involved in design. In the process of generating ideas about design, a group of strangers came together to form friendships and a support group, the bedrock of community. The resulting physical structure exhibited the organic qualities associated with the unplanned settlement.

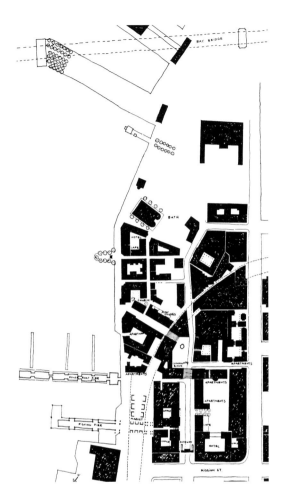

Figure 5.15 Alexander: organic design process, final stage of the process.

The fourth case study is the Norwegian Ecological City. The ideas taken from nature have been developed in Norway and applied to the city as a whole. A number of features of the Ecological City are examined using 'Gamle Oslo' and Bergen as the main examples.

DESIGN FOR ECOLOGICAL SUSTAINABILITY ON AN EIGHT-ACRE SITE IN SURREY, UK
This private residence which is linked to Construction Resources, Ecological Building Centre,

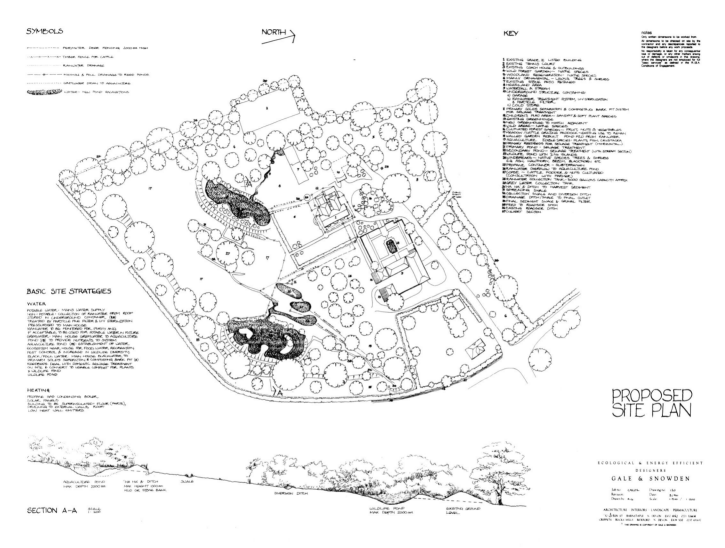

Figure 5.16 Design for ecological sustainability in Surrey, by Gale and Snowden. Plan.

16 Great Guilford Street, London SE1, was designed by Gale and Snowden, an architectural practice based in Barnstaple and specializing in ecological and energy efficient design.

The main concept for the site is the integration of building and landscape to provide the occupants with shelter, energy, food and water in an ecologically sustainable way. The principles of design follow the philosophy of permaculture. An existing seventeenth-century building, when completed and refurbished can, together with the landscape, provide a robust, efficient, self-perpetuating, balanced ecosystem (Figures 5.16 to 5.19). The building will use on-site renewable energies including passive solar heat and coppiced wood, along with effective superinsulation. Sympathetic energy-efficient window and door detailing, draught proofing, passive ventilation and low-energy appliances

Figure 5.17 Design for ecological sustainability in Surrey.

are also features of the design. All materials and products used in the building will be 'healthy', that is, those products and materials which minimize pollution and energy use in manufacture, on the site and in transport.

The landscape is laid out strategically in zones related to their frequency of use, the topography and micro-climate. Planting is mainly native perennial and self-seeding annual vegetation with appropriate introduced species. The aim, over a short period of time, is to increase the diversity of stock of native woodland, plants and animal species. To achieve this, the landscape scheme is designed to increase habitat-diverse micro-climates by the planting of windbreaks, the development of the hedgerow system, the creation of ponds, marsh areas and meadows.

The landscape has also been designed for food production. Low maintenance forest gardens provide fruit, nuts, salads and vegetables. In addition to food production and shelter for wild life the forest garden's other function is to build soil structure for the herb and vegetable gardens surrounding the house. An aquaculture pond and associated marsh area is a feature of the landscaping, producing food in the form of a variety of fish, crustacea and water plants. In addition, the landscape could be organized to support chickens, geese and ducks which are all essential to the ecosystem.

All waste will be recycled on site, creating cyclical systems which mimic the natural ecosystem. Rainwater is used in the home, grey water taken to the aquaculture pond, sewerage is treated by biological means in carbon-filled (wood chips) collection

chambers (bark pits), reed beds and in the ponds on site: the foul water will be converted into usable compost. Compost will be formed by planting nutrient-absorbing species onto sediment collection bunds situated next to the forest garden. Rainwater will be collected and some treated for use as drinking water and for kitchen use. The bulk of the rainwater will be stored in a subterranean tank, purified, and introduced into the building under pressure for WCs, washing machine and dishwasher.

The wildlife pond, being at the end of all aquaculture systems, acts as a large buffer for all water systems. In the summer, a solar PV panel pumps water from the wildlife pond to the aquaculture pond to prevent adverse conditions affecting the various species in the pond. The wildlife pond benefits from fluctuations in depth, as water is pumped to the aquaculture pond permitting a unique habitat to be formed, supporting species which otherwise would not exist on the site.[23]

This is a holistic concept for building and landscape based upon ecological sustainability. The individual elements interact to form the complete ecosystem. It is a concept designed to change and develop as the users come to terms with, and form a symbiotic relationship with, the plants and creatures which also occupy the site. The project designed by Gale and Snowden is a practical application of the principles of permaculture as developed by Mollinson: 'The philosophy behind permaculture is one of working with, rather than against nature; of protracted and thoughtful observation, rather than protracted and thoughtless action; looking at systems in all their functions: and of allowing systems to demonstrate their own evolutions'.[24]

Figure 5.18 Design for ecological sustainability in Surrey.

Figure 5.19 Design for ecological sustainability in Surrey.

THE RAILWAY COTTAGES, DERBY
(Designed by Derek Latham & Company Limited)
Two decades after their conservation was undertaken, the Railway Cottages in Derby (Figure 5.20) are a thriving urban village and a fine example of sustainable living. The village is not a self-sufficient community according to the strict definition by Mollinson. It does not, for example, produce its own food or energy but it has other features associated with sustainable development. There is a well-formed community which has been actively involved with the development. The community lives within walking distance of the city centre and a few yards from the railway station. While some of the residents own cars, the development is not dependent on the car for its continued existence. The Railway Cottages are located in an area where

there are many workplaces and job opportunities. The development also sets a high standard both for conservation practices and for environmental design, two criteria for defining sustainable development. The Railway Cottages in Derby are a particularly appropriate case study, illustrating the practical development of an urban village which adheres to many of the precepts associated with sustainable development.

The Railway Cottages were built in 1840 and are the earliest known railway company cottages in the world. They are adjacent to Derby's station outside the Borough boundary. Despite a campaign to save the cottages by Derby Civic Society, the Council in Derby was not persuaded to rescue them for council housing. They were scheduled for demolition, being on the line of a proposed inner relief road. The only

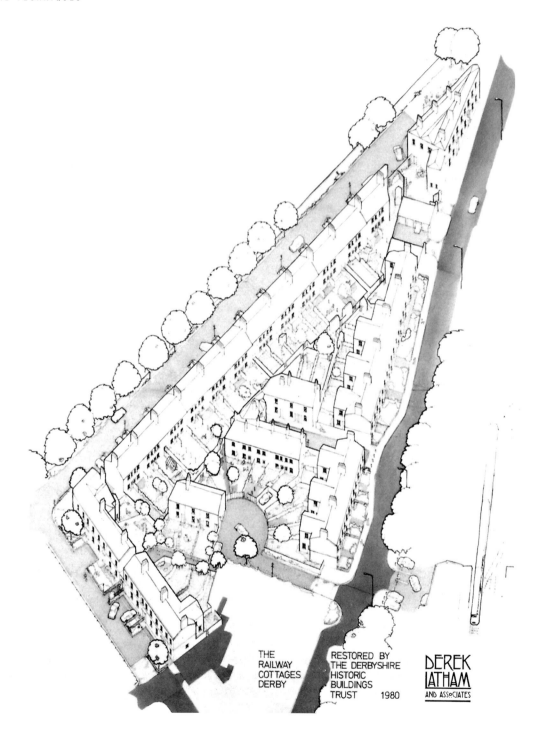

THE
RAILWAY
COTTAGES
DERBY

RESTORED BY
THE DERBYSHIRE
HISTORIC
BUILDINGS
TRUST   1980

DEREK
LATHAM
AND ASSOCIATES

Figure 5.20 Railway
Cottages, Derby.
Axonometric.

Figure 5.21 Railway
Cottages, Derby. Sketch.

reasonable alternative to council housing was the rehabilitation of the cottages for sale on the open market. With this in mind the cottages were bought by Derbyshire Historic Buildings Trust.

Agents advised that there was no market for terraced housing in Derby. The professional view of Estate Agents was that people in Derby wanted either detached or semi-detached houses. In 1979, at the start of the development process, the value of an unimproved terraced house was £5000, and £8000 when improved. After rehabilitation, it was estimated that there would be a shortfall of £2000 per house. This was not a particularly favourable market prediction.

'The key to this conundrum lay in identifying what the market need was and delivering a product that satisfied that need in a unique manner.'[25] The

market identified was for conveniently located dwellings which were attractive two- and three-bedroom houses of compact form but not of minimum size. They were to have generously proportioned rooms, were to be economic to heat, set in an attractive surrounding with a defensible space outside the front door, a decent sized garden and adjacent car parking space. The result of this market research informed the project programme and set the design objectives.

The project was declared a General Improvement Area which made it possible to seek ways to improve the physical context of the properties. Roads on the edge of the site and within it were closed or part closed. This permitted the introduction of gardens with railings and some dedicated car parking space allocated to specific properties. These

Figure 5.22 Railway
Cottages, Derby. Before
rehabilitation.

Figure 5.23 Railway
Cottages, Derby. After
rehabilitation.

improvements increased the rehabilitation costs to £11 500 per house, requiring a new sale price of £12 750. The new sale price was reluctantly accepted as a reasonable valuation by one potential building society which enabled the sale of the first six houses. The demand for the properties increased in the later phases of the project, raising the selling price to £13 500, so creating a project surplus. Ten years on from the original sale, the price of properties had increased by a factor of five.

The project for the Railway Cottages in Derby is a sensitive rehabilitation of fifty-five traditional nineteenth-century dwellings: materials from three cottages demolished to improve daylight in others were re-used; sensitive landscaping and street furniture have been introduced into the area; the development has its own street pub, the original Railway Inn which was also part of the rehabilitation process and now forms a social focus for an active resident group. All this has been achieved in a free market which makes the case study a most promising example for those interested in promoting sustainable development (Figures 5.20 to 5.24).

MILLGATE, NEWARK IN NOTTINGHAMSHIRE (The Nottingham Community Housing Association) Participation in the design process is fundamental for the theories of both sustainable development and permaculture. Both movements aim to empower people so that they are able to take control of the environment in which they live. A theoretical structure for the role of public participation in design and planning was outlined in *Urban Design: Street and Square*, see also *Creating Community Visions*, and *Community Participation in Local Agenda*

Figure 5.24 Railway Cottages, Derby. After rehabilitation.

Figure 5.25 Millgate, Newark, entrance to the site.

PARLIAMENT STREET

21.[26] It is proposed here to illustrate in greater detail some of the techniques which enable people to take part actively in the design process. A case study from Newark, Nottinghamshire, is used to discuss the techniques of participation.

The impetus for the project in Newark came from Mark Vidal-Hall, the Vicar of Chellaston in Derbyshire. He maintained that architects and planners were quite wrong in the methods they use to create communities. His criticism was that as professionals involved in the building industry we placed too much emphasis on physical structures: in effect we were starting from the wrong place. By designing and building the physical structures and then expecting people to move into those structures and form a community we were 'putting the cart before the horse'. His thesis involved a reversal of this process. Vidal-Hall suggested that 'community building' should be completed before the design and construction phase. Adopting this approach means that the group meets, forms a

community, then the group decides the shape of the physical structures necessary to house the community and to meet its needs and fulfil its aspirations. With this elegant idea in mind the Newark experiment was set in motion. The Nottingham Community Housing Association who had been commissioned to build about twenty-five homes on a small site of under one hectare agreed to work on this experiment with the Projects Unit of The Institute of Planning Studies of the University of Nottingham (Figures 5.25 and 5.26).

A description of the project was placed in the local paper with an invitation to a public meeting for families wishing to design their own homes. About fifty families arrived at the meeting from which twenty-five families fitting the requirements of this type of social housing and who were keen to participate were selected. The families ranged from young single people, young married couples, a single-parent family, married couples with older children, and retired single people. The range of

Figure 5.26 Millgate, Newark, the site.

Figure 5.27 Millgate, Newark, design meeting on the site.

5.28

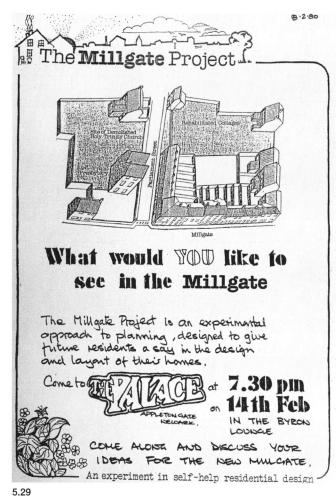

5.29

Figure 5.28 The Millgate project: broadsheet.

Figure 5.29 The Millgate project: broadsheet.

family types, while not statistically representative, nevertheless could be described as balanced. This was the group given the task of forming a community.

The group met in a room close to the site to introduce themselves, to meet the design team and to participate in the arrangements for additional design meetings (Figure 5.27). At the first meeting it was decided to produce a weekly broadsheet listing the forthcoming activities and the latest news about

the project (Figures 5.28 and 5.29). The second meeting was a walk about in the town conducted by architects from the local authority. The task of the architects was to try to show to the group features of Newark which make it so special and, in particular, to look in detail at the visual context of the streets surrounding the site. After these preliminary meetings aimed at building group confidence and solidarity the first design session took place. A model of the site outline was presented to the

Figure 5.30 The Millgate project: working round the model.

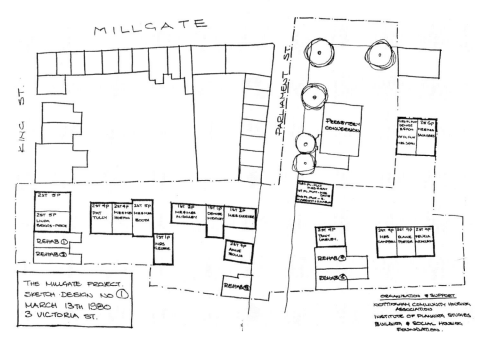

Figure 5.31 The Millgate project: sketch plan.

group by the research team together with a set of model homes made to the same scale. The model homes were made to represent bungalows, flats and two-storey houses of various floor sizes. Each family unit chose a home of a size compatible with the number of people in the family. Each family then printed its name on the bottom of the model home (Figure 5.30).

Right from the initial meeting the group divided into two sub-groups. One sub-group always located their homes to the north of the road dividing the site while the other group chose to locate their homes to the south of the site. Within each sub-group, particular families insisted on locating on adjacent plots. A group of unmarried young people insisted on being together in a block of flats while a married couple with three young children and a single widowed woman wished to be next-door neighbours. The couple intended to take care of both gardens and the older woman was to be the resident baby sitter: during the design process the older woman became an adopted granny. A group of elderly people wished to occupy bungalows on adjacent sites while the single-parent mother with a piano always located on the fringe of the site with the 'room for the piano' facing away from the neigh-bours. The community-building exercise did not precede the design process as we envisaged, but proceeded along with the design. Both processes were in fact parallel. Within three weeks, a plan was prepared showing the position of each family home. It was given to the local authority for comment and, while there were no objections, much greater detail of the project was required (Figure 5.31).

The next stage in the process was to enable individual families to design their own homes. For this purpose each family was asked to describe and,

Figure 5.32 The Millgate project: visit to Milton Keynes.

Figure 5.33 The Millgate project: visit to Milton Keynes.

Figure 5.34 The Millgate project: house model.

5.35

5.36

Figure 5.35 The Millgate project: house model.

Figure 5.36 The Millgate project: house design.

if possible, make a sketch plan of their current home, listing its good and bad features. In addition, a field trip to Milton Keynes was arranged for the group to view a range of house types. The bus trip and pub lunch was part of the community-building process even though the primary purpose of the visit was to widen the group's knowledge-base (Figures 5.32 and 5.33).

The task of home designing was facilitated by the use of another large-scale model. The model consisted

5.37

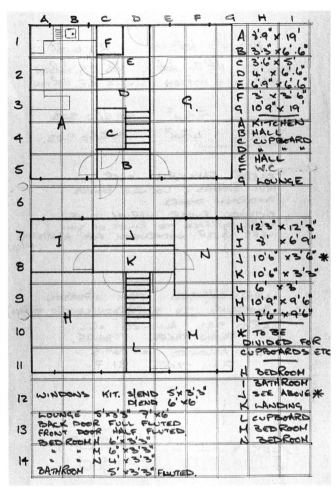

5.38

of a thick chipboard base with deep grooves marking out a checkerboard pattern enclosing 1-m squares at a scale of 1:20. Into these grooves partition walls, window or door units could be placed (Figures 5.34 to 5.37). A thick perspex sheet with a pattern of grooves similar to those on the base represented the first floor. The two floors were separated by pegs at the corners being kept apart at the scale height of the floor. In addition to the wall panels, model staircases of different forms, and furniture and fittings were provided. Each family worked with an architect to design the home of their dreams. The family was allocated the number of squares permitted by the standards for its family size. The architects' role was a difficult one of giving advice only when it was requested. At all times the aim was to try to place control in the hands of the families. The architect could intervene only if he or she could see mistakes of a structural or geometrical nature. Within a three-hour evening session, most families had prepared a

Figure 5.37 The Millgate project: house design.

Figure 5.38 The Millgate project: house plan.

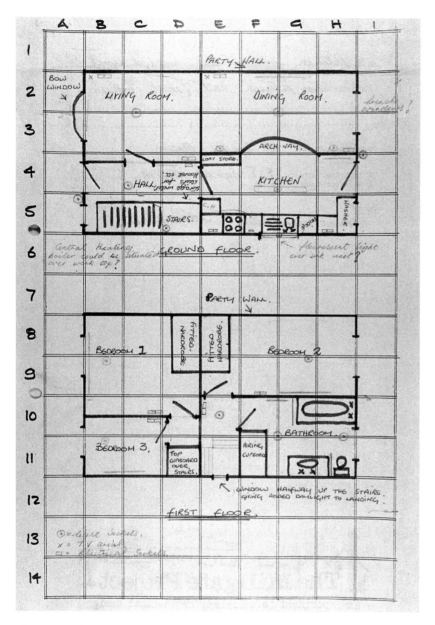

Figure 5.39 The Millgate project: house plan.

5.39). They were also encouraged to give important dimensions for the rooms. The game was described as great fun 'as good as telly'.

The sketches were interpreted by the Projects Unit's architect Dan Bone and redrawn in a professional style. The group, together with the professionals in the team, analysed the drawings, comparing them with the original layout (Figure 5.40). From this critique, anomalies such as windows in party walls were thought about again. Then, for the final design phase, a large-scale polystyrene model of the whole layout was made (Figures 5.41 and 5.42). The purpose of this design phase was to organize the use of the space between and around the buildings. A further group visit was organized to illustrate the landscaping possibilities in the design of this little street. It was decided to take the group to Norwich, which was noted for some of its urban landscaping schemes. The visit to Norwich also became another community-building exercise, cementing friendships in a relaxed atmosphere (Figures 5.43 and 5.44).

The final people's plan was presented to the Housing Association three months after the start of the project and within the time allocated for the exercise (Figure 5.45). The probable cost of the project was determined and found to be about 10 per cent over the limit set by the then Government cost yardstick. The Association's architect, in consultation with the community group, reorganized the scheme to meet the cost yardstick without detriment to the design or the process. Unfortunately, the then Conservative Government placed a moratorium on all 'new build' housing. Two years later the site was developed, the design being based closely on the ideas of the people taking part in the exercise (Figures 5.46 to 5.49).

The project in Newark shows quite clearly that people can become involved in the detailed design of their homes and surrounding environment. It also shows that the process is conducive to the creation of a 'community', taking the form of emerging friendship patterns. Furthermore, the process

design to their satisfaction. They were then asked to transfer the design to squared paper following the checkerboard pattern of the model (Figures 5.38 and

Figure 5.40 The Millgate project: critique of house plans.

Figure 5.41 The Millgate project: large-scale model.

mirrors closely the natural evolution of settlements where myriad decisions produce an environment of great complexity, as opposed to the bland and often inhuman imposition of grandly designed housing estates. For the purpose of public participation in urban design, the model at all scales plays a vital role and, together with educational visits to projects of a similar nature, it becomes a powerful tool in the process of empowerment.

THE ECOLOGICAL CITY: CASE STUDIES FROM NORWAY

Norway can, in many ways, be regarded as the birthplace of sustainable development. Clearly, there are other claims to be first in the field for this particular environmental movement. A number could be made with some justification. But when a leading national politician such as Norway's Brundtland puts her name to a seminal international report on the environment, it indicates active national political support for the idea.[27] For this reason, it is appropriate for a book whose theme is sustainable development to review current ideas in Norway about environmental protection. The planning concept reviewed in this case study is the concept of an Ecological or Environmental City.

The Ministry of Environment, Norway in 1992-1993 initiated a project to promote environmentally sound development in five cities: Fredrikstad, Kristiansand, Bergen, Tromsø and the part of Oslo known as 'Gamle Oslo', or Old Oslo

Figure 5.42 The Millgate project: large-scale model.

Figure 5.43 The Millgate group in Norwich.

Figure 5.44 The Millgate group in Norwich.

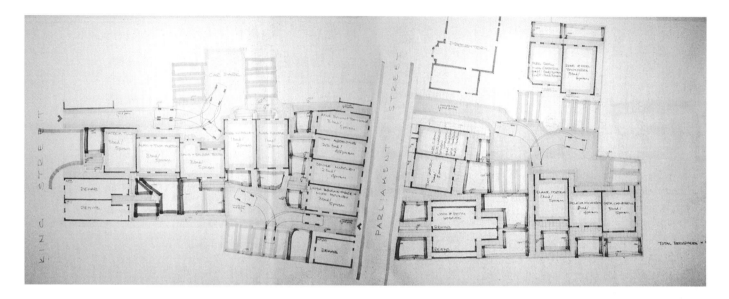

Figure 5.45 Millgate, the people's plan.

Figure 5.46 Millgate. Completed project.

Figure 5.47 Millgate. Completed project.

Figure 5.48 Millgate. Completed project.

Figure 5.49 Millgate. Completed project.

(Figures 5.50 to 5.53). The populations of the project areas range from 19 000 in Gamle Oslo to about 215 000 in Bergen. The objective of the project is to arrive at models for sustainable development while laying the foundation for jobs, improving the environment for children and adolescents and improving the conditions for all people living in the cities.

The project is designed to develop a holistic approach to city planning and design by exploring an ecological vision for the city. The project derives much of its core philosophy from the work of the Brundtland Commission.[28] The main features and priority areas for action in the proposed environmental cities are:

1   Co-ordinated land-use and transport planning with priority being given to environmentally friendly transport, environmental improvement in the cities and an increase of densities in the built-up areas. The land-use pattern is being concentrated and co-ordinated with the transport system in order to reduce consumption from nature, including energy, and to reduce the need for transport. New residential and commercial areas will be concentrated along main corridors and at nodes in the public transit system.

2   Policies have been developed to strengthen the centre as a meeting place for commercial, social and cultural activities. The centre is planned to include a mixture of dwellings, work places, commercial, civic and cultural land uses, so bringing back life to the city centre. The activities in the centre will be reached by environmentally friendly means of transport, which will

reduce the need for out-of-town shopping centres along the highways served by cars.

3   An important feature of the environmental city in Norway is the development of the idea of the 'living neighbourhood' which will have a good quality residential environment and be served by all necessary local services. The living neighbourhood is designed to satisfy many of the residents' needs for services and leisure activities, thereby reducing the need for unnecessary movement in the city.

4   Norway is a country which is well-endowed with a rich natural environment and some magnificent scenery. It is not surprising, therefore, to find that the love of nature plays a prominent part in the planning of the environmental city and in the design of its main components. The aquatic environments and green areas are to be safeguarded for the purposes of recreation, to preserve biological diversity and to ensure that residents will have a close contact with green areas and nature in the vicinity of their homes. The green structure for the city will form part of the network for pedestrians and cyclists, while improving the micro-climate in the city.

5   The responsible management and recycling of waste is fundamental for the development of the ecological city in Norway. For this purpose, the different kinds of waste from households, industry and commercial establishments are sorted at source. Sorting at source leads to smaller quantities of waste, increased recycling, and by example and practice, to a more responsible management of the remaining waste.

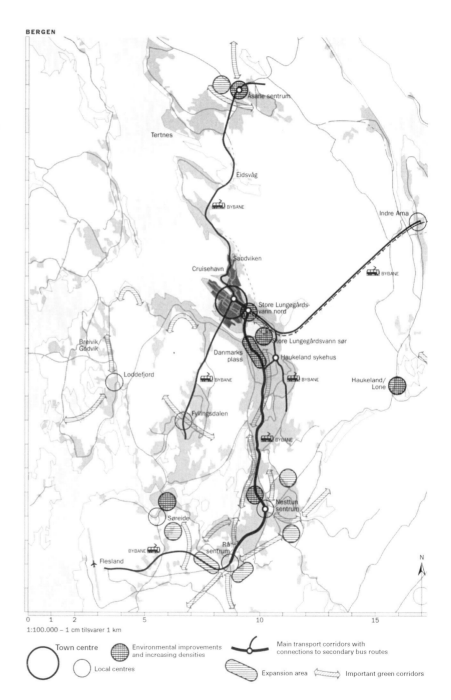

Figure 5.50 Development plan for Bergen, Norway.

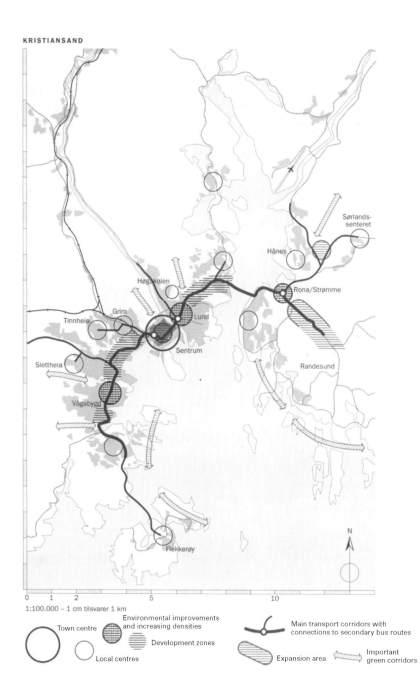

KRISTIANSAND

0   1   2   5   10

1:100.000 – 1 cm tilsvarer 1 km

Town centre

Environmental improvements
and increasing densities

Development zones

Local centres

Main transport corridors with
connections to secondary bus routes

Expansion area

Important
green corridors

6   Finally, the design of the built environment is
    given priority in the management of Norway's
    environmental cities. The aim is to achieve good
    design of the physical environment through the
    protection of the built environment, the devel-
    opment of public places and the preservation of
    the cultural heritage, making such sites and
    buildings more accessible to the public. As a
    whole, the environmental city should make the
    resident community aware of its identity and
    historic roots.[29]

Each of Norway's environmental cities, while following the overall aims of the project, has adapted the
concept to its own particular site and local conditions. The application of the six priority areas has
produced a different result in each location. In
Gamle Oslo, the environmental city covers a run-
down inner city area where the aims are: to rejuve-
nate the local economy; to upgrade a degraded
environment; and to encourage an inner city population to take effective community action. The project
is building upon developmental possibilities inherent
in its historic setting. For example, an extensive
area of archaeological remains is being developed as
a park which is an attraction to tourists in addition
to being a valuable green area for residents. An
existing school, once closed for administrative and
financial reasons, has been reopened in response to
community pressures. This is seen as a major reversal in the fortunes of the neighbourhood, providing
a new focus for local activities. Perhaps the most
interesting feature of this project is the removal of
through traffic by the unusual procedure of reducing the width of major roads and converting the

Figure 5.51 Development plan for Kristiansand.

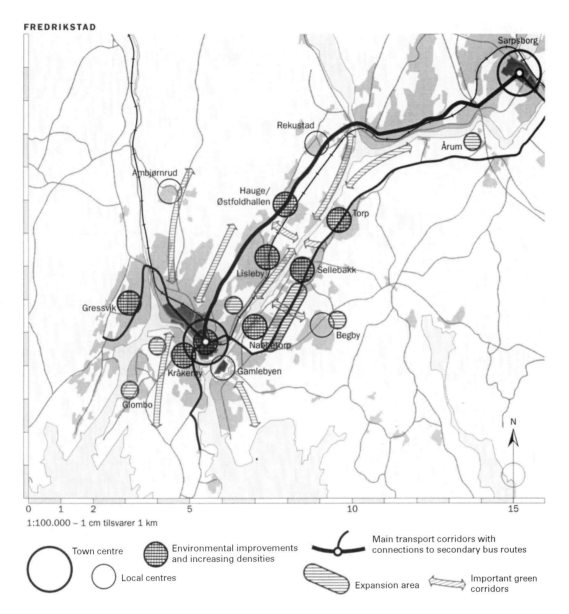

FREDRIKSTAD

Figure 5.52 Development plan for Fredrikstad.

1:100.000 – 1 cm tilsvarer 1 km

○ Town centre

◎ Environmental improvements and increasing densities

○ Local centres

Main transport corridors with connections to secondary bus routes

Expansion area

Important green corridors

Figure 5.53 Development plan for Tromsø.

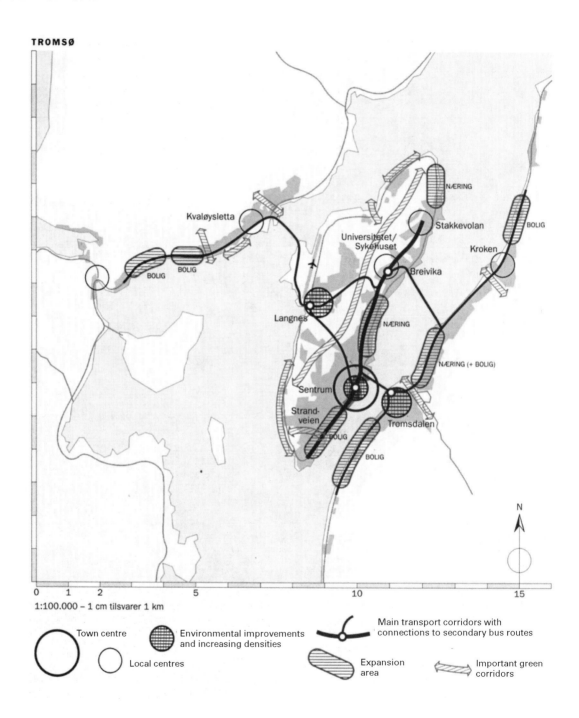

TROMSØ

Kvaløysletta

BOLIG

BOLIG

Universitetet/
Sykehuset

NÆRING

Stakkevolan

BOLIG

Kroken

Breivika

Langnes

NÆRING

NÆRING (+ BOLIG)

Sentrum

Strand-
veien

BOLIG

Trømsdalen

BOLIG

N

0   1   2   5   10   15

1:100.000 – 1 cm tilsvarer 1 km

○ Town centre

⊙ Local centres

▦ Environmental improvements
and increasing densities

⬭ Expansion
area

Main transport corridors with
connections to secondary bus routes

Important green
corridors

closed carriageways into linear parks (Figures 5.54 to 5.58). Bergen and Kristiansand are cities with a fine architectural heritage (Figures 5.59 to 5.61). Both cities are intent on maintaining that heritage. In Bergen the old market area Bryggen is undergoing extensive but sensitive rehabilitation using traditional materials and employing traditional construction methods (Figures 5.62 to 5.65). The older parts of Bergen are also undergoing extensive and impressive upgrading. The streets are being returned to the pedestrian, following the principles of the Dutch *woonerf*, which aims to reduce traffic speeds by the introduction of ramps and chicanes. These areas are still served by the motor car but its requirements no longer dominate the urban landscape (Figures 5.66 to 5.70). Kristiansand, in addition to its wonderful timber street architecture kept in immaculate condition, also boasts a state-of-the-art sewerage treatment facility, which is buried deep in the hill side. A key to Norway's plans for

the environmental cities is the development of transport strategies, thereby reducing the need for movement which relies on the private car. The concept of the ecological city is well-developed in Norway but it still remains for the Norwegian Government to take the politically difficult decision of reducing the expenditure on roads considerably and to divert those resources to developing mass public transport systems.

DESIGN CONCEPTS DRAWN FROM HISTORY

History can be a useful source for design ideas. The past, with its many wonderful examples of city development, can be a source of great inspiration. Even misinterpretation or misunderstanding of past events can provide a fruitful mine of ideas for analogy and concept formation. John Wood the Elder, when replanning Bath in the eighteenth

Figure 5.54 Gamle Oslo: environmental upgrading.

Figure 5.55 Gamle Oslo: archaeological park.

Figure 5.56 Gamle Oslo: reopened inner city school.

Figure 5.57 Gamle Oslo: conversion of major road into a linear park.

Figure 5.58 Gamle Oslo: conversion of major road into a linear park.

Figure 5.59 Kristiansand.

Figure 5.60 Kristiansand.

5.61

5.62

century, wished to return to that city's great Roman past for inspiration. He wrote in grand terms of building gymnasia, a circus and a Roman town of splendour. This was his vision. The reality was somewhat different. His circus, a lovely three-storey housing development is, as Summerson points out,

the Roman Circus turned inside out and, furthermore, would fit many times into its great precursor in Rome (Figures 5.71 to 5.73). Wood may have misinterpreted the scale and grandeur of ancient Rome, but using this idea as a starting point he produced a masterpiece of urban design. It was a

Figure 5.61 Kristiansand.

Figure 5.62 Byggen, Bergen.

5.63

5.64

Figure 5.63 Byggen, Bergen.

Figure 5.64 Byggen, Bergen.

design for speculative housing for the wealthy middle class, visiting or living in an eighteenth-century spa town.

The difficulty and danger for the designer using history rather like a collector of flotsam from a beach, is choosing examples from which can be developed concepts relevant for today. Any design concept taken from history, or indeed from any

source, must be relevant for the present concern with environmental protection and resource conservation. The concept of the city as a three- or four-storey solid form enclosing and enfolding urban space has much to commend itself as an energy efficient form: so too, is the Medieval concept of linear development with long deep lots on both sides of an access road, which maximizes the

Figure 5.65 Byggen, Bergen.

Figure 5.66 Old Bergen, traffic calming.

Figure 5.67 Old Bergen, traffic calming.

Figure 5.68 Old Bergen, environmental improvements.

5.69

5.70

number of units per given length of infrastructure.[30] In assessing the utility of a concept for sustainable development, its aesthetic value is not critical: more important is the concept's compatibility with the organic model of the city.

CONCLUSION

The organic metaphor for the city has certain limitations. The city is not a tree.[31] Cities do not grow, reproduce and heal themselves. The agents for

Figure 5.69 Old Bergen, environmental improvements.

Figure 5.70 Old Bergen, environmental improvements.

Figure 5.71 Bath, The Circus.

Figure 5.72 Bath, The Circus.

5.71

5.72

change are men and women: humankind with its greed, its intelligence, as well as a sometimes surprising degree of generosity. Describing the city in terms of its heart, lungs and arteries does not help in the analysis of the problems of city centre decline, pollution and gridlock on city streets. Such terms for the parts of the city based on human anatomy, however, may have value in suggesting ideas for problem solution through analogy.[32] For analytical purposes, the most fruitful metaphor from nature is the ecosystem, particularly the tropical rain forest. The rain forest is a stable arrangement of flora and fauna, delicately balanced, requiring no inputs of energy and capable of dealing with its own pollution. Such open systems can be analysed and their components defined in terms of their relationship to other components. Systemic analysis, which need not necessarily be mathematical modelling, is the test for the validity of concepts today where the ethos is the

Figure 5.73 Comparison of The Circus at Bath with the Coliseum, Rome.

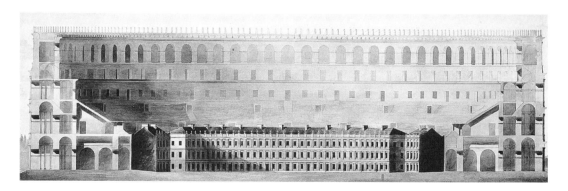

necessity to find solutions to urban problems which add no further burden to a global ecosystem under considerable strain.

REFERENCES

1 Lynch, K. (1981) *A Theory of Good City Form*, Cambridge, MA: MIT Press.

2 Le Corbusier (1946) *Towards a New Architecture*, London: Architectural Press; (1948) *Concerning Town Planning*, London: Architectural Press; (1967) *The Radiant City*, London: Faber and Faber; (1971) *The City of Tomorrow*, London: Architectural Press. Leger, F. (1975) The machine aesthetic: the manufactured object, the artisan and the artist, *Bulletin de l'Effort Moderne*, Paris, and quoted in T. Benton and C. Benton with D. Sharp, eds, *Form and Function*, London: Granada (1979). Sant'Elia, Antonio (1914) The new city, *Nuove Tendenze*, Exhibition Catalogue, Famiglia Artistica, Milan, May–June, and quoted in *Form and Function, ibid.*

3 Moughtin, J.C. (1996) *Urban Design: Green Dimensions*, Oxford: Butterworth-Heinemann.

4 Geddes, P. (1949) *Cities in Evolution*, London: Williams and Norgate; Mumford, L. (1938) *The Culture of Cities*, London: Secker and Warburg; (1946) *Technics and Civilization*, London: George Routledge; (1961) *The City in History*, Harmondsworth: Penguin.

5 Kopp, A. (1970) *Town and Revolution*, trans. T. E. Burton, London: Thames and Hudson.

6 Lloyd Wright, F. (1957) *A Testament*, New York: Horizon Press; (1958) *The Living City*, New York: Mentor Books.

7 Alexander, C. (1975) *The Oregon Experiment*, New York: Oxford University Press.

8 Lovelock, J. (1995) *The Ages of Gaia: A Biography of Our Living Earth*, Oxford: Oxford University Press, 2nd edn.

9 *Ibid.*

10 Mollinson, W. (1992) *Permaculture: A Designers' Manual*, Tyalgum, Australia: Tagari Publications.

11 *Ibid.*

12 *Ibid.*

13 Moughtin, J.C. (1996) *op. cit.*

14 Both quotes are taken from Mollinson, W. (1992) *op. cit.*, The first is from Koestler (1967) and the second is from Newsweek (1977).

15 Mollinson, W. (1992) *op. cit.*

16 Moughtin, J.C. (1996) *op. cit.*

17 McKie, R. (1974) Cellular renewal, *Town Planning Review*, Vol. 45, pp. 274-290.

18 Alexander, C. (1975) *op. cit.*

19 Alexander, C., Neis, H., Anninou, A. and King, I. (1987) *A New Theory of Urban Design*, Oxford: Oxford University Press.

20 *Ibid.*

21 Moughtin, J.C. (1996) *op. cit.*

22 Alexander, C. *et al.* (1987) *op. cit.*

23 Mollinson, W. (1992) *op. cit.*

24 Based on letters from David Gale.

25 Taken from a personal communication, Derek Latham and Company Limited, November 1997.

26 Moughtin, J.C. (1992) *Urban Design: Street and Square*, Oxford: Butterworth-Heinemann; The Local Government Management Board (LGMB) (1993) *Community Participation in Local Agenda 21*, Luton: The Local Government Board; and LGMB (1996) *Creating Community Visions*, Luton: LGMB.

27 World Commission on Environmental Development (1987) *Our Common Future: The Brundtland Report*, Oxford: Oxford University Press.

28 *Ibid.*

29 Norway, Ministry of Environment (1994) *Five Environmental Cities: A Short Description of a Development Programme*, Oslo: Ministry of Environment.

30 Moughtin, J.C. (1996) *op. cit.*

31 Alexander, C. (1965) A city is not a tree, *Architectural Forum*, April, pp. 58-62, May, pp. 58-61.

32 De Bono, E. (1977) *Lateral Thinking*, Harmondsworth: Penguin, and Gordon, W.J.J. (1961) *Synectics: The Development of Creative Capacity*, New York: Harper Row.

PROJECT EVALUATION

6

INTRODUCTION

Moderate- to large-scale urban design projects are aimed at improving social, economic and infrastructure conditions rather than focusing on the single objective of physical urban renewal. For instance, projects aimed at regenerating inner cities are planned as a series of interrelated actions in which the increase of employment levels is interlinked with sustainable improvement in general. For this type of project the issue of methods and techniques needs to be considered from an economic and social perspective. There is the need to integrate the traditional urban design evaluation instruments with methods and techniques which can give an insight into the social, economic and environmental impacts the project is intended to produce.

ECONOMIC EVALUATION TECHNIQUES

A range of measurements and economic appraisal techniques are required to assess the economic viability of a project. This section focuses on a number of techniques with which to determine the monetary values of those projects. In the interest of brevity the techniques are summarized and some of their applicability discussed.

The methodological approach, common to all the economic appraisal techniques, is that of discounting, which enables streams of costs and benefits to be compared on an equal footing by reducing both streams to their net present value (NPV) for the years in which they occur. Net present value forms the basis of evaluation techniques such as cost-effectiveness and cost-benefit analysis. Whatever technique is applied, in economic terms the chosen method should assist in ascertaining the most economically efficient way of meeting the objectives of the project. Where the project has no quantifiable benefits, the cost-effectiveness approach is the main one to apply. This technique calculates all the costs, both capital and revenue of a project, applying the appropriate shadow prices and discounting the resulting stream, to obtain an NPV of costs. This procedure is repeated for the main alternative ways of carrying out a project, and the one with the lowest present value is chosen. This approach assumes that all the alternatives being compared can carry out the project equally well and that there are no quality differences in the services being supplied.

Another well-known technique used to judge the monetary value of a project is cost-benefit analysis (CBA). Cost-benefit analysis uses three main decision techniques, namely the internal rate of return (IRR) approach, the net present value (NPV) and the benefit-cost ratio (BCR). The IRR, as defined in previous chapters, is the percentage discount rate used in capital investment appraisal which brings the cost of a project and its future cashflow into equity. Projects with a higher IRR are to be preferred to those with a lower IRR. The IRR method has the convenience that it enables a comparison to be made between the rate of return of a project against the rate of return on other feasible investments. Thus, an organization may set minimum target rates of return of, for instance, 10 per cent. The IRR approach enables it to accept and reject projects that result in rates, above and below 10 per cent, respectively. The IRR can also be defined as that discount rate at which the NPV of a project is zero. The IRR and NPV are consequently linked by definition. The NPV is simply the difference between the discounted streams of benefits and costs. It is the value, discounted to the present, of doing the project rather than not doing it. For example, a sum of £100 today is worth £100; a sum of £100 receivable in one year's time is worth less, because £100 in hand could earn interest at perhaps 10 per cent. Therefore, at an interest rate of 10 per cent, the net present value of £100 one year from now would be approximately £90.91.

NPVs are usually worked out from a pre-determined discount rate and tables such as Parry's Valuation Tables[1] show present values of £1 for periods of 0-15 years at differing rates percentages. The most common approach though, is to set a more or less arbitrary rate (normally 8 per cent) and apply it to each project, choosing that with the highest NPV. However, a better approach is to estimate what real rate of return is available on investments in the private sector, and to require all public investments to achieve at least the same.

The benefit-cost ratio (BCR) is the ratio between discounted total benefits and costs. Thus, if discounted total benefits are £120 and discounted total costs £100 the benefit:cost ratio is 1.2:1. If the ratio is positive then the project is viable. The ratio also allows to distinguish projects whose NPV is high because of its magnitude from projects that have a genuinely high rate of return (IRR). In most cases the IRR, NPV and BCR will give the same result and will produce the same ranking of projects according to their attractiveness. There will be few cases where the use of IRR on one hand and the NPV and BCR on the other will produce different results. In general, where organizations are using some sort of target rate of return on capital, maximizing NPV should be the approach, with BCR as a supplementary check.

ECONOMIC EVALUATION OF URBAN DESIGN PROJECTS

As discussed above, the most important technique used to carry out an economic evaluation of urban design projects is cost-benefit analysis. This assessment is necessary when there are several alternative proposals among which decision-makers have to choose or where they have to appraise the feasibility of one single project.

The overall objectives to be achieved through the project are the starting point of this assessment. As stated in Chapter 1 the goals of urban design are threefold: 'to design and build urban developments which are both structurally and functionally sound while at the same time giving pleasure to those who see development'. These three main goals are guided by the main aim of sustainable development. These general principles are then to be tailored to the local situation. For the successful achievement of project objectives these objectives should be defined in measurable terms.[2] Ill-defined objectives can produce a misunderstanding about what the programme is meant to achieve. Widespread problems arise when objectives are presented in a vague form. When the objectives are stated in a clear and measurable form an *ex-ante* assessment in terms of cost-benefit analysis can be carried out more easily.

The cost-benefit analysis is an evaluation method based on the estimation of costs and benefits a specific project produces, in relation to the stated objectives. The cost-benefit ratios of several projects are compared in order to choose the most economically efficient project, that is the one which produces the lowest ratio.

The types of costs and benefits vary according to the type of project. For instance, costs and benefits involved in transportation projects differ from those of housing renewal schemes. According to Schofield the benefits of urban renewal include increased site productivity, neighbourhood spillovers and reduced social costs, while costs comprise site acquisition cost and expenditure to redevelop the site.[3] Of all these estimates of cost, the most difficult to measure are the social costs, such as crime reduction.

In *Urban Design: Street and Square*, there is a case study of urban design from Belfast.[4] The main objective of the Markets Area project 'was to provide a pleasant residential environment for the existing people of the Markets ... In specific terms it meant the rehousing of 2200 people on at least 9.5 ha (21 acres) of land in two- and three-storey terraced housing ... Other goals included the rehabilitation of some of the better-quality housing, to relocate small industries in the area, to minimize pedestrian-vehicular conflict and the physical separation of the Upper and Lower Markets, to provide a shopping centre to act as a focus and, finally, to provide a primary school campus'.[5] For each of these goals the costs

and benefits involved were different. The choice between two alternative options to achieve the same goal was based on the grounds of economic efficiency. For instance, the sinking of Cromac street was abandoned in favour of the simple widening of the street at ground level because of the prohibitive costs involved in the first option.

Zoppi carried out a cost-benefit analysis of the Central Artery/Third Harbour Tunnel project in Boston.[6] The costs of the project were distinguished in fixed and variable costs. The former includes land costs, development costs, construction costs and administration costs, what Schofield calls project resource costs; while the variable costs are those which are sustained for maintenance during the project's life time.[7] The benefits of the project were calculated as intrasectoral and intersectoral benefits. Among the intrasectoral benefits there are the reduced vehicle operating costs, a decrease in the number of accidents and the reduced costs in travelling time for the transportation of goods and passengers; these are user benefits, while the increase in regional income is an intersectoral benefit.

Central to the cost-benefit analysis is the selection of the appropriate discount rate to make costs and benefits calculated at different years comparable. This rate is the level at which future costs and benefits are converted into present-day values.[8]

Table 6.1 Results of the cost–benefit analysis.

Discount rate (%)	Fixed costs (in 1987 millions of dollars)	Difference between benefits and variable costs (net benefits) (in 1987 millions of dollars)	Difference between net benefits and fixed costs (in 1987 millions of dollars)
5	4842	6795	1953
6	4970	4364	−606
7	5110	3938	−1172
8	5246	3388	−1858
9	5385	2594	−2791
10	5521	1651	−3870

Source: Zoppi, 1994.

Table 6.1 presents Zoppi's results of this analysis. It is apparent that the results change radically in relation to the selected discount rate. While with a discount rate of 5 per cent the project is economically efficient because the difference between net benefits and fixed costs is positive; with a discount rate equal to or greater than 6 per cent the project is not economically viable. Another important issue in cost-benefit analysis is the assessment of the intangibles, i.e. those elements for which it is difficult to quantify their value, for instance 'the quality of life'. In conclusion, cost-benefit analysis is an important tool in the assessment of the economic viability of a project. At the same time, it is difficult to account for those elements which improve the individuals' well-being. The Balance Sheet Method and the Goals Achievement Matrix are two techniques which derive from, and improve on cost-benefit analysis.[9] The two techniques are not explained here as they are based on the same principles as cost-benefit analysis; the interested reader can consult the above-mentioned literature.

ENVIRONMENTAL IMPACT ASSESSMENT

Central to sustainable development is the assessment of urban projects in terms of their environmental and social impacts, as a study of the economic viability of the project would give only a partial picture of the project's impacts. It is recognized that the term 'environment' should include both physical and socio-economic dimensions. According to Glasson *et al.*, the consideration of physical elements exclusively, as is the case with the Department of Environment checklist of environmental components, is too restrictive.[10] Table 6.2 shows both types of components to be

Table 6.2 Environmental assessments: components.

Physical environment (adapted from DoE 1991)	
Air and atmosphere	Air quality
Water resources and water bodies	Water quality and quantity
Soil and geology	Classification, risks (e.g. erosion)
Flora and fauna	Birds, mammals, fish, etc.; aquatic and terrestrial vegetation
Human beings	Physical and mental health and well-being
Landscape	Characteristics and quality of landscape
Cultural heritage	Conservation areas; built heritage; historic and archaeological sites
Climate	Temperature, rainfall, wind, etc.
Socio-economic environment	
Economic base – direct	Direct employment; labour market characteristics; local/non-local trends
Economic base – indirect	Non-basic/services employment; labour supply and demand
Demography	Population structure and trends
Housing	Supply and demand
Local services	Supply and demand of services; health education, police, etc.
Socio-cultural	Lifestyle/quality of life; social problems (e.g. crime); community stress and conflict

taken into account when trying to assess the full extent of project impacts. For instance, an urban regeneration project can have potentially negative effects (increasing air pollution), and beneficial socio-economic effects (increasing levels of local employment) or vice versa. The inclusion of both components implies that techniques that deal with the assessment of both types of impact are needed.

A tool to determine potentially negative environmental effects is Environmental Impact Assessment. The term environmental impact assessment implies a package of methods aimed at both identifying any impact of policies, programmes, plans and projects, and assessing their effects on the environment and human health.[11] Environmental impact assessment is defined as a process through which significant environmental impacts are assessed and taken into account in the planning, design, authorization and implementation of all relevant types of action. As can be seen from Figure 6.1, this process supports decision making through the screening, scoping, identification, prediction and evaluation of key impacts of projects, and through the preparation and review of environmental impacts statements.

A similar process can be applied to policies, plans and programmes, which is called 'strategic environmental assessment'. The aim of this assessment is to ensure that consideration of environmental impacts is taken into account at the decision-making level, that is when policies and plans are formulated. This assessment will ensure that alternative approaches can be taken into consideration before a definitive decision is made about a particular project.

Environmental impact assessment is normally applied to certain kinds of development categories in relation to three features, viz. type of development, scale of development and the site of the development. The European Community Directive 337/85 on environmental impact assessment specifies in its Annex I the types of project for which the elaboration of an environmental impact assessment is mandatory. These projects include oil refineries, power stations but also construction of

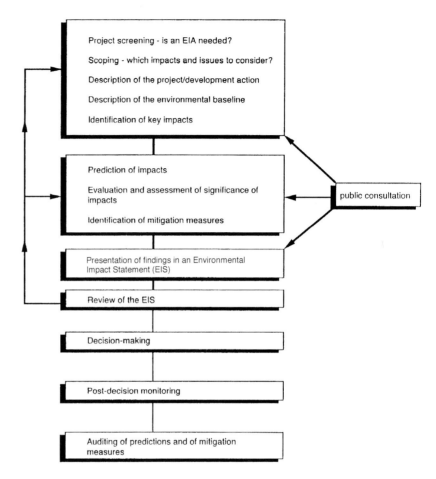

motorways, express roads and trading ports which are more often part of an urban design project. Annex II lists the projects which are submitted to environmental impact assessment only if the regional authorities require it. This second Annex includes infrastructure projects which have more relevance for the types of project considered in this book, such as urban-development projects, and tramways for passenger transport. This second Annex has created controversy because of the possibility that potentially harmful projects are overlooked if the decision of EIA is left to local authorities.[12] In the UK, the European Community

Figure 6.1 The EIA process.

Figure 6.2 Checklist for assessing impacts of urban developments.

1 **Local economy**
   Impact on public finances
   Impact on businesses
   Impact on employment
   Change in land values
   Impact on support grants of other agencies
   Impact on land tenure
2 **Local environment**
   Impact on air quality
   Impact on water resources (surface/ground)
   Changes in noise and vibration
   Impact on greenbelt and open spaces
   Impact on natural habitats, species and vegetation
   Changes in land use and densities
3 **Aesthetic and cultural values**
   Impact on urban patterns
   Visual impacts and effects on buildings
   Impact on cultural heritage and designated areas
   Impact on amenity and personal security
   Impact on community cohesion and identity
   Impact on minority groups and equal opportunities
4 **Infrastructure**
   Impact on public utilities
   Impact on public services and facilities
   Impact on emergency services
   Impact on traffic conditions
   Impact on public transport
   Impact on health and safety

Directive was implemented by Section 71A of the *Town and Country Planning Act 1990* and Section 26B of the *Town and Country Planning Act* in Scotland, and the *Town and Country Planning Regulations 1995*. The publication of Directive 97/11/EC has led to the Town and Country Planning (Environmental Impact Assessment) (England and Wales) Regulations 1999.[13] The Regulations broaden the range of development projects that need an EIA and introduces some important changes to EIA procedures. An EIA is always required if the proposed development is included in Schedule One of the Regulations. This includes motorways and express roads, oil refineries, power stations and chemical works within certain capacities. An EIA is always required if the project is included in Schedule Two of the Regulations; or if threshold criteria are met; or the project is situated in a 'sensitive area'; and is likely to produce in either circumstances 'significant' environmental effects. The Schedule Two development relevant for urban designs includes shopping centres, car parks, multiplex cinemas, leisure centres and sports stadiums. Moreover, one important innovation of the 1999 Regulations for urban design is the introduction of statutory size thresholds which have been reduced to half a hectare.

Where an EIA is required the 1999 Regulations have introduced the following changes to environmental assessment procedures.

- A developer may submit an application to the Local Planning Authority for a scoping opinion on what should be added in the Environmental Statement.
- An applicant should now give information on the main alternative considered and reasons for the chosen development option.
- For all Schedule Two developments, the Local Planning Authority must adopt its own formal determination of whether or not an EIA is required either before or after a planning application has been submitted. The opinion must be placed on the Planning Register.

IDENTIFICATION OF IMPACTS

The classification of environmental impact assessment techniques can relate to their organizational characteristics or to the distinction between magnitude and significance of impacts. Magnitude refers to the size of the impacts, while significance is related to the importance of impacts for decision making. There are five main categories of assessment techniques: checklist, matrix, overlay, network and quantitative methods.[14] These techniques are normally utilized to identify the impacts of different types of projects on the environment. The following is a short description of the techniques; this will not be exhaustive of all aspects of the techniques. How these techniques fit within the field of urban design method and techniques will be examined.

The *checklist technique* (Figure 6.2) consists of constructing several lists which enumerate the expected impacts of the project. It can be qualitative or quantitative. Qualitative checklists show the expected impacts in relation to several environmental aspects. Quantitative checklists use coefficients and formulae to assess the impact made upon the environment.[15] Different types of checklists can be recognized, from purely descriptive to more quantitative in the identification of expected impacts.[16] The limitations of a checklist approach are due to its generality, and for this reason it is employed when a full and in-depth analysis of impacts is not required. The types of project which can be assessed using the checklist technique are, for instance, those involving water resources, for example housing projects which might alter natural water habitats. Leone and Marini recommend the use of indices to describe the ecosystem situation before and after project implementation.[17]

The *matrix technique*, allowing cross-analysis between the activities of the projects and the environmental characteristics of the area where the project is to be implemented, includes the consideration of the cause and effect relationships. The differences between matrices are due to the quantity and quality of variables included in the matrices. The environmental characteristics are usually classified in three categories: physical and chemical features, biological characteristics and social variables. Matrices have been used to assess the environmental impacts produced by large scale projects such as airports or major urban regeneration schemes.

The *overlay technique* is a cartographic method. Several thematic maps are overlaid in order to describe the environmental quality of the area and to verify whether the project is compatible with the characteristics of the area. The techniques developed by McHarg can be included in this category.[18] The basic procedure is based on the preparation of several maps, showing the environmental components which are expected to be affected by the development project. Each map is shaded according to the degree of impact caused by the project on the environmental component considered. The shadow will range from the lightest tone to indicate no impact to the darkest tone for significant negative impacts. Then these maps will be superimposed showing the areas in the darkest tone as unsuitable for the proposed development. This technique has been further improved with the development of Geographical Information Systems (GIS), which allow the handling of a great deal of data. In addition, the use of GIS enables the construction of several hypothetical scenarios of development in a shorter time than doing it manually. The limits of this method are threefold. Firstly, it does not assess secondary impacts. Secondly, there is no distinction between reversible and irreversible impacts. Finally, it does not take account of whether the impact takes place or not. Despite these limitations, this technique is suitable in the case of new urban housing developments, for instance, to give information on the types of soils or the natural habitats affected by the development.

Methods of impact identification based upon the use of *networks* try to estimate project impacts using, as the starting point, the single actions which form the project. Each action generates direct, indirect and primary and secondary impacts, which this technique tries to depict. According to Glasson *et al.* this technique can only be used to nominally identify impacts, since it does not give insight into the magnitude or significance of impacts.[19]

Quantitative techniques are based on the production of indices to measure the changes caused by the project. The technique developed by the Batelle Columbus Laboratories identifies a score for each of the four components of the environmental impacts to be assessed, namely: ecology, environmental pollution, aesthetics and human interest. The aim is to assess through mathematical functions the changes induced by the project. If the new score is greater than the original one there is a negative impact.[20]

The important issue is which technique is relevant for urban design schemes. This question is very much related to the nature of the project. A new housing development, an urban renewal scheme, or a transport-related project are assessed through the employment of different techniques. Not only is the choice of the technique determined by the nature of the project but also by the size of the project, whether a moderate- or a large-scale project, and last but not least, by time constraints in preparation of the assessment.

CASE STUDY: NOTTINGHAM LRT

The Nottingham Express Transit Project is a light-train transportation project. The line links Nottingham City Centre and the northern part of the Nottingham conurbation.[21] The objective of the project was to serve the transport needs of the area without jeopardizing the equilibrium between environment and economy. The project was enclosed in Annex II of the 1988 Town and Country Planning Regulation on the assessment of environmental effects. However, a full environmental impact assessment was carried out because the preparation of such an assessment is required for all projects presented in Parliament. The project was granted Royal Assent in 1994, but the process itself started in 1988. It included the preparation of feasibility studies which examined several of the projects' features, such as engineering feasibility, cost, road congestion and the potential environmental impacts. Public participation was sought to define the Nottingham Express transit route. A checklist technique was used to carry out the assessment. The

project impacts, assessed both at the construction and operation stage, were: transport and traffic, noise and vibration, land use and planning, contaminated land, spoil and waste, air quality, visual intrusion and landscape, community issues, water quality and ecology. Significant impacts on the environment at the construction stage were identified and a series of mitigation measures in terms of good construction practices were suggested. The study identified a number of concerns. In particular, consideration was given to the implications of land-take of open space, the visual impact in areas of high scenic value, and noise and vibration in tranquil residential areas. The study found considerable scope for mitigating impacts through engineering solutions, changes to layout, modification to operating specifications, and by rigorous control of certain aspects of detail design. The study concluded that the positive beneficial effects outweighed the negative impacts which were reduced to a minimum by the mitigation measures. The environmental impact study was not concerned with secondary impacts because these were considered far beyond the scope of the environmental assessment. The Nottingham Express Transit Project has gone through the several steps of an environmental impact assessment process from screening to project approval. It would, however, be of use to carry out an *ex-post* assessment to evaluate the extent to which the environmental impact assessment was correct in predicting project impacts and in preventing irreversible damage to the environment.

PREDICTION OF ECONOMIC IMPACTS

To predict economic impacts, mathematical models can be employed.[22] For instance, using several techniques based on regional multiplier theories, the effects that a new injection of investment produces on an economy can be predicted. Three types of analysis can be carried out: economic base analysis, regional multiplier analysis and an input-output analysis. These analyses are linked to three regional multiplier theories. These three main theories, namely, economic base theory, regional trade multipliers and input-output models, can be used to explain the income and employment effects in an economy owing to an exogenous change such as a financial investment. For instance, an urban regeneration project produces direct, indirect and induced economic impacts.

The economic base theory is based on the distinction made between basic and non-basic economic activities. The first type of activity is oriented towards export, which is assumed to be the main factor in creating or supporting a wealthy economy. The second type of activity serves a local market and it primarily constitutes services for local residents. This theory assumes that an investment in basic activities will have a positive income and employment effect on non-basic activities, thus benefiting the local economy. The main limitation of this theory is that it overlooks the role of imports. It does not take into account that the beneficial effect of an investment in basic activities can be limited by the leakages of expenditure in the form of imports. Other limitations concern the difficulty of defining the distinction between basic and non-basic activities, and the difficulty of selecting and defining the study area.

The regional trade multiplier theory considers that an investment of a certain amount into an economy will increase the income of the economy, determining an increase in consumption. In turn, this increase in consumption is transformed into someone else's income which will be again spent. This chain of effects will take place several times before the effect of the initial injection ends. The termination of these effects is due to the three main leakages that this theory takes into account. These are: savings, taxation and imports. For instance, an initial investment in the construction sector will spread to other economic sectors such as manufacturing and industry, because of goods and services bought from these sectors by the agriculture sector

Input-output models trace the impact of an

investment in one sector of the economy through the income and employment repercussions in all the other economic sectors. Input-output analysis can be used as a descriptive tool. This breaks down an economy into its sectoral components and gives information on the transactions taking place between them. The main problems related to the use of input-output analysis are data limitation and the assumption about the constant coefficients.

Input-output analysis is a descriptive tool and also gives an insight into those industrial sectors which produce the highest economic effects as a result of investment. Economic base analysis and regional multiplier analysis are based on a highly aggregated approach which does not give account of specific economic sectors and inter-industry relations. In the light of these considerations, the rest of this section will give a closer insight into input-output analysis.

Input-output analysis is one technique which can give, at the appraisal phase, an insight into an equitable distribution of the economic effects caused by development programmes. The first practical work on input-output analysis is due to Wassily Leontief. The aim of this technique was the analysis of the structural interdependence within an economy. According to Richardson, input-output tables perform two main functions.[23] On the one hand, they provide a descriptive tool for highlighting the relationship between input and output, and between industries and sectors of an economy. On the other, they offer an analytical approach for measuring the impact of a change in final demand on the output and income of an economy.

A conventional input-output transactions table is divided into four quadrants (Figure 6.3). The first records the intraregional transaction taking place within an economy between the several economic sectors. The second quadrant shows the sales by each sector to the final demand which indicates the ultimate destination (i.e. consumption, export) of production for each economic sector. The third quadrant contains the cost of inputs to the economic

Figure 6.3 Simplified input–output transaction table.

FROM \ TO	Purchasing sectors			Local final demand			Export	Total gross output
	1 .... j .... n			House-holds	Private invest-ment	Govern-ment		
1	X_{11} .... X_{1j} ...... X_{1n}			C_1	I_1	G_1	E_1	X_1
i	X_{i1} ...... X_{ij} ...... X_{in}			C_i	I_i	G_i	E_i	X_i
n	X_{n1} ...... X_{nj} ...... X_{nn}			C_n	I_n	G_n	E_n	X_n
Labour	L_1 ...... L_j ...... L_n			L_C	L_I	L_G	L_E	L
Other value added	V_1 ...... V_j ...... V_n			V_C	V_I	V_G	V_E	V
Imports	M_1 ...... M_j ...... M_n			M_C	M_I	M_G	-	M
Total gross outlay	X_1 ...... X_j ...... X_n			C	I	G	E	X

sectors of an economy. The final quadrant represents the utilization of primary inputs by final demand.

The first, top left-hand quadrant shows the inter-action of the processing sectors. The purchasing sectors are shown across the top of the table, while selling sectors are listed down the left side. The horizontal rows indicate the destination of the output of the sector in the left-hand column to all other sectors named on the column headings. In this first quadrant all endogenous sectors are included, the term 'endogenous' referring to sectors which are shaped by the internal structure of the economy.

The second, top right-hand quadrant contains sales by each sector to the final demand. This is the autonomous sector. Changes which occur in the final demand spread their effects to the rest of the table. It is basically composed of four columns which indicate exports, government purchases, gross private capital formation and household.[24] The export column shows the level of export of each sector during the period examined by the table. The government purchases column represents the level of purchases by government from each of the sale sectors. The gross private capital formation show the quantities of sale purchased by buyers who use them for private capital formation. Finally, the household column shows the purchases for private consumption from each of the selling sectors.

In the third, bottom left-hand quadrant, the

payments sector shows the cost of inputs for each of the purchasing sectors. Usually, five basic rows comprise this quadrant: gross inventory depletion, imports, payments to government, depreciation allowances and household. The gross inventory depletion row shows the amount of stored final goods or raw materials which have been used by the sector named at the top of the table. Similarly, the imports row shows the amount of imports purchased by each sector. The payments to government row represents the purchases by each sector of government services. The depreciation allowances row approximates the cost of plant and other equipment used up in the production of goods. Finally the household row can be expressed as the value-added portion in each sector, such as wages, salaries, interest; in other words, it can be thought of as the payments of labour input by the economic sectors.

The fourth, bottom right-hand quadrant expresses the level of primary inputs used by final demand. This quadrant shows the links between the exogenous sectors so defined because they are not determined by the local economy. This fourth quadrant is usually utilized as a balancing element to equal total output to total inputs. For this reason it does not hold an important role in input–output analysis.

A tool of this type is helpful as a regional analytical framework but also at an urban level to calculate income and employment effects of a new injection of investment. For instance, the measurement of the economic effects expected to be generated by the Integrated Mediterranean Programme of Calabria, in Southern Italy, has been calculated using an input–output analysis.[25] The Programme, a five-year project, came into force on 1 January 1988 and ended on 31 December 1992. The European Union financed 40.37 per cent of the total investment and the Italian State 59.63 per cent of the total budgetary resources. The Integrated Mediterranean Programme for Calabria comprises five sub-programmes: agriculture, industry, tourism, fisheries and programme implementation. The main purpose of the analysis was to assess how far the programme's economic effects benefit the more deprived areas of the Region at the construction stage. The analysis has shown that the direct, indirect and induced income to be produced in the more deprived inland areas was far less than that produced in the relatively wealthier areas where most of the urban renewal projects were located. This was mainly because the investment was channelled towards those economic sectors which did not represent the larger income multipliers and which could cause greater economic effects locally.

The main limitations in using an input–output analysis are due to the high costs in building survey-based input–output tables and the overestimation of multipliers in non-survey-based tables.

Nevertheless, Batey *et al.* have utilized an input–output analysis to assess the socio-economic impacts of the construction of an airport upon a local economy.[26] Since the use of input–output analysis is a costly operation, it is probably best reserved for large-scale projects.

CONCLUSION

The assessment of alternative urban design projects or of a single project requires the investigation of numerous aspects of projects' impacts, from a cost-benefit analysis to a complete environmental impact assessment of the project. The attention was focused on the use of techniques and methods which allow such an assessment. The results of these assessments support decision makers as any project requires a trade-off between economic, environmental and social impacts. An important element is the involvement of the public as soon as possible in the assessment process. Since the project will affect those who live in the area where the project is to be implemented, it is essential to involve the public at an early stage of the assessment process, and to give them the opportunity to trade-off between alternatives.

REFERENCES

1 Davidson, A.W. (1978) *Parry's Valuation Tables*, Tenth Edition, The Estates Gazette Ltd.

2 United Nations (1978) *Systematic Monitoring and Evaluation of Integrated Development Programmes: A Source Book*, New York: Department of Economic and Social Affairs.

3 Schofield, J. (1987) *Cost-benefit Analysis in Urban and Regional Planning*, London: Allen & Unwin.

4 Moughtin, J.C. (1992) *Urban Design: Street and Square*, Oxford: Butterworth-Heinemann.

5 *Ibid.*

6 Zoppi, C. (1994) *The Central Artery*: Third Harbour Tunnel Project, in Schachter, G., Busea, A., Hellman, D. and Ziparo, A. (Eds) *Boston in the 1990's*, Rome: Gangemi.

7 Schofield, J. (1987) *op. cit.*

8 Bateman, I. (1991) Social discounting, monetary evaluation and practical sustainability, *Town and Country Planning*, June, pp. 174-176.

9 Lichfield, N. (1975) *Evaluation in the Planning Process*, Oxford: Pergamon.

10 Department of the Environment (1989) *Environmental Assessment. A Guide to the Procedures*, London: HMSO; and Glasson, J., Therival, R. and Chadwick, A. (1994) *Introduction to Environmental Impact Assessment*, London: UCL Press.

11 Munn, R.E. (1979) *Environmental Impact Assessment*, Chichester: Wiley.

12 World Wide Fund for Nature (1989) *Reform of the Structural Funds. An Environmental Briefing*, Godalming: WWF-International.

13 Commission of the European Communities Council Directives 97/11/EC of 3 March 1997.

14 Ziparo, A. (1988) *Pianificazione Ambientale e Trasformazioni Urbanistiche*, Rome: Gangemi; Thompson, M.A. (1990) Determining impact significance in EIA: a review of 24 methodologies, *Journal of Environmental Management*, Vol. 30, No. 3, pp. 235-250; Glasson, J.R. *et al.* (1994) *op. cit.*

15 Bruschi, S. (1984) *Valutazione dell'Impatto Ambientale*, Rome: Edizioni delle Autonomie.

16 Glasson, J.R. *et al.* (1994) *op. cit.*, and Ziparo, A. (1988) *op. cit.*

17 Leone, A. and Marini, R. (1993) Assessment and mitigation of the effects of land use in a lake basin, *Journal of Environmental Management*, Vol. 39, pp. 39-50.

18 McHarg, I.L. (1969) *Design with Nature*, New York: The Natural History Press.

19 Glasson, J.R. *et al.* (1994) *op. cit.*

20 *Ibid.*

21 Nottinghamshire County Council (1991) *Greater Nottingham Light Rapid transit Environmental Statement*, Nottingham: Nottinghamshire County Council.

22 Glasson, J.R., *et al.* (1994) *op. cit.*

23 Richardson, H.W. (1972) *Input-Output and Regional Economics*, London: Redwood Press Ltd.

24 Miernyk, W.H. (1965) *The Elements of Input-Output Analysis*, New York: Random House.

25 Signoretta, P.E. (1996) *Sustainable Development in Marginal Regions of the European Union. An Evaluation of the Integrated Mediterranean Programme Calabria, Italy*, Unpublished Ph.D. Thesis, University of Nottingham.

26 Batey, P.W., Madden, M. and Scholefield, G. (1993) Socio-economic impact assessment of large-scale projects using input-output analysis: a case study of an airport, *Regional Studies*, Vol. 27, No. 3, pp. 179-191.

PRESENTATION

7

The communication of ideas is central to the design process. Ideas, however good they may be, remain still-born until they are expressed in terms which engage the support of key actors in the development process. For this purpose, ideas which infuse an urban design project, together with a supporting argument, have to be expressed with clarity, economy and enthusiasm. The presentation of urban design proposals often involves reports and sets of documents similar in form and content to those prepared for planning projects. Urban design reports may include a description of the survey, its analysis and a fully evaluated final proposal with its cost. This written material is accompanied by maps, drawings, photographs and models. The proposal may then be presented in a number of arenas and defended at Public Inquiries and planning appeals.

The style adopted for report writing is of the utmost importance. One can use this written report as an opportunity to sell the idea to client and public. For this purpose a simple, straightforward text is the most effective. The main reason for any report is 'to get an idea as exactly as possible out of one mind into another'.[1] Sir Ernest Gowers' book *The Complete Plain Words* remains one of the best guides to the process of writing: *The Complete Plain Words*, together with Fowler's *Modern English Usage, Roget's Thesaurus* and *The Shorter Oxford English Dictionary* should be essential reference material for the report writer.[2] The report writer's job is to convey his or her ideas to others in the most efficient and economical form. Writing is, for the professional designer, simply, an instrument to make the reader apprehend readily and precisely the meaning of a report.

There are features, commonly found in report writing, which obstruct this process of precise communication. One such feature is the long shopping list of points, the text moving from one boring list to the next, putting to sleep even the most avid report reader. It may be more appropriate to place such lists of points in boxes or tables, referring only to their main features in the text. Using this approach, the list of items does not interrupt the main thrust or flow of the argument, which should be presented in readable prose. Emphasis, in the form of emboldened lettering; asterisks, often referred to as 'bullet points' in some management texts; or underlining, should be used infrequently. Points of emphasis should be evident from the text. Verbosity is a common fault found in report writing. The art of writing is to express the idea with the utmost economy of words. The basic rules for good writing are: to use one word rather than many; to use, where possible short words rather than long ones; to avoid both jargon and colloquialisms, since both of these tend to confuse rather than to clarify. Robert Louis Stevenson said that: 'The difficulty is not to write, but to write what you mean, not to affect your reader, but to affect him precisely as you wish'.[3]

Language is in a state of constant change, possessing a momentum which is quite irresistible. It is impossible to stop the progress of language. During the progress of language the meanings of words change, new words become fashionable and are accepted into standard speech while others become moribund and disappear from the language. In Britain, unlike France, there is no committee of wise people which ratifies the addition of new words to the English language nor does such a body sign the death certificate for a word, finally consigning it to history. Public opinion decides all these questions. This country's vocabulary is part of its democratic institutions. What is generally accepted will ultimately be accepted as correct. Choosing the right word to convey a precise meaning using a language which is always changing is an art form, the practice of which requires regular revision and updating. Even some of the details in Gowers' excellent book, *The Complete Plain Words*, as he himself would admit, must be read with care. The book, however, is important for the principles of good writing which it presents. For this reason, it is essential reading for the writer of professional reports: '... it is the duty of the official in his use of English, neither to perpetuate what is obsolescent nor to give currency to what is novel, but, like a good servant, to follow what is generally regarded by his masters as the best practice for the time being. Among his readers will be vigilant guardians of the purity of English prose, and they must not be offended. So the official's vocabulary must contain only words that by general consent have passed the barrier, and he must not give a helping hand to any that are still trying to get through, even though he may think them deserving'.[4] Report writing for urban design projects is conservative in its approach to language, being more like the prose of the Civil Service than that of the novel or even the text book where the use of English may be more innovative.

Reports are written in sentences. They are not presented in notes taking the form of unfinished phrases separated by a multitude of dashes and structured with interminable asterisks or 'bullet points'. Good prose is a careful mixture of long and short sentences. Most sentences, however, should be short. The short sentence is less confusing for the reader than the long sentence. It can therefore express the writer's meaning more precisely. The *Oxford English Dictionary* defines a sentence as: 'A series of words in connected speech or writing, forming the grammatically complete expression of a single thought ... such a portion of a composition or utterance as extends from one full stop to another'.[5] For those wishing to make their meaning clear the sentence should express one idea. This is most easily achieved using the short sentence. Long sentences tend to attract verbiage and end as a meandering stream of words.

Reports would be unreadable if they were not divided into paragraphs. A paragraph is essentially a unit of thought. Paragraphs should be composed with sentences having ideas which illuminate its main thought. The paragraph should have a beginning, a middle and an end. The first sentence of the paragraph introduces the main thought. Sentences in the middle of the paragraph expand the theme. The last sentence in the paragraph restates and rounds off the particular unit of thought. The chief thing to remember is that paragraphing is used to make the text readable and to facilitate precise understanding. Paragraphs of one sentence are unusual and should only be used to give emphasis to a particularly important statement. Generally, however, the use of the single sentence paragraph should be avoided and it should never be used in series. At the other extreme, paragraphing loses its point if the paragraphs are excessively long.

The report is arranged into sections. A section of the report is the equivalent of a chapter of a book. A section is a significant part of the report. It is usually an account of a particular step in the design process, such as a description of the survey or an account of its analysis. The section, like the paragraph, has a beginning, a middle part and an end. The first paragraph sets out the content of the section. The middle part is composed of paragraphs, each of which develop one theme of the section. The concluding paragraph summarizes the main contents of the section and points the way to the next section. The reason for structuring the report into sections is to present information in manageable and cohesive units for clarity and ease of reading. Before starting to compose a particular section it is useful to list the themes which will form the basis of the paragraphs. The list of these ideas should be organized so that one topic leads logically to the next. If the author cannot state the idea in each paragraph simply then it is unlikely that the reader will understand what he reads. If the idea in each paragraph is unclear, or if each paragraph does not lead rationally to the next idea then the text is unlikely to present a coherent and precise account to the reader.

The detailed structure of an urban design project may take a number of forms: it varies to suit the requirements of the type of project. Normally, however, it contains information on three main subject areas. The first subject is a description of the survey or investigation. The second main subject area covers the analysis of the survey material. The final subject area is the synthesis of ideas leading to the proposed solution. Urban design is an iterative process, that is, the designer does not follow the stages of the process in a linear fashion, completing the survey, then proceeding to its analysis, followed by synthesis or design. The nature of the problem may at first be unclear. The definition of the problem may be discovered by confronting the limited evidence available with a number of partial solutions. Both problem definition and solution unfold together during this process of iteration. To describe this cyclical design process blow by blow would result in a confused and confusing report. For the sake of brevity and clarity the design process is presented as if it were a linear progression from project inception to the distillation of the solution. All the return loops and untidy abortive endeavours which are inevitable in the design process are simplified.

The report starts with an abstract, sometimes called an executive summary. This is the part of the report which most people read. It should therefore be composed with great care. The executive summary is written particularly for the busy politician who wants to know the key information in the report without taking time to read the full document. Others may read the executive summary and then turn to read particular sections of the report which they believe are of interest or are of greatest significance. Sir Winston Churchill is reported as saying that an idea which cannot be summarized on one side of foolscap is not worth considering. This may be an extreme position to take on this subject, nevertheless, the core of the idea should appear at the start of the executive summary. It should be brief and preferably

- EXECUTIVE SUMMARY
- CLIENT'S BRIEF including goals, objectives and programme
- INVESTIGATION including site surveys and study of design precedents
- ANALYSIS of the survey and other evidence gathered
- PROBLEM STATEMENT including generation of alternative solutions
- EVALUATION OF ALTERNATIVES
- DEVELOPMENT OF THE PLAN
- IMPLEMENTATION including cost, delivery of the plan, phasing and arrangements for monitoring

Figure 7.1 Urban design report: list of contents.

Figure 7.2 Report layout: Leicester City Council.

expressed in one paragraph. The executive summary, however, may extend to several pages depending on the length of the report. It may summarize each section and end with a paragraph on cost, phasing and other details of implementation.

The report may take a number of forms. Figure 7.1 shows one possible structure. In addition to the substantive matter in the various sections, information has to be given to the reader so that he or she can find a way round that information. For this purpose a short introduction describing the format of the report and indicating the content of each section is most useful. The report should also contain the usual list of figures, bibliography, sources of information, appendices and index.

CASE STUDY: LEICESTER CITY COUNCIL

If the report is written for a local authority by officers working for that authority there will be documents which give guidance about the style and content of reports. Leicester City Council, for example, has a *Report Writer's Guide*, and a *Guide to Plain English*. This latter booklet is produced by the Policy Unit of the Chief Executive's Office and gives advice on 'how to express yourself clearly and simply and how to avoid **jargon** and **officialese**'.[6] The first document gives practical information about content, the requirements of reports prepared for particular committees and references to Codes of Practice, Standing Orders, or Financial Regulations. This, or a similar document prepared by another local authority, is essential reading for those working in the field of urban design in the public sector.

Figure 7.2 gives a list of contents for a typical report presented to a committee of a local authority. The advice given in Leicester is to keep the report short: 'The Elected Members are busy people who, in most cases, have to perform their Council duties in addition to their everyday jobs. As their time is precious, they appreciate receiving committee

---

1 Summary

2 Recommendations (sections 1 and 2 may be combined)

3 Equal Opportunities Implications

4 Policy Implications

5 Details of Consultations

6 Background Papers

7 Report

8 Director of Personnel and Management Services' Comments

9 Director of Computer Services' Comments

10 Cycling Implications

11 Environmental Implications

12 Reason for Referral to Policy and Resources Sub-Committee*

13 City Treasurer's Comments*

14 Reason for Treating the Report as Confidential**

*   Only required for reports which have financial implications.

** Only required for reports recommended for consideration in private in accordance with the *Local Government (Access to Information) Act 1985*.

7.2

---

reports which are short, clear and concise.' Report writers are further advised: 'to make the fullest possible use of plans/diagrams where these are appropriate. These can often explain issues more easily than words'. The aim at Leicester is to keep the report to no more than five double-sided pages. Anything larger than that is presented as a short covering report and the full text attached as an appendix.

Reports in Leicester start with a summary and recommendations, the key to understanding the main content. Other sections which are of particular significance are: the policy implications; support for the ideas from other officers after consultation; the implications of the proposals for special areas of concern which in Leicester include equal opportunities, cycling and the environment. Finally the financial implications of the proposal have to be made clear, together with the views of those responsible for budget control. The aim at Leicester is to prepare quality reports efficiently and only in numbers necessary for effective communication between Officers, Elected Members and general members of the public. The first advice to the would-be-writer is: 'Satisfy yourself that a report is needed and that the matter cannot be dealt with in any other way'.

VISUAL PRESENTATION

A project report is usually accompanied and supported by visual material. In the case of urban design the visual material explaining the project is as important as the written report: in many cases it is more important. The old saying that a drawing is worth a thousand words is particularly apposite for the practice of urban design. There are a number of ways that an urban design project can be illustrated using visual material. The most usual method of illustrating ideas in urban design is the drawing in all its many different forms. The drawing has a long tradition as a means of illustrating townscape and town developments and is still the main means of communicating ideas in urban design. Canaletto, for example, developed tremendous skill in depicting the street scenes of Venice. His drawings and paintings remain an inspiring model for those wishing to illustrate the modern city (see, for example, Potterton, *Pageant and Panorama, The Elegant World of Canaletto*[7]). The drawings may be accompanied and supplemented by models, photographs, colour slides, video and tape recordings. The choice of presentation technique depends very much on the audience at which it is aimed, the type of project and venue for display.

There are four main types of drawings used in urban design. They are: those drawings used to record information; those used in analysis; those used for the presentation of ideas; and finally those drawings used to implement a particular action. The choice of drawing style and technique depends, in part, upon the function of the drawing in the design process. It also depends upon the way in which the drawing will be read, that is, it depends upon, for example, the distance of the observer from the drawing or the surroundings and occasion on which the drawing will be seen.

The photograph is probably the quickest and most efficient way to record both the street scenes and the architecture of the city. The freehand sketch, however, presents the author with the opportunity to select and emphasize those elements in the townscape which are important for the particular project. There are a number of techniques which can be used for the freehand sketch. This variety of sketching techniques and the ability to select and edit material from the townscape gives the designer control over the presentation of the thought process leading to the design solution. Figures 7.3 to 7.5 illustrate the meticulous record of scenes in the landscape.[8] They should be contrasted with Figure 7.6 where a careful choice has been made about those features of the townscape which the draughtsman wished to emphasize.[9] There is considerably more editing than in the two earlier drawings. The drawings by Cullen in Figures 3.36 and 3.37 have been edited in a most rigorous, even dramatic manner to illustrate spatial movement through urban space. The city is considered by Cullen to be almost a stage-setting through which the observer moves, appreciating the environment in serial vision, each view being presented as a picture or theatre set.[10] The wonderful drawings by Wiltshire (Figure 7.7) show a natural gift for editing which enables the artist to capture the essential character of the place.[11]

Design drawings for presentation are of three main types. There are those drawings for public

Figure 7.3 Landscape
drawing.

MALHAM

Upper Dambrook Beck
(near Potholes)
Deep incision of upper part of Great Scar Limestone
22.3.57

Figure 7.4 Landscape
drawing.

Figure 7.5 The foot of Wastwater.

exhibition or for board room presentations. There are those drawings for reproduction in report form and finally those used to make slides for projection. It is sometimes possible, but not always desirable, to use the same set of drawings for all three purposes. This course of action certainly avoids duplication of work but drawings designed to be seen at a distance of two metres may not reduce well for reproduction in a report which is designed to be read at less than half a metre. The three techniques of presentation require different styles of drawing. The drawing for exhibition is large in size and scale. It uses bold techniques with weighty lines, heavy tones, panels of large lettering, and possibly also the

Figure 7.6 Siena by
Francis Tibbalds.

27th october 1985

notre dame.

stephen wiltshire

Figure 7.7 Drawing by Wiltshire.

Figure 7.8 Axonometric by
Francis Tibbalds.

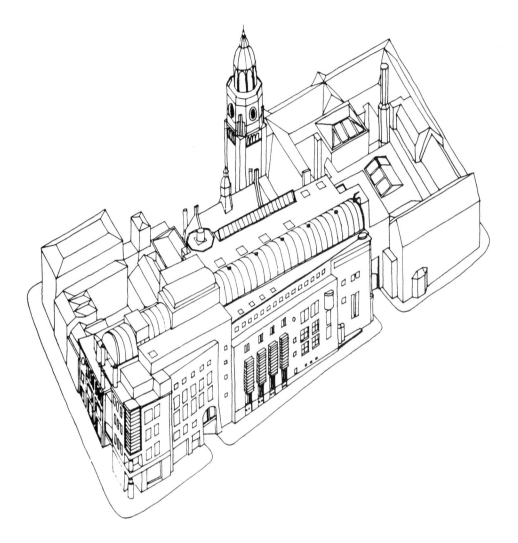

limited use of vivid colour. The aim of the drawing
is to catch and hold the attention of an observer
moving about in a large space. It is meant to be
viewed at a distance of one to two metres and is
designed to have an impact at that distance. The
illustration for a report is small in size and scale. It
is often in black and white for ease of reproduction
and is designed to be read as a page of a book, that
is, at a distance of about twelve inches or thirty

centimetres (see Figure 4.9; Tibbalds *et al.*, 1991).[12]
Both drawing types are often unsuitable for slide
presentation. Some information included in
drawings for reports cannot be read on a slide at
normal seating distances for such presentations.
Such material only tends to confuse the observer
and obstructs communication. Large-scale drawings
for exhibition, if bold enough in style, may be
converted into effective slides, provided they

Figure 7.9 Axonometric by Francis Tibbalds.

contain little written information. Before deciding on the techniques to be used in the preparation of the final design drawings, the method of presentation should be determined. If the presentation is to include a public exhibition, an illustrated report and a talk accompanied by slides, ideally, three sets of drawings would be required.

A set of design drawings normally includes a location map showing the site in relation to the city or its region; a layout of the site showing access points, internal vehicular and pedestrian circulation, the main building blocks and the landscaping; sections through the site and its buildings showing the relationship of the floors and the positions of

Figure 7.10 Piazza del
Popolo, Todi. Drawing by
J.H. Aronson.

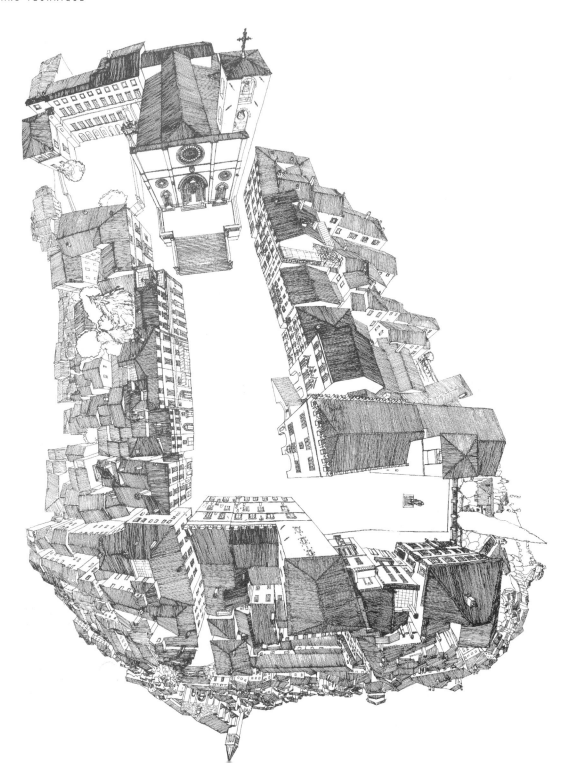

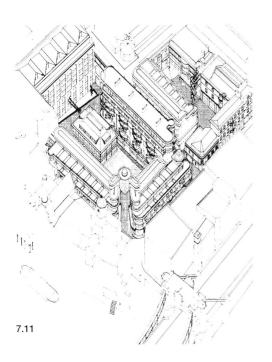

7.11

the vertical circulation; outline elevations relating the building blocks to each other, to the planting and to the buildings surrounding the site. In addition, axonometric drawings, aerial perspectives and ground-level perspectives accompany the main drawings to illustrate the three-dimensional form of the development (Figures 7.8 to 7.11). Design drawings may also be accompanied by scale models, which is a particularly appropriate technique for communicating design ideas to the layperson (Figures 7.12 to 7.15). A technique currently being developed involves the three-dimensional modelling of the city, using computer graphics (Figures 7.16 and 7.17). The observer sitting at the computer terminal can set a path through the development and create moving images of the city as he or she moves along the path. In this way, it is possible to simulate movement through the city's urban spaces where the observer can see the shape of the buildings, their relationship to each other and to appreciate the general quality of the city environment.

Figure 7.11 Horselydown Square designed by Julyan Wickham.

Figure 7.12 Student model: School of Architecture, The University of Nottingham, photograph by Glyn Halls.

Figure 7.13 Student
model: School of
Architecture, The University
of Nottingham, photograph
by Glyn Halls.

Figure 7.14 Student
model: School of
Architecture, The University
of Nottingham, photograph
by Glyn Halls.

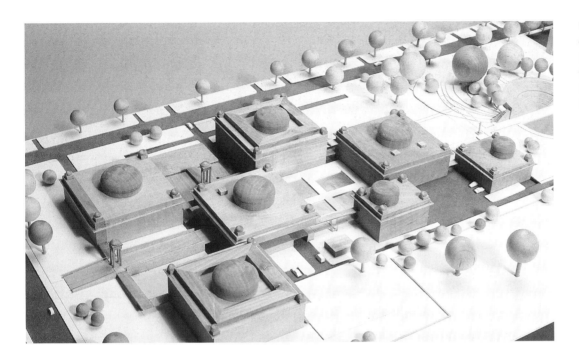

Figure 7.15 Model of competition entry for The Indira Ghandi Cultural Centre, Delhi, India. Design by Moughtin and model built by John Stone.

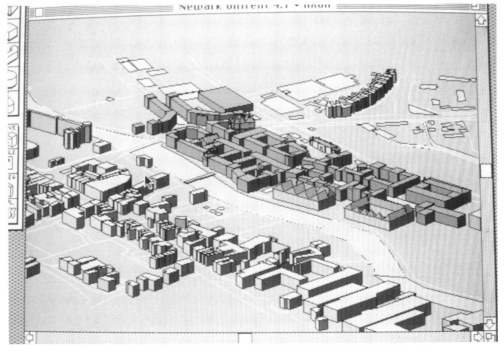

Figure 7.16 Computer model of Newark, Nottinghamshire: student project, The Institute of Planning Studies, The University of Nottingham, by Peter Whitehouse.

Figure 7.17 Computer
model of Newark,
Nottinghamshire: student
project, The Institute of
Planning Studies, The
University of Nottingham,
by Peter Whitehouse.

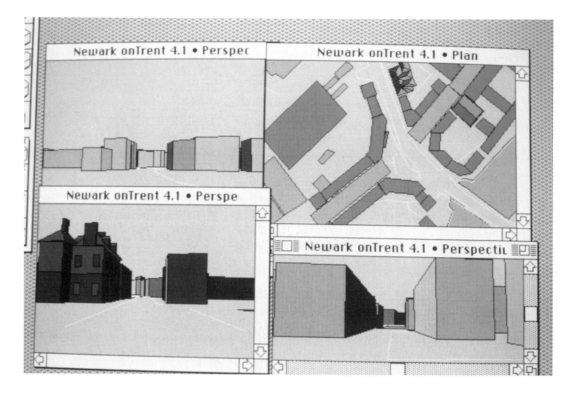

Figure 7.17 Computer model of Newark, Nottinghamshire: student project, The Institute of Planning Studies, The University of Nottingham, by Peter Whitehouse.

Such computer simulations of the city will soon be as important to urban design as computer-simulated flight to the pilot. A three-dimensional computer model of Bath includes the whole of the Georgian city, the commercial and business centres, a large part of the residential area and a three-dimensional terrain model of the surrounding countryside. The model is made up of 150 sub-models, each of which is about the size of a city block. An important use of the model is in development control where the effect of any proposed development can be examined to determine how it affects neighbouring buildings, public space or the rural skyline, which is so important in Bath's setting (Figure 7.18).

The urban computer model presents a way of analysing the present form of development, the impacts of proposed developments and assessing future possibilities. It is also potentially a technique whereby the whole community can 'focus and articulate its thoughts on how urban growth and change can be accommodated'.[13]

The preparation of drawings, reports and models is the responsibility of professional architects, planners and urban designers. At this stage in the design process, the role of members of the public is to receive information, to hear the evidence, to understand the main arguments for the proposal and to see the implications of the proposed development. This understanding may be impaired for those with defective vision. An estimated 250 000 people in Britain have a partial, but nonetheless disabling, loss of vision which cannot be corrected by ordinary spectacles. This may even include senior decision makers whose vision is failing through age. For this section of the community the task of reading documents and visual displays can

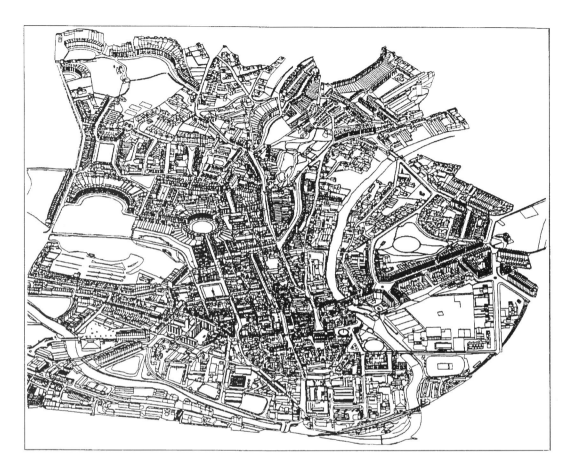

Figure 7.18 Bath computer model.

become difficult and confusing if the information presented is unclear and lacks consistency.

The minimum size of lettering that is required for displays varies according to distance. Research has established that the relationship between letter height and viewing distance is linear. As a general rule, letters and numbers should be at least 10 mm high for every metre of viewing distance. No lettering should be less than 22 mm in height while texts used in overhead projector slides should not be smaller than 18 point. Considerable research into legibility has led to the design of typefaces suitable for presentations. It was found that a mixture of upper and lower case letters can be read more easily

and recognized more quickly than words consisting entirely of capital letters. People usually recognize words by their shape, so for example Nottingham can be recognised more easily than NOTTINGHAM. Typefaces such as Helvetica, Arial, Universe and Times are usually considered to be easy to read rather than over-stylized designs. Legibility depends upon text spacing and, where possible, splitting the text around illustrations should be avoided.

Because an estimated 9.3 per cent of the population is colour blind (leading to a particular confusion between red and green), and 8 per cent significantly affected by colour confusion, contrast is more important than colour for achieving legibility.

The high-contrast combination of black letters on a yellow background is legible at three times the distance as a low contrast combination of green and red. Some partially sighted people, however, find that white or pale colours on a dark background give a high degree of legibility.

If the public has been involved with the project throughout the earlier design stages, a strong consensus may have developed giving legitimacy and a strong political authority to the proposals. Complete consensus is unlikely and there will be those individuals and groups whose interest is threatened. At this stage they will, no doubt, be advised to lobby political representatives in the hope of having the project rejected or, at least, having it amended favourably. Such groups, depending on the type and scale of the project, may then formally object at a planning appeal, hearing or inquiry. Since it is possible that groups of objectors may employ professional advisors it is wise for those preparing an urban design project to have considered the main alternatives to the proposal and to have at their disposal pertinent arguments for the rejection of any alternative. A failure to defeat such arguments could lead to the loss of the project or the development of an unsatisfactory compromise.

Assuming a successful outcome to the public consultation process, then further drawings are necessary to instruct legal advisors on land conveyancing for land assembly or subdivision and to instruct contractors to carry out the work. These specialist production drawings for project implementation will usually be prepared by architects, landscape architects, engineers and land surveyors and not necessarily by the urban designer. While the urban designer may not be directly involved with the preparation of working drawings for buildings, roads or planting, he or she should know when they are required, what form they take and be able to read and understand their content. The content of such drawings has to be related to the general proposal in order to determine points of conflict.

Most designers are called upon, from time to time, to make a presentation to members of the general public, colleagues or the client. Such presentations are often used to sell the idea of the project and to seek support for the project. Presentations may also be used to elicit information from the public and to seek ideas. The presentation should be organized with a view to its purpose and the audience to whom it is directed. A series of public meetings, such as those described in the Newark study in Chapter 5, are quite different from a presentation to a large formal gathering or even to a small intimate group of colleagues. Common to all such presentations is a sound preparation, a thorough knowledge of the subject matter and an enthusiasm for the project. If the speaker does not believe in the project and its vision then clearly neither will the audience. Some hints at presentation are listed in Figure 7.19.[14]

Figure 7.19 Good practice in the presentation of projects.

1 Consider the audience and its needs.
2 Assemble the facts in the light of (1) above, taking into account the complexity of the material.
3 Develop sufficient and suitable visual aids.
4 Make available supporting information such as drawings and photographs.
5 Introduce the subject by outlining its content. End in the same way by reminding the audience of the main points discussed.
6 Be enthusiastic about the subject.
7 Be natural.
8 Maintain eye contact with the audience.
9 Be prepared for questions during and at the end of the session.
10 Involve your audience.

CONCLUSION

The presentation of urban design ideas takes a number of forms depending upon the information to be communicated and to whom. When dealing with the public, such information, whether written or visual, should be simple and direct. Britain is a multi-cultural society where several minority languages are spoken. Projects sited in areas where such languages are spoken should consider the preparation of important project information in the locally spoken minority languages. This is a common feature of most planning work in local authorities. It is an example allied professions and private developers might follow. Drawn communication for the implementation of projects requires precision. Such drawings are needed for the calculation of land areas, volumes of materials and the precise physical location of each element of the project. The preparation of production drawings requires a number of different professional skills. These skills are seldom found in the same person and they are often not found in the same urban design team. Clearly, production drawings should conform to both the spirit and purpose of the project design. It is, therefore, in the interest of those working in the field of urban design to be conversant with the varied forms of maps and drawings used for the purpose of project implementation.

REFERENCES

1   Gowers, Sir Ernest (1962) *The Complete Plain Words*, Harmondsworth: Penguin.

2   Fowler, H.W. (1981) *A Dictionary of Modern English Usage*, 2nd Edn, Revised by Sir Ernest Gowers, London: Book Club Associates; Roget, M. (1962) *Roget's Thesaurus*, Abridged R.A. Dutch, Harmondsworth: Penguin.

3   Gowers (1962) *op. cit.*

4   *Ibid.*

5   Little, W., *et al.* (1952) *Shorter Oxford English Dictionary*, Revised Edn, C.T. Onions, Oxford: The Clarendon Press.

6   Leicester City Council (undated) *Report Writer's Guide* and *Guide to Plain English*, Leicester: Leicester City Council.

7   Potterton, H. (1978) *Pageant and Panorama, The Elegant World of Canaletto*, London: Book Club Associates.

8   Wainwright, A. (undated) *A Lakeland Sketchbook*, Kendal: Westmorland Gazette, and Hutchings, G E. (1960) *Landscape Drawing*, London: Methuen.

9   Tibbalds, F. (1962) *Making People-Friendly Towns*, Harlow: Longman.

10 Cullen, G. (1961) *Townscape*, London: Architectural Press.

11 Wiltshire, S. (1989) *Cities*, London: Dent and Sons.

12 Tibbalds, Colbourne, Karski, Williams in association with Touchstone (1991) *National Heritage Area Study: Nottingham Lace Market*, Nottingham: Nottingham City Council.

13 Day, A. (1994) New tools for urban design, *The Urban Design Quarterly*, No. 51, July.

14 Cole, G.A. (1996) *Management: Theory and Practice*, London: D P Publications.

PROJECT MANAGEMENT

8

INTRODUCTION

This chapter returns to the theme of structuring the design process to ensure a successful outcome, but it approaches the subject from a slightly different view point. The material for this chapter is derived from business studies but, where appropriate, those ideas have been adapted and applied to the built environment. This chapter focuses on the basic concepts of project management. The practices and techniques that can assist in transforming ideas into real undertakings are discussed, together with an assessment of the software currently available. Of key importance is the difference between the traditional approach to project management and the model advocated here which focuses not only on the intrinsic management process but on the external factors which affect the development, management and implementation of any project.

DEVELOPMENT OF PROJECT MANAGEMENT

Managing projects is an activity which dates back to the early history of man. Great projects, such as the pyramids, the building of ancient cities, the planning of the Great Wall of China and other wonders of the ancient world, required careful planning and implementation. Project management then was used as a powerful way of controlling communities and to coerce them towards a clearly established goal. The ancient projects involved enormous numbers of people, with extremely high ratios of labourers to managers. Ancient megastructures such as the Mayan Ceremonial Centres with their majestic temples were built with the involvement of the whole community, guided by the vision of secular and sacred authorities. The length of time taken to build these great structures covered several generations. The focus on the ultimate goal, however, was never lost.

The building of ancient cities required proper management in order to achieve complex and detailed specifications. How, for example, did the Incas erect so accurately the massive walls of Machu Picchu (Figure 8.1)? How were the gigantic Hindu temples at Angkor built in such close conjunction to its complex of waterways? All these undertakings required detailed specifications of the work to be carried out, the material to be used, as well as guarantees and methods of organizing the

Figure 8.1   Machu Picchu

used in an essentially unaltered form. Critical path analysis developed by Wright in 1918 to show the relationships between activities is another example of a technique which plays an essential role in modern management.[1]

Although many of the early codifications of principles and practices were developed in the first half of the twentieth century, project management in its modern form extends back only thirty to forty years. The project management processes and techniques used in the Manhattan Atom Bomb project (1940-1945), became the model for the management of later projects such as the Polaris Missiles (1955-1960) and the Apollo Moon Programme (1960-1970). The evolution of project management and its new role as a defined professional discipline in its own right is now universally apparent as new roads or bridges open, as major buildings rise, as new computer systems come on line or as spectacular shopping centres and urban projects unfold. The use of its principles and practices can assist in the elimination of the need to rely on luck to attain a successful outcome for a project.

PROJECT MANAGEMENT TECHNIQUES AND PRACTICES

The Code of Practice for Project Management of the Chartered Institute of Building[2] defines project management as:

> the overall planning, co-ordination and control of a project from inception to completion aimed at meeting a Client's requirements in order to produce a functionally and financially viable project that will be completed on time within authorised cost and to the required quality standards.

In other words, a 'project' is a process of creating a specific result; a means to an end. Project management deals with the co-ordination and integration of the process. A project can be further defined as a non-routine activity; a separate undertaking having

distribution of tasks. Clearly, these projects were procured with great consciousness of the importance of time, cost and quality which are the cornerstones of project management.

There are numerous examples of the achievements of project management throughout history; the Medieval cathedrals representing the dominance of faith over territories, the architecture of the eighteenth century representing classic perfection, or the great triumphs of urban planning in the late nineteenth century representing the steady increase of engineering sophistication. It was, however, the great wars in the twentieth century which gave new impetus to the development of scientific ways of organizing and undertaking complex operations. New project planning techniques emerged as well as new approaches to general management. Henry Gantt's bar chart used for production scheduling at the Frankfort arsenal in 1917 became an essential tool for project management and it is still widely time, cost, quality constraints and objectives. A project usually involves multiple disciplines in new and complex activities with clear start and end dates. It involves greater risks than operations which are simply 'business as usual' and can become an agent of change.

Paralleling the method outlined in previous chapters for urban design, the life cycle of a specific undertaking in project management terms can be subdivided into four major stages, namely: 'Project Definition Stage', 'Project Planning Stage', 'Project Implementation Stage' and 'Project Closure Stage' (Figure 8.2). These stages and the activities that take place at each stage are described below.

PROJECT DEFINITION STAGE

Most projects emerge from a strategic objective or investment aim established by an individual or an organization. In project management terms the individual or the organization responsible for formulating the preliminary project concepts is referred to as the client or project sponsor. The client is responsible for defining the business requirements; justifying funding; setting success criteria; reviewing progress and project environment; and ensuring that the project benefits are realized.

At the early stages of a project the client develops a set of basic assumptions in answer to the following questions:

- Why is the project being considered?
- What are the benefits to the business or the organization?
- What are the minimum achievements which must be attained?
- What are the constraints?
- What are the success criteria?
- What are the relative priorities in terms of time, cost, and quality/performance?

Once the strategic or investment aims and project objectives are understood, the activities that are necessary to bring about the implementation of the

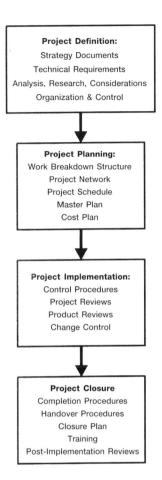

Figure 8.2 Project stages.

project can be determined. With this in mind, the first step in the project definition stage is for the client to establish a clear statement of purpose. In project management terms this strategy document is known as client requirements definition (CRD). The definition of the client's requirements is the client's formal statement of the aims of the particular enterprise and the project objectives. It provides an outline definition of the project scope, and more importantly, defines the essential requirements to be met. The definition of the client's requirements outlines the reasons for the project.

Figure 8.3 Client requirements.

- Client's aims, performance specifications and project description
- Project's business priority or strategic objective
- Project objectives (time, cost and quality) and their relative priorities
- Constraints and success criteria

Figure 8.4 Project requirements.

- Project scope
- Project deliverables
- Functional requirements, to meet the performance specifications
- Acceptance criteria of end product
- Project identification and coding
- Assumptions required to deliver end product

Once a clear statement of the client's requirements is formulated, the client has to focus on implementing the project. Depending on the size of the venture, it is usually at this stage that a project manager is appointed with the specific responsibility of establishing the route which best meets the client's aspirations, within the constraints that are set. The project manager will discuss with the client the available options and initiate feasibility studies to determine the best route to be adopted. The Code of Practice for Project Management emphasizes that the project manager, both acting on behalf of, and representing, the client has the duty of providing a cost-effective and independent service, selecting, correlating, integrating and managing different disciplines and expertise, to satisfy the objectives and provisions of the project brief from inception to completion. The services provided must be to the client's satisfaction, safeguard his/her interests at all times, and, where possible, give consideration to the needs of the eventual user of the completed project.[3] The local community may be the eventual user or purchaser of the project. Ways must be found to involve the community positively in the development of a project, particularly if they are likely to be the users. This issue was discussed in earlier chapters.

In the field of urban design the project manager may, of course, be the person leading the design work, although much will depend on the nature of the project or the client's available expertise and interests. The project manager, who may be educated in any of a number of disciplines, has the continuous duty of exercising control over project time, cost and performance. To achieve such control it is important to produce a project brief,

Figure 8.5 Relationship between scope for change and cost of change.

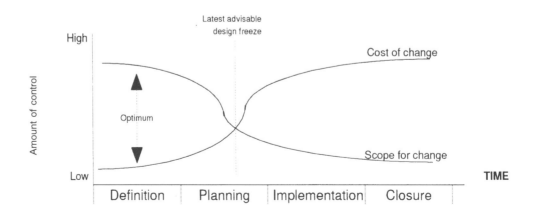

referred to in project management terms as the Project Requirements Definition (PRD) document.

The Project Requirements Definition is the full definition of what the project is about. It includes the items shown in Figures 8.3 and 8.4. The items in Figure 8.3 follow directly from the client's requirements while those in Figure 8.4 are concerned primarily with the definition of a successful outcome.

This vital strategy document is used by the project manager to obtain the client's decision and full authorization for the project. It provides a contract between the client and the project manager and forms the baseline for changes. It provides the starting point for developing a detail project plan and provides a reference point for review and audits at later stages of the project. The term 'Project Requirements Definition' is used in business jargon; in many ways it is equivalent to the agreed design brief to which the urban designer works. The rigour of the design brief and programme in urban design would be greatly enhanced by the inclusion of measurable criteria for determining a successful outcome.

As project development progresses, the control over project outcome decreases and the cost of saving time, or removing errors, increases. The value of early definition and the relationship between scope for change and the cost of change, set against the timescale of a project, is described graphically in Figure 8.5.

It is useful, at this stage, to undertake a thorough analysis of project risks. The technique for identifying and quantifying aspects of the project that could lead to losses is known as Risk Analysis. Risk can be defined as exposure to adverse consequences. Risks exist in all forms of project and are normally of a physical or financial character. Physical risks relate to loss of, or damage to, goods and property, and financial risk relates to loss of money. Most projects, including those in urban design, are business ventures; the risks are therefore concerned with financial losses rather than physical hazards. Where physical risks are involved the project manager

- The project goal: it may be too ambitious
- The project plan: the activities may be poorly perceived and the interactions not well understood
- The project organization: it may be poorly staffed and managed badly
- The project methods: they may fail to provide adequate controls

Figure 8.6 Internal risks.

- The client: support can be withdrawn or interference with the running of the project can take place
- The market environment: market preferences may change and make the project less attractive
- The supporting links: suppliers can be unable to deliver according to schedule or may be affected by industrial disputes
- The competition: competitors may instigate rival bids or projects in adjacent areas

Figure 8.7 External risks.

should consider taking out insurance cover. The analysis of risk gives an increased understanding of the project. It allows the formulation of more realistic plans, in terms of both cost estimates and timescales. It identifies the party best able to handle a risk and leads to the use of the most suitable form of procurement strategy. It also allows the assessment of contingencies that actually reflect the risk.

Risk may be internal or external to the project. Some examples of internal risk are shown in Figure 8.6. External risks are shown in Figure 8.7.

It is helpful to identify both the internal and external risks and their potential impact on the project objectives. External risks are always much harder to deal with than internal ones. A project manager can usually control internal risks, but can only react to external ones. Where risks can be identified, the project manager can take action to

Figure 8.8 Risk analysis table.

Risk Description	Risk Assessment			Cost Implications			Risk Class	Proposed Management of High Risk
	High	Average	Low	High	Average	Low		
Planning permission refused		Yes		Yes			5	Contract experienced planner
Construction delays	Yes			Yes			6	Seek compensation clause within contract
Construction accidents			Yes		Yes		2	Ensure insurance policies exist
Unforeseen ground conditions			Yes	Yes			3	Undertake adequate survey of ground conditions

lessen their impact on the project. This can be done firstly, by identifying and assessing risk; secondly, by managing the risk to minimize the adverse effects, and thirdly, by monitoring and evaluating the risks. Risk assessment helps in quantifying or ranking the risks according to how likely they are to arise and in predicting their effect. This can be done by producing a risk assessment table which not only identifies the risks most likely to occur, but also outlines the actions which will contain or eliminate them (see Figure 8.8).

As most risks are ultimately measured in financial terms, the techniques usually used for assessing risks are of a monetary nature.[4] They include:

Figure 8.9 Risk management strategies.

- Addition of contingencies; by adding extra budget allocations to cover risks if they arise
- Avoidance of risk; by passing on risks to sub-contractors or the client
- Reduction of risk; by including testing and other project activities that will discover technical risks before the project is completed
- Insurance against risk; by taking out insurance if the risks have a known statistical nature

- break-even analysis;
- cost–benefit analysis;
- multiple criteria analysis.

Some of these techniques have been described in earlier chapters. Having analysed risks, it is wise to prepare strategies that minimize the adverse effects on the project if the risks materialize. This is known as risk management.

Some examples of risk management strategies that can be developed are shown in Figure 8.9.

It is good practice to closely monitor activities which have a high risk classification. Special attention should be given to exceptional issues, milestones and target achievements. Some monitoring techniques are described later in this chapter. Risk analysis is an iterative process. Therefore, risks are reassessed at least once during the project's life cycle when changes to the likelihood or the seriousness of risks might require amendments to the risk analysis and contingency plans.

The project definition stage provides the framework that enables the effective execution of the project. Issues such as the project brief, organization, control systems, analysis of risk and project interfaces are established. Time and money spent, at this stage, will be repaid in the overall success of the project.

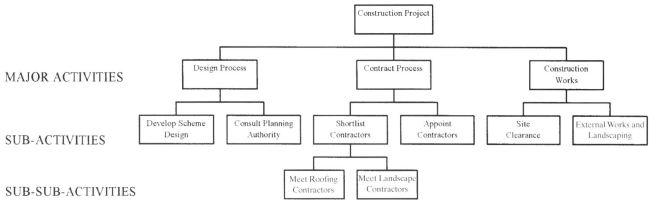

MAJOR ACTIVITIES

SUB-ACTIVITIES

SUB-SUB-ACTIVITIES

Figure 8.10 Work breakdown structure.

PROJECT PLANNING STAGE

The objective of the project planning stage is to translate the overall project aims into a series of identifiable activities which can be set out in a logical way that will achieve the desired end. Project requirements such as schedules, deadlines, resources, as well as budget and cost constraints, have to be clearly defined. The ultimate objective of the planning stage is to produce a total project plan. To do this it is necessary to develop in a methodical way the key elements that form the project plan; these are the 'work breakdown structure', the 'project network', the 'project schedule', and the 'cost plan'.

The work breakdown structure is a list of all major activities and sub-activities that form the project. It has built-in levels to allow a clear identification of the actual work that must be performed to meet the project requirements. Each major activity is divided into sub-activities and sub-sub-activities helping in this way to completely define the project scope. The work breakdown structure assists in relating all the elements of work to each other and to the project. It also helps in defining work packages, establishing cost breakdown structures, organizational breakdown structures and project estimates, permitting the development of the project network and programme. The work breakdown structure should specify clear deliverables for each activity. In practice, when all the activities identified in the work breakdown structure are finished, the project is completed. The work breakdown structure assists in establishing in detail 'what' has to be achieved in terms of meeting the project requirements. It also helps in identifying 'who' is accountable for achieving it, 'how' it is going to be achieved in terms of detailed action and 'when' it is going to be achieved in terms of milestones and target dates (see Figure 8.10).

The critical path is one of the techniques most commonly used in building a project network. Once all the detailed activities have been identified, it is possible to create a network which shows the dependencies of activities and work packages. A critical path shows the sequence of the project activities and how they depend on each other. It also reveals those activities which are critical for completing the project on time. This sequence of activities, known as the critical path, determines how long the project will take to complete. Any delays to the activities on the critical path will delay the overall completion of the project.

With simple projects it is possible to find the critical path by ascertaining the duration of the activities that form the project and the sequential path that these activities follow. With more complex projects, project management software is used to undertake these arithmetic calculations. By

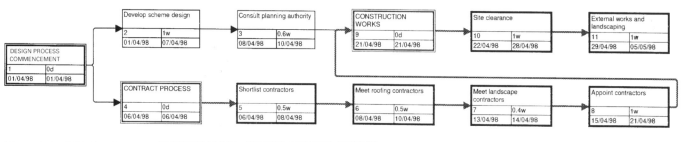

Figure 8.11 Critical path diagram.

networking the activities of the project it is possible to have a clearer understanding of the critical activities which can constrain the project's success. It also enables the project duration to be optimized by focusing on the activities that form the critical path, as it is these that can affect the progress of the project (see Figure 8.11).

Once the work breakdown structure has been defined and the network has been established, it is possible create the project schedule. The project

schedule contains key information regarding the viability of completing the work in the given timescales with the given resources. It identifies key events which, if late, could delay the programme and the project milestones or those points against which progress can be monitored.

Gantt charts or bar charts are particularly useful for displaying a schedule of project activities in a cascading form, whilst showing in a graphical way their durations and their start and finish dates

Figure 8.12 Gantt chart for a building project.

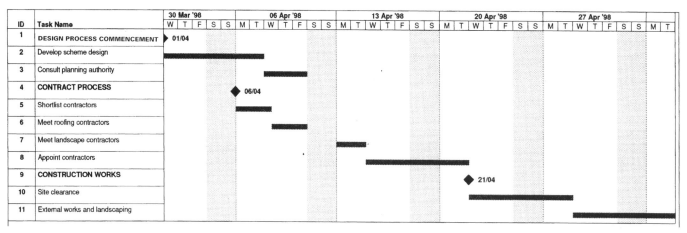

(Figure 8.12). Gantt charts are also useful for illustrating who is responsible for given activities and for displaying key events and project milestones. They can be used as a powerful communication tool for improving the understanding of a project and for providing management focus. Gantt charts are used as project master programmes as they permit the organization of even the most complex project in manageable and measurable chunks of activities.

The project plan needs to be complemented by a cost plan. The objective of a cost plan is to provide the best estimate of the final cost of the project. It assists in planning when money will be spent and on what. It is the basis of the final budget and the limit of expenditure. The cost plan should include a cash flow plan and payment profile based on the master programme. It should allow for contingencies, professional fees, direct costs and other operational costs. It also aids in setting up detailed cost control procedures for all stages of the project.

In planning a project it is important to realize that the involvement of the project team in the planning process is as important as the plan produced. John Harvey-Jones, recollecting the experiences of a UK firm and a Japanese firm each charged with the responsibility of constructing chemical facilities for ICI of similar size and complexity, recounts that the UK firm's construction had reached the roof at eaves level before the Japanese team began site construction work. Yet, the Japanese team handed over a fully operational plant before the UK team finished. While the UK team was busily building the Japanese were still planning. A possible explanation of what was happening can be related to the planning system of 'Ringi' used by the Japanese.[5] In this system, a proposal is passed around the responsible team, each member of the team being free to amend any part of the proposal. Every time the proposal is amended it is recirculated around the whole team, with each still able to amend in each iteration. The proposal is not finally adopted until every member of the team is able to subscribe fully to the proposal. When it is finally adopted, each is committed fully to its implementation.

Whatever implementation system is used, it is clear that effective teams lead to successful projects. Although project management is strongly associated with control systems, project management is also about integrating a group of people, gaining their commitment and motivating them towards clearly established goals. The project team, on the other hand, should be geared towards supporting the project manager in carrying out his/her responsibilities. For a project team to function properly, it is necessary that the project team concept is conveyed to all concerned. Clearly defined and measurable project objectives, as well as clearly identified roles and responsibilities of each team member, provide the formula for a successful team.

Team members are often unaware of how their contributions affect the project and on many occasions team members tend to become defensive and keep to themselves any problems they may have with the project. They then solve their own problems in an independent way. This can be avoided by conveying a common understanding of the project and ensuring that the team members are aware of the inter-relationship between all tasks and activities. The use of the work breakdown structure, the project network and critical path as communications tools can illuminate everyone's contribution to the project objectives. It is wise to promote teamwork by involving the project team in problem solving and brainstorming, undertaking social activities, encouraging feedback within the team, carrying out regular performance reviews of all team members and developing the team through team-building exercises. The promotion of a working environment which encourages an interchange of ideas and shared responsibility will ultimately benefit the project.

It is recognized above that setting clear objectives is the first step in ensuring that the project team operates as an effective and focused unit. Objectives should therefore be realistic, challenging, worthwhile, agreed and written down. The acronym

Figure 8.13 Project
handbook content.

- **Financial information**; including contracts of authorization, project expenditure, billing, budget and cash-flow records
- **Planning and control information**; including top-level project plan, master programme, schedules and quality control review records
- **Standards**; including specific project standards and authorization for changes and deviations from agreed standards
- **Project personnel information**; including details of project personnel with key dates, experience, contact information
- **Logs and records**; including project diary and log recording position statements, key decisions, key events, review reports and project statistics
- **Project documents**; including the client's requirements definition (CRD) and project's requirements definition (PRD), design reports, technical specifications, test specifications and correspondence
- **Other documentation**; including documentation relevant to specific issues not allowed in the above sections. For example, leases of office equipment, portakabins and communication connections.

SMART is used to describe an approach to objective setting. It is used to ensure that objectives are properly set. SMART stands for: specific, measurable, achievable, relevant (to the project objective), and timed (with clear timescales and deadlines). A high level of commitment is best achieved when all members of the team are involved in the setting of clear and measurable objectives.

To ensure that all the details concerning the project and key documentation are kept together it is normal practice to create a project handbook. The project handbook provides a central point of reference for up-to-date project documentation and should be accessible to any person authorized by the project manager. All details concerning the project should be maintained in the project handbook, properly organized into relevant sections. Some of the sections that a project handbook should include are shown in Figure 8.13. The project handbook should be established at the beginning of every project and should be kept up-to-date throughout a project's life cycle.[6]

PROJECT IMPLEMENTATION STAGE

The key to successful project management is to actually follow the project plan and keep track of how the project is progressing. This is achieved through leadership, team commitment and by making the achievement of required progress and success highly visible. To assist the implementation of the project, it is worthwhile to look at the various forces that will, or could, affect implementation. These can be split into the 'driving forces' which are likely to support key events leading to project completion, and the 'restraining forces' or those aspects which could restrict or hamper progress towards set milestones. When this analysis is completed, actions can be identified to reduce the influence of the restraining forces and increase the influence of the driving forces (see Figure 8.14).

Projects rarely go exactly as planned and an important part of project control is keeping the project plan up-to-date. The project plan is updated so that the effects on the critical path of changes and delays can be assessed. Projects can suffer changes resulting from a variety of reasons. Some of the more common ones are: inaccurate initial estimating; unforeseen price rises of material, labour or services; changes to the original plans/specifications; overruns of time and cost.

In order to make certain that the project is proceeding as scheduled, it is necessary to monitor and evaluate project progress to ensure the comple-

Driving Force	Proposed Action
1 Political support	1 Lobby politicians
2 Project suppliers	2 Agree common strategy for promoting project
3 Community which benefits	3 Create community consultative panel
Restraining Force	**Proposed Action**
1 Pressure groups	1 Improve information to other stakeholders and clarify misconceptions
2 Cashflow limitations	2 Review payment profile
3 Team members' apathy	3 Undertake team building exercise

Figure 8.14 Driving and restraining force table.

tion of the work as planned. There are two levels of monitoring and evaluation that need to be considered, namely 'progress review' and 'product review'.

The aim of the 'progress review' is to measure project progress and compare it with the plan. Variations from the plan should be evaluated and corrective action considered. Actions resulting from the progress review should aim to correct any variations rather than attempting to manage the consequences. After identifying a problem in the progress review it is good practice to obtain general agreement on the nature of the problem and appoint a member of the team with the specific task of solving the problem within an agreed timescale and with a specific mechanism for reporting back.

'Product reviews' can involve a number of people from a variety of professions. A review of a specialized design, for instance, may involve the project manager, the designer, an external expert. The timing of the product review is dependent on the project schedule. A product is available for reviewing when the activity involved in producing that product, or part of the product, is completed. Product review can be tied to the payment profile as assurances are required that the work has been completed to specific requirements before it is accepted. Product review allows early identification of risks, weakness and errors, as well as major product deficiencies. Projects in the field of urban design are usually structured in a number of phases linked to the termination of specific tasks, such as analysis, drawings, models. Major progress reviews occur at the end of each phase so that deficiencies in project design and management can be amended in the light of experience.

The project manager, acting for a client or for the designer, is responsible for ensuring that the final product meets the technical specifications and for determining whether the work is completed satisfactorily so that the next phase may proceed. In some instances, changes would need to take place to allow the project to progress. Changes, however, have to be managed rigorously to ensure that the project progresses to plan. If left uncontrolled, the rate of change will exceed the rate of progress, with further effect on budgets and funding. Uncontrolled change often results in loss of project confidence and a loss of morale amongst the project team members.

A strict and formal procedure is required to enforce identification and definition of changes, justification for changes and evaluation of change requests. Formal authorization or rejection of change needs to be well documented and fully authorized by the client. It is the responsibility of the project manger to ensure that change control procedures are in place and that the implementation of change is closely monitored. Once a change has been accepted the project requirement definition document and the project plan need to be updated.

Figure 8.15 Change order form.

Change Order Form

Project ID:	Date:

Client ID:	Distribution list
Project Name::	

Description of change:
"What":

Requested by:
"Who":

Reasons for change:
"Why":

Authority for change:	Discretionary/Non-discretionary:

Cost and time implications:

Change to be paid by:

Recommended action:

Client Authorization:	Dated:

Master plan and cost plan amended on:

Change implemented on:

Change control documentation should include a change request form (Figure 8.15), a change appraisal form and a change register document. Change control is crucial to project success and should be properly catalogued and filed to avoid unfunded disputes and litigations at later phases of project implementation.

To aid control of the project implementation stage, project progress meetings take place at relevant intervals to review achievements against targets on all aspects of the project and to initiate action by appropriate parties to ensure adherence to the project plan. It is good practice to produce proper agendas and effective minutes to ensure follow-up action by those concerned.

PROJECT CLOSURE STAGE

As stated earlier in this chapter, the ultimate aim of project management is to achieve a co-ordinated and satisfactory completion of all work phases within time, cost and quality requirements. The project closure stage includes activities such as the termination of contracts with external suppliers and contractors, the production of a final financial statement of the project and the completion of the project handbook.

The practical completion and handover procedures should be detailed by the project manager in the project closure plan covering aspects of acceptance of works, completion of unfinished or deficient works, commissioning and test reports, maintenance schedules and working instructions. Proposals for training project operators and users should also be included.

A key activity of the project closure stage is ensuring that a plan for 'post-completion project evaluation' is in place to allow feedback from those that took part in the project. The post-implementation review process is designed to examine the entire project retrospectively, with the purpose of identifying what lessons can be learned through its management and the process followed, and whether or not the original client requirements were met in full, or

in part. The results of the review are usually put into a report. In many cases, a review cannot examine whether the strategic or business objectives have been met, since many of these are long-term objectives spanning several years. However, the strengths and weaknesses of key project plan elements can be assessed, so that future benefits for other projects can be derived. However, the most important aspect of this final stage of the project cycle is to ensure that the project closure is properly celebrated in order to acknowledge the efforts of everyone who contributed to defining, planning and implementing the project. Celebrating achievements demonstrates that people's work is valued.

THE ROLE AND USE OF PROJECT MANAGEMENT SOFTWARE

The extensive use of computer applications as tools to assist most project management functions has become a usual occurrence. It is therefore essential to keep abreast of developments in this area in order to select and recommend appropriate packages for use on a project. It is particularly important to make sure that systems used by project team members are compatible to facilitate electronic exchange of data. E-mail and teleworking are examples of new ways of facilitating and accelerating communications exchange between parties.

Project management software can assist in managing time and cost aspects of projects. It can provide a consistent approach to project planning and can provide management focus by illustrating the various stages of the project in graphical form. When selecting a particular software package, it is necessary to consider how user-friendly and functional the application is and to what extent staff training is necessary. Consideration should also be given to quality and performance standards and the value for money that it provides.

The most popular project management software currently available in the market includes CA Superproject, Microsoft Project, Timeline, Project

Manager Workbench and Schedular. Most of these packages offer good value for money and provide useful function cover. Microsoft Project is probably the most user-friendly and provides the ability to visualize projects very effectively. It links to spreadsheets, databases and it is powerful enough to deal with complex projects. Software is updated regularly and new versions can offer improvements, therefore the buying of software requires much thought and research. Before committing a project to a particular software package, it is important to ensure that a number of packages have been tried and demonstrated and that the training and support offered is to the project manger's satisfaction.

MANAGEMENT OF PROJECTS: THE NEW MODEL

As described earlier in this chapter, the evolution of project management has been closely related to engineering management processes and the development of system engineering in the defence and aerospace industry. These systems have been complemented by developments in modern management theory, particularly in organizational design and team building. Quantum leaps in computer technology and the simplification of its use for all professions have also benefited the general running of projects. Notwithstanding these great advances, the concepts and techniques of project management described in this chapter are often not sufficient for the overall task of managing projects successfully. The successful accomplishment of projects may well require detailed attention to other factors not addressed by the traditional project management approach.[7] The management of political forces; the timing of decisions, which is something quite different from the theory and practice of project scheduling; the role of effective negotiation; consultation processes, environmental issues; sustainability strategies are subjects frequently ignored by some pragmatic project management professionals. The new model currently emerging for the successful management of projects which may be more appropriate for urban design, focuses on broader areas which go beyond the more narrowly defined areas of 'project management'. The change of emphasis from 'project management' towards 'management of projects' requires this emergent professional discipline to address not only the traditional core project management topics such as scheduling, cost control, work breakdown structures and team building, but also the new dimensions of the subject such as strategy, politics, ethics, standards and the environment. Ultimately, these are the variables which enable a project to happen.

CASE STUDY: BIRMINGHAM'S EASTSIDE REGENERATION PROGRAMME

Birmingham is a leading example of urban renaissance in progress, resulting from the application of efficient project management. Transformation of the city centre's Eastside quarter is seen as the next phase in the city's renaissance after the successful regeneration of Brindley Place, a canal-side redevelopment. The Eastside redevelopment is one of the largest regeneration programmes in Europe, bringing forward new commercial, retail, leisure and residential developments, linked to learning, technology and heritage-related attractions and activities.[8]

After more than 15 years of false starts and failed plans, a partnership of landowners, universities and regeneration agencies was formed to bring over £800 million of investment to create a new city centre quarter. Guided by a master plan that covers a 40 hectares site (Figure 8.16), the Eastside regeneration project sets out locations for a number of major redevelopments, including the new Millennium Point (Figure 8.17) - a £113 million centre for science, technology, engineering and learning - which opened in 2001. The physical hub of the scheme is a new municipal park, the first of its kind in Birmingham city centre since the late nineteenth century. Located next to Millennium Point, the park will be part of a string of pedestrian

Figure 8.16 The Eastside
Regeneration Area.

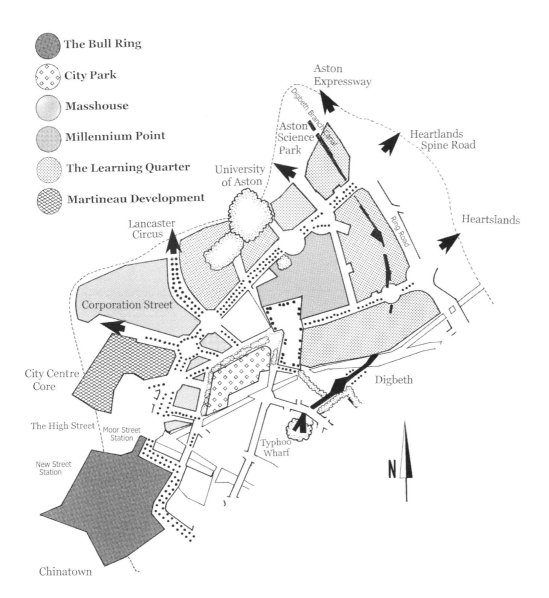

Key:
- The Bull Ring
- City Park
- Masshouse
- Millennium Point
- The Learning Quarter
- Martineau Development

Aston Expressway

Digbeth Branch Canal

Aston Science Park

Heartlands Spine Road

University of Aston

Ring Road

Heartslands

Lancaster Circus

Corporation Street

City Centre Core

Digbeth

The High Street

Moor Street Station

New Street Station

Typhoo Wharf

N

Chinatown

routes which link outlying neighbourhoods in the Eastside area to the city centre through an extensive pedestrian parkland network. The park will assist in extending the city centre, providing opportunities for a number of new landmark buildings, including the Curzon Street Station (Figure 8.18), a Grade 1 listed building, which will reclaim its rightful status as a focal point in a parkland setting.

Integral to the vision of Eastside, and the drive to diversify Birmingham's economic base, is the

8.17

8.18

Figure 8.17 Millennium
Point.
Figure 8.18 Curzon Street
Station.
Figure 8.19 Bull Ring
Redevelopment.

proposal to create a world-class learning quarter.
The existing facilities of Aston University and the
University of Central England, complemented by the
new city library landmark building, will provide the
foundations for the development of a knowledge-
based environment, encompassing all aspects of
education. A central element of the learning quarter
is to stimulate new links between inner city schools
and city centre businesses, encouraging pupils to
use local initiatives as a stepping stone to training
and eventual employment. The Eastside regeneration
area is being linked to Birmingham city centre
through the redevelopment of Masshouse Circus, a
notorious ring road 'concrete collar', which has
stifled redevelopment and investment for many
years. New development opportunities, including
the introduction of a major urban boulevard, will be

8.19

facilitated by the removal of the elevated sections of the ring road. Other plans for the area include the redevelopment of Birmingham's 1960s 'Bull Ring' (Figure 8.19) to be replaced by a series of streets, offering new open public areas, revitalized markets and restoration of the historic landmark St Martin's Church. This £400 million project will provide an imaginative solution to one of Birmingham's worst urban eyesores and will offer over 10 hectares of retail, leisure and public space. The project is due for completion in 2003 and is expected to create 8000 jobs.

Through these major redevelopment projects, Birmingham will be able to reap the rewards of a well-defined vision, transformed into a properly coordinated programme. The programme has followed the key stages of project management outlined previously in this chapter, including project definition, project planning, project implementation and project completion. This approach could see the city developed into one of the most exciting in Europe, bringing about sustainable economic regeneration and development. Eastside provides a model for future European urban regeneration and offers a good example on how a tired industrial zone can be transformed into a high quality development, which will create new jobs, new homes and new investment.

CONCLUSION

This chapter has examined some of the issues involved in the implementation of projects. Project management methods and techniques can complement the gentler aspects of design method discussed in this book, such as generating ideas, co-operation, participation, environmental protection and conservation in general. Implementation, of its nature, often requires a brusque approach overriding objections once goals have been agreed. This rather aggressive manner of working originated from war-time experiences. Martial terminology, reflecting a military

origin, was transposed into business management culture which appears as: attacking the problem, the thrust of strategy, marshalling resources, the target, aim and even bullet points. Implementation cannot be neatly separated from the stages prior to the construction gangs entering the site. This chapter accepts this wider view of implementation and has therefore examined the subject through the eyes of the project manager. The dilemma facing the urban designer is how to achieve a productive marriage between the creative nature of the design process and the harsher realities of making a project happen within the constraints of market value, profit margin and value for money. Aiming at the right target, which in this book is defined as sustainable development, is more sensible than pursuing a misguided objective, however effective the strategy. Nevertheless, the hard-headed techniques of the project manager are needed to ensure delivery of the community's environmental objectives.

REFERENCES

1   Urwick, L. and Brech, E. (1970) *The Making of Scientific Management*, New York: Pitman.

2   Chartered Institute of Building (1996) *The Code of Practice for Project Management*, London: CIOB and AW Longman Ltd.

3   *Ibid*.

4   Brigadier, G. and Winpenny, J. (1987) *Planning Development Projects*, London: HMSO.

5   Bevan, O. (1991) *Marketing and Property People*, London: Macmillan.

6   Morris, P. (1994) *The Management of Projects*, London: Thomas Telford.

7   Nottinghamshire County Council (1993) *Project Management Framework Document*, Nottingham: Nottinghamshire County Council.

8. Birmingham City Council (1999) *Eastside Story - Developing the Future*.

CONCLUSION

9

This book is a discourse on the process of urban design for sustainable development and its method. It is not an exhaustive account of the techniques used in urban design. Where techniques have been included in the text they are used to illuminate the process and method. A short book of this type, inevitably, raises more questions than it answers. Readers are invited to consider for themselves some of the apparent contradictions and paradoxes raised by this text. The book makes no claim to be the definitive study of urban design method. It is an introduction to the subject and therefore requires the reader to consider, for himself or herself, the role and scope of method in urban design.

The terms method and technique were defined in Chapter 1. Urban design method was then set within a theoretical framework. The method advocated in this book assumes a synoptic approach to planning and urban design which presupposes a rationalist view of problem solving where alternative solutions are assessed against a set of criteria derived from the project goals and objectives. The method outlined in this book has its origins in rationalism and utilitarian philosophy; nevertheless, the process has been adapted to take account of the difficulty of seeking solutions to ill-defined design

problems. Solving such problems involves a dialectical process of confronting problem and solution in a dialogue. In this iterative process problem definition is refined by posing part solutions. The method outlined in the book is based on a process which includes: the definition of goals and objectives; a survey and its analysis; a synthesis or the generation of alternative solutions; evaluation of alternatives; the process of implementation. It is recognized, however, that when dealing with design, this process is not linear, it is cyclical, possibly requiring several return loops to reassess the validity of design objectives, gather additional information, carry out further analyses and adjust the direction of the search for a solution.

The synoptic approach to planning and urban design is a 'top-down' process where goals and objectives are derived from a higher tier of authority, whether it is from the Government, a regional authority or a city council. The design or plan is organized so that it conforms with these larger-scale requirements. Public participation is central to sustainable development, which is a goal of urban design. Public participation, particularly where a degree of power has been delegated to the public, implies a decentralized administration and a 'bottom-up' planning or design style. The dilemma which arises when rational synoptic planning is used for planning a city and a participatory approach is adopted for the design of a neighbourhood in that city is illustrated in the case study of the Markets Area, Belfast, mentioned in Chapter 6 and, in passing, in Chapter 1.[1] There is no easy resolution of this conflict between a synoptic and a participatory process of urban design. This remains an area of potential conflict which is perhaps best resolved pragmatically for individual cases.

The process involved in negotiating the brief is explained in Chapter 2. This is the starting point in the design process for many consultants in the field. A visit to the local authority to assess the potential for development in the area and the requirements placed upon a potential site is, or should be, an early investigation for a developer. For the local authority and its design staff, however, the preparation of advice for developers may be the result of a long process of planning investigations and site analysis. The design brief clarifies the goals and particular objectives for the development, together with a schedule showing the way in which the land will be used in the project. An agreed design brief at an early stage in the planning of a project can remove some of the difficulties associated with development control. An agreed strategy for development between developer and local authority holds out the prospect of reduced conflict and a more effective project implementation. Effective project implementation also depends on an early understanding of the cost implications of, and the necessary procedures for, land assembly together with an appreciation of the need for sound financial backing for the development. Chapter 2, therefore, outlines the procedures that relate to land assembly, acquisition of land, compulsory purchase orders, valuation of development sites, financial appraisal, and the current use of public, private finance initiatives.

Chapters 3 and 4 outline the procedures and techniques used in the gathering and analysis of information which is directly relevant for the development project. Chapter 3 deals with site investigation, including the history and development of the site, townscape analysis, urban legibility, permeability studies and visual analysis. The precise nature of the project determines the scope of the survey and the emphasis given to individual aspects of the investigation. Of particular concern for sustainable development is the conservation of the built environment and the creation of a local environment of quality which is largely self-sufficient in terms of energy use and daily requirements. Surveys which explore the possibility of retaining existing structures and those which aim to understand the cultural heritage of the local community are of particular significance. Also important is the perception of the environment held by residents in the area. Attempting to gain an understanding of the image of a place and its legibility is a fundamental investigation for most urban developments. Two other analytical techniques for understanding a place in its urban context, which are reviewed in Chapter 4, are Geographic Information Systems (GIS) and Space Syntax.

Appropriate development results from an understanding of present conditions, future possibilities, together with a knowledge of constraints which limit the nature and extent of any development. With this in mind the analysis of the problems of an area are sharpened by a study of its strengths, weaknesses, the threats it faces and the opportunities that may unfold for sustainable development.

Chapter 5 discusses the techniques used for generating ideas for alternative design solutions. Foremost amongst these is the art of developing appropriate analogies. The organic metaphor for the city is the most useful generic model for sustainable development. The eco-system is possibly the idea which generates the most practical suggestions for urban design and city planning. A number of case studies are described which illustrate the use of the organic analogy in urban design, including the eco-city in Norway, a landmark for studies in sustainable development. Participation is fundamental for sustainable development. A case study from Newark, Nottinghamshire, is analysed to illustrate the ways in which the public can be involved in the design of the local environment. The generation of design concepts has been the province of the professional designer. The invasion of this, the core of design, by the lay person poses some difficult questions for the professional working in this field. These questions include: whose opinion prevails in case of dispute? What if the popular view excludes from the design process others on grounds of race or religion? Who arbitrates in the case of rival communities with conflicting goals? What is the role of the designer if it is not design?

Some of the techniques used to evaluate plans for urban design projects such as 'Payback Method', 'Rate of Return', and 'Discounted Cash Flow' are outlined in Chapter 6. The material in the chapter is limited to those techniques of evaluation normally associated with the social sciences, such as cost–benefit analysis, the planning balance sheet, environmental impact studies and economic input–output analysis. Technical evaluations for urban design normally associated with the architectural and engineering professions, such as daylight, noise and wind studies, though important, cannot be adequately dealt with in this short book.

The physical, social and economic benefits of developments resulting from urban design projects benefit some groups in the community while the costs of that development may be imposed on other groups. Costs of development, often unaccounted and unrecognized, are sometimes imposed upon the environment in the form of pollution, the misuse of non-renewable resources or the destruction of valuable flora and fauna. The equitable distribution of development costs and benefits between generations and within the same generation is a fundamental consideration for those working towards sustainable development. One of the goals of sustainable development is the pursuit of inter- and intra-generational equity. Chapter 6, therefore, ends with a brief account of a case study from southern Italy.

The case study assesses the distribution of benefits accruing from the Integrated Mediterranean Programme for Calabria. It showed quite clearly that the income generated by the Programme was far less for the poorer upland areas of the region than for the relatively more prosperous towns along the coast. Since the Programme was widening the income gap between the poor and the better off in the region, then according to this criterion, the Programme did not fulfil a central goal of sustainable development.

The implementation of urban design projects is the theme of Chapters 7 and 8. Chapter 7, a relatively short chapter, deals with communication. Ideas and schemes for development and city improvement remain dreams until they are implemented. Fundamental to the implementation of visions for the future is the ability of the designer to express those ideas with great clarity, imagination and enthusiasm, so that others in key positions in the development industry will give support to the vision. Chapter 7 outlines the tools available for expressing urban design ideas. It discusses, in particular, the style of report writing, effective public speaking, the use of drawings, three-dimensional material and the computer in the presentation of the urban design project.

Chapter 8 is also concerned with implementation and outlines project management techniques. The chapter stresses the need to consider implementation from the start of the project. Thought given to the setting-up of the project greatly facilitates implementation at the construction stage of the process. In some ways, Chapter 8 mirrors the whole process of design method outlined in Chapter 1 and also returns to emphasize the theme of Chapter 2 which considered that the early agreement of a broad development agenda gave a necessary overview of the complete development process which facilitates implementation. The chapter ends with a case study, the Eastside of Birmingham, an examination of successful regeneration resulting from a dynamic management process.

This chapter does raise the question about the control of the design process. Should control remain with the designer in the traditional architect–client relationship? Alternatively, is a further layer of management control so vital to achieve cost-effective environmental sustainability that a professional in this field is needed to organize the whole process for the client? The chapter raises this whole question of the composition of the design and development team and the roles adopted by its members.

Project management is goal-directed: it is the aggressive pursuit of the project vision by adopting the most direct strategy. The single-minded dedication of the project manager contrasts with the softer, gentler, non-directive approach out of which visions are born. The aggressive pursuit of ends also contrasts with attitudes more appropriate at other phases of the design process. There are times when collaboration, consultation and negotiation are necessary for the successful implementation of the project. At such times skills, in tact, diplomacy and political bargaining, are appropriate. Successful urban design method probably results from the marriage of these opposite characteristics, that is, the need to imagine or to see in the mind's eye a dream of how the world may be and the discipline necessary to achieve that desired future.

REFERENCE

1   See also Moughtin, J.C. (1992) *Urban Design: Street and Square*, Oxford: Butterworth-Heinemann.

FIGURE SOURCES

The author and publishers would like to thank those who have kindly permitted the use of images in the illustration of this book. Attempts have been made to locate all the sources of illustrations to obtain full reproduction rights, but in the very few instances where this process has failed to find the copyright holder, apologies are offered. In the case of an error, correction would be welcomed.

Fig. 1.1 Moughtin, J.C. (1992) *Urban Design: Street and Square*, Oxford: Butterworth-Heinemann, based on a drawing in Markus and Maver.

Figs 1.2, 1.4, 1.5, 3.3, 3.4, 3.5, 3.9, 3.10, 3.25, 3.26, 3.27, 5.9, 5.10, 5.71, 5.72 Moughtin, J.C. (1992) *Urban Design: Street and Square*, Oxford: Butterworth-Heinemann.

Figs 1.3, 1.4 Moughtin, J.C. (1992) *Urban Design: Street and Square*, Oxford: Butterworth-Heinemann, based on drawings in Wallace, W. (1971) *The Logic of Science in Sociology*, Chicago: Aldine-Atherton, p. 18.

Table 1.1 Naess, P. (1994) Normative planning theory and sustainable development, *Scandinavian Housing and Planning Research*, No. 11, pp. 145–167.

Figs 3.9 and 3.10 Wilford, M. (1984) Off to the Races or Going to the Dogs? *Architectural Design*, Vol. 54, No. 1 / 2.

Fig. 3.17 Barley, M.W. and Straw, I. F. (undated) Nottingham, in *Historic Towns*, Ed. M. D. Lobel, London: Lovell Johns-Cook Hammond P. Kell Organization.

Figs 3.18, 3.22 Beckett, J. and Brand, K. (1997) *Nottingham, An Illustrated History*, Manchester: Manchester University Press.

Figs 3.30, 3.31 Moughtin, J.C., Oc, T. and Tiesdell, S. (1995) *Urban Design: Ornament and Decoration*, Oxford: Butterworth-Heinemann.

Fig. 3.35 Bentley, I. *et al.* (1985) *Responsive Environments: A Manual for Designers*, London: Architectural Press.

Figs 3.36, 3.37 Cullen, G. (1961) *Townscape*, London: Architectural Press.

Figs 3.38, 7.10 From *Design of Cities* by Edmund Bacon. Copyright © 1967, 1974 by Edmund N. Bacon. Used by permission of Penguin, a division of Penguin Books USA Inc.

Fig. 3.39 Gibberd, F. (1955) *Town Design*, London: Architectural Press, Revised Edition.

Fig. 3.42 Holford, W. (1956) St Paul's: Report on the surroundings of St Paul's Cathedral in the City of London, *Town Planning Review*, Vol. 27, No. 2, July, p. 61.

Figs 3.43, 3.44 Holford, W. (1956) St. Paul's: Report on the surroundings of St Paul's Cathedral in the City of London, *Town Planning Review*, Vol. 27, No. 2, July, p. 62.

INDEX